## Praise for Katherine Pangonis

'Pangonis's combination of familiar and unfamiliar places is one of the great attractions of the book... This is a vividly written book to savour and enjoy, whether criss-crossing the Mediterranean or lounging in an armchair dreaming of it.'

David Abulafia, *Spectator* on *Twilight Cities*

'An anecdote-stuffed tour of lost cities that ruled the ancient world, then collapsed... Pangonis writes in a lively style... she is an amiable literary travelling companion.'

*The Times* on *Twilight Cities*

'Luminous... Both – sophisticated and delightfully wide-ranging.'
Daisy Dunn, *Daily Telegraph* on *Twilight Cities*

'The subjects of this important and inspiring book have regularly been resigned to the footnotes of history. But the *Queens of Jerusalem* are history-makers, game-changers. Delight in their company in this seminal and scintillating debut.'

Bettany Hughes on *Queens of Jerusalem*

'Beautifully constructed, highly intelligent, perceptive, humane and empathetic, this wonderful book turns the forgotten women rulers of Jerusalem from powerless broodmares into complex actors with agency, ingenuity and fascinating lives.'

William Dalrymple on *Queens of Jerusalem*

'Fascinating, intriguing, exciting and authoritative. Here are the female rulers of the crusader states as shrewd politicians, warrior queens and mothers and wives, holding their own against male crusader states and Islamic warlords in the ruthless arena of the Middle East.'

Simon Sebag Montefiore on *Queens of Jerusalem*

**Also by Katherine Pangonis**

*Twilight Cities*

*Queens of Jerusalem*

# A HISTORY OF FRANCE IN 21 WOMEN

Katherine Pangonis

A Oneworld Book

First published by Oneworld Publications Ltd in 2026

Copyright © Katherine Pangonis, 2026

The moral right of Katherine Pangonis to be identified as the Author of this work has been asserted by her in accordance with the Copyright, Designs and Patents Act 1988.

All rights reserved
Copyright under Berne Convention
A CIP record for this title is available from the British Library

ISBN 978-1-83643-070-4
eISBN 978-1-83643-071-1

Typeset by Geethik Technologies
Printed and bound in Great Britain by Clays Ltd, Elcograf S.p.A.

No part of this publication may be reproduced, stored in a retrieval system, or transmitted, in any form or by any means, electronic, mechanical, photocopying, recording or otherwise, or used in any manner for the purpose of training artificial intelligence technologies or systems, without the prior permission of the publishers.

Image credits: p. 6, Statue of Balthild in the Jardin du Luxembourg, Paris / JPLC / Wikimedia Commons; p.18, *Queen Eleanor* by Frederick Sandys, 1858 / Wikimedia Commons; p. 34, 'The Temptation of Lechery' / PICRYL; p.49, Christine de Pizan from 'The Queen's Manuscript' / PICRYL; p. 64, *Johan of Arc* by Georges Spetz, c. nineteenth century / Wikimedia Commons; p. 80, *Portrait of Caterine de' Medici, Queen of France*, attrib. Germain Le Mannier, c. 1547–1559 / Wikimedia Commons; p. 100, Émilie du Châtelet, engraving, 1751 / Wikimedia Commons; p.114, Olympe de Gouges, watercolour, 1793 / Wikimedia Commons; p. 130, Detail from *Joséphine in Coronation Costume* by Baron François Gérard, c. 1807–8 / Wikimedia Commons; p.152, *Portrait of George Sand* by Auguste Charpentier, c. 1837–1839 / Wikimedia Commons; p. 172, Louise Michel during her exile in New Caledonia, anonymous, c. 1873–1880; p. 188, Portrait of Berthe Morisot by her sister Edma, 1865 / Wikimedia Commons; p. 206, *Sarah Bernhardt dans Gismonda* by Theobold Chartran, c. 1900 / Library of Congress; p. 226, Colette and Mathilde 'Missy' de Morny, anonymous, c. 1900; p. 242, Coco Chanel, unknown photographer, early 1950s / PVDE. All rights reserved 2026 / Bridgeman Images; p.258, Photograph of Paulette Nardal and her sisters, unknown photographer, 1935; p.274, Josephine Baker by Walery, 1926 / Wikimedia Commons; p. 288, Edith Piaf singing / Everett Collection / Bridgeman Images; p. 304, Simone Veil at the Élysée Palace, 26 May 1977 © AGIP / Bridgeman Images; p. 316, Djamila Boupacha, unknown photographer, 14 March 1963 / Wikimedia Commons; Brigitte Bardot in *La femme et le pantin* by Julien Duvivier, 1959 © Dear Film Produzione / Gray-Film / Progéfi / Diltz / Bridgeman Images.

Every reasonable effort has been made to trace the copyright holders of material reproduced in this book, but if any have been inadvertently overlooked the publishers would be glad to hear from them.

The authorised representative in the EEA is eucomply OU,
Pärnu mnt 139b–14, 11317 Tallinn, Estonia
(email: hello@eucompliancepartner.com / phone: +33757690241)

Oneworld Publications Ltd
10 Bloomsbury Street
London WC1B 3SR
England

Stay up to date with the latest books,
special offers, and exclusive content from
Oneworld with our newsletter

Sign up on our website
oneworld.co.uk

For my parents.

# CONTENTS

| | | |
|---|---|---|
| | Introduction | 1 |
| 1 | Balthild of Chelles | 7 |
| 2 | Eleanor of Aquitaine | 19 |
| 3 | Béatrice de Planisolles | 35 |
| 4 | Christine de Pizan | 49 |
| 5 | Joan of Arc | 65 |
| 6 | Catherine de' Medici | 81 |
| 7 | Émilie du Châtelet | 101 |
| 8 | Olympe de Gouges | 115 |
| 9 | Empress Josephine | 131 |
| 10 | George Sand | 153 |
| 11 | Louise Michel | 173 |
| 12 | Berthe Morisot | 189 |
| 13 | Sarah Bernhardt | 207 |
| 14 | Colette | 227 |
| 15 | Coco Chanel | 243 |
| 16 | Paulette Nardal | 259 |
| 17 | Josephine Baker | 275 |

| 18 Édith Piaf | 289 |
| 19 Simone Veil | 305 |
| 20 Djamila Boupacha | 317 |
| 21 Brigitte Bardot | 333 |
| | |
| Conclusion | 349 |
| Acknowledgements | 353 |
| Key Sources and Suggested Reading | 355 |

# INTRODUCTION

The 'history of France', in the popular imagination at least, stands as a parade of kings, conquerors, cardinals, revolutionaries, renegades and sometimes (only sometimes) their wives and mistresses. A lot of Louises, Philippes, a few Napoleons and maybe Charles de Gaulle spring to mind. The women that manage to elbow their way in are generally limited to Marie Antoinette and Joan of Arc, variously vilified and sanctified, and in both cases violently executed.

In truth, the history of the sprawling European nation – the hexagon and scattering of overseas islands and territories that make up France – is marked by the lives of many extraordinary women. Women whose lives, actions and courage have shaped the country and its culture in profound ways, yet are too often relegated to the margins of history. This book, *A History of France in 21 Women*, seeks to shed light on the achievements of *some* of these women, and their impact on the times they lived in. While not widely recognised, women helped to shape the Renaissance, the Enlightenment and the revolutionary periods in France, and their contributions have been left in the shadows for far too long.

In July 2024, Paris celebrated the opening ceremony of the Olympic Games in style on the River Seine. Female performers and athletes took centre stage in the celebrations: a silver *chevalière* – a cloaked female figure astride a silver horse – galloped down the ribbon of the Seine, evoking both Joan of Arc and Sequana, the mythic spirit of the river. Paris and the world collectively wept when Céline Dion sang out Édith Piaf's greatest masterpiece 'Hymne à l'amour' from the Eiffel Tower. Still more directly, a segment specifically titled 'Sororité' ('Sisterhood') launched a powerful tribute to ten women who had a significant impact on French history and French feminism. As the Seine transformed into a stage, golden statues of these women were unveiled, rising from the empty plinths that lined the river, hailed as heroines of France. The moment moved me: seven of the ten selected women were ones I had already chosen to include in this book. These moments for me brought this book to life and confirmed to me the need for these stories to be told now.

I have spent years living in France – basking in sunny cafés, researching in the archives of the Bibliothèque Nationale, struggling with accents and exploring the historical layers of this country. With its diverse array of regions like Brittany, Occitanie and Aquitaine, France is a country where history is ever-present – whether in the heaving streets of Paris or in the quieter corners of medieval towns. The influence of women in these stories is clear, from legendary figures like Joan of Arc to lesser-known, yet equally significant, women who navigated the complexities of their time with resilience and brilliance. But their memories are fainter than those of men.

I have always been shocked to see how systematically women are excluded from the national narrative. One of my favourite museums in France, the Musée Carnavalet, reopened after a

## INTRODUCTION

major renovation in 2021, but it still presents a narrative history of Paris that overwhelmingly excludes women.[1] Sure, the curators share information on St Genevieve in their sections on Lutetia, Paris's Gallo-Roman predecessor, but in their rooms on the Enlightenment they have only been enlightened enough to include one small engraving of Émilie du Châtelet. Furthermore, on my last visit they had not even captioned the portrait, nor do they provide visitors with any information about her work. A visitor might pass through the exhibition and glance at her portrait, register her beauty, but never learn her name, or what she did for science in France. This is too often the case in how women have been treated in history over the centuries, reduced to decorative objects, rather than recognised as active agents.

My aim in this book is to do more than simply recount achievements, seeking instead to explore the sweeping history of France through the lives of twenty-one women. These women are not two-dimensional heroines or icons; they were flawed, human; rebels, reformers and, sometimes, traitors and zealots. Each chapter is designed to capture the spirit of a particular era, focusing not only on the individual but also on the historical, social and cultural context that shaped their lives.

Choosing only twenty-one women was an incredibly difficult task. Countless others deserve to be included. The suffragettes who fought tirelessly for women's right to vote, like Marguerite Durand and Hubertine Auclert, should have their own chapters too. Marie Curie may also feel conspicuously absent from these pages, but her life has already been covered in other excellent books in this series. Pioneers like Simone de Beauvoir and Gisèle Halimi, whose activism transformed women's rights in the twentieth century, should have had dedicated chapters – but at the same time I don't think they would have minded being cast as supporters for one of the women they won justice for: Djamila

---

[1] Or at least it was on my last visit in 2024.

Boupacha, whose own life is essential to understanding a darker side of French history. Beyond this, they have had reams and reams written about them already. And what of the courageous women who played pivotal roles in the Haitian Revolution, fighting against the brutality of colonialism? These women have made significant contributions to French history, and to feminist history and theory, but in the interest of offering a broad narrative sweep, I had to make difficult choices. The goal was to avoid focusing too heavily on any single period or movement and to provide a diverse overview of France's history and culture, while still including some of the most important figures. That said, in describing the Revolution, I have chosen to do so through the life and work of Olympe de Gouges, rather than the perhaps more popular Marie Antoinette. I just felt that, in anglophone circles at least, Olympe de Gouges might be more surprising, more interesting, more revelatory. After all, Sofia Coppola hasn't made a film about her (yet).

What connects the women in this book is not only their historical significance but also their shared spirit of determination. Nearly all were self-made, often defying the expectations and limitations imposed on them by their circumstances and their time. Balthild of Chelles rose from slavery to queenship, using her newfound power to advocate for the abolition of the slave trade in the Frankish kingdom. Émilie du Châtelet defied societal norms to publish ground-breaking works in mathematics and physics. Coco Chanel, from humble beginnings, revolutionised women's fashion, while Josephine Baker, an African-American entertainer, became a decorated spy for the French Resistance during the Second World War. These women were go-getters and visionaries who refused to accept the constraints of their circumstances.

The lives of the women featured in this book are also intended to offer unexpected perspectives on major historical events. For example, the chapter on Empress Josephine provides a more

## INTRODUCTION

intimate view of Napoleon's rise and fall, while Paulette Nardal's story opens a window into the endeavours of Black intellectuals in early-twentieth-century Paris, connecting the Harlem Renaissance to the burgeoning Négritude movement in France.

The stories in this book are as diverse as France itself. By exploring the life of Béatrice de Planisolles, we delve into the Cathar heresy and the brutal Albigensian Crusade that tore the south of France apart. Through Olympe de Gouges, we witness the fervour of the French Revolution and the high cost of advocating for equality in an era of radical change. Meanwhile, in the chapters on George Sand, Berthe Morisot and Colette, I intend to offer glimpses into the artistic and literary movements that redefined French culture in the nineteenth century and Belle Époque. For centuries, France has been one of the world's great cultural and intellectual powerhouses, shaping art, literature, music, philosophy and political thought far beyond its borders. Its influence is inescapable – and the cultural and intellectual advances made by French women are woven into the fabric of world history. For better or worse, France's history is not just a national story, but a global one.

This book is also an acknowledgement of the countless women who are not included in its pages – those who fought bravely, lived courageously and left their mark in quieter, often undocumented ways. Ultimately, *A History of France in 21 Women* is a testament to the resilience, intellect and bravery of women who dared to change the course of history. The history of France, like any great story, is incomplete without the voices of the women who helped shape it.

These are their stories.

Statue of Balthild, in the Jardin du Luxembourg, Paris.

# 1

# Balthild of Chelles

## c.626–30 January 680

In 1983, archaeologists discovered an unexpected grave in the town of Chelles, just east of Paris. When they started digging, they were not hopeful of finding much. The chances of uncovering an intact royal grave were minuscule: during the French Revolution royal and holy graves were desecrated – broken open and the remains thrown into quarries and rivers and pits. The quiet town of Chelles and its eponymous abbey were not, however, so thoroughly ransacked as the royal tombs in the Basilica of Saint-Denis, and they hoped they might find *something* at least – a coin perhaps, or a prayer book, maybe some fragments of fabric.

What they did find exceeded even their wildest expectations. Dusting away the earth and debris, their brushes and trowels uncovered bones. Ribs, hands, feet, a skull – the complete skeletal remains of a petite woman, clad in elegant, high-status clothing and still with an intact plait of hair. She was richly dressed in a pink and yellow silken cloak with rounded edges, made of more than three metres of cloth – a luxurious item indeed – and embellished with a metal brooch and silk woven straps adorned with playful animal designs. Remarkably, they had found the body of Balthild, queen of the ancient kingdom of Neustria, and Catholic saint.

# A HISTORY OF FRANCE IN 21 WOMEN

This grave alone tells us much about Balthild, giving a remarkable glimpse into what she looked like and her personal style – details that are almost always impossible to glean about medieval women. When Balthild died and was laid to rest in Chelles, she had golden hair streaked with silver, was clad in costly silks, and was five feet tall.

Balthild was the starting point of this book – depicted as she is among the statues of illustrious ladies of the Jardin du Luxembourg in Paris. I have visited this famous garden in the 5th arrondissement many times, but only a few years ago paused to properly look at the statues. It is the only place in Paris where statues of women stand alone in a prominent public place – twenty of them positioned in a circle around the octagonal basin in the centre. Thousands pass these statues every day, without paying any attention to their faces. Tourists and Parisians alike come and sit on the green metal chairs arranged around the fountain, eating macarons, reading books, scrolling – while older people play chess nearby. As a teenager I did the same. But it is rare for people to look up into the face of Balthild or Clotilde and think about their stories.

These statues are known as *Les Reines de France et Femmes Illustres* and were commissioned by King Louis-Philippe in 1843 and have stood there in serene splendour ever since. Mystifyingly, no information plaques have been placed alongside them. St Balthild is the first of these and was sculpted by Victor Thérasse in 1848. She is depicted as tall, with a steely gaze locked ahead of her. Long plaits coil around her face, under a modest veil, surmounted by a Germanic crown. In one hand she grasps a scroll, presumably a law book or writ that she has seen passed, and in the other she grasps her long, curved cloak, as though to remind her subjects of her status. Her waist is cinched with a girdle, and around her neck is a beaded necklace, from which hangs a simple, large crucifix. The queen presented is a powerful, devout one, unafraid to take the law into her own hands.

## BALTHILD OF CHELLES

Balthild was no ordinary Queen of France. In fact, France did not yet exist as one unified nation. She was born in East Anglia, England, sold into slavery in Francia – the ancestor of modern France – and through her wits, beauty and virtue found her way to the throne. The story of her life offers a unique insight into Francia during the time known as the Dark Ages. It was a time before 'France' had formed, as either a nation or a concept, but when its foundations were being laid.

'Francia' – the ancestor of modern France and kingdom of the Franks – had not existed as a concept under Roman rule. The region was simply 'Gaul', and the Franks one tribe of many that would come to populate the vast fields that spread from the broad sands of Normandy to the Alps and Pyrenees.

The end of Roman Gaul is usually dated to 486 CE, when Clovis, hailed as the first King of the Franks, defeated the last Roman governors in the region, conquering their territory. The western fringes of the Roman Empire had been harried for some time by the 'barbarian' tribes, among which the Franks were counted, alongside Vandals and Visigoths, and the empire was crumbling from within, in a century marked by serious internal power struggles and conflicts with local rulers. The decisive Battle of Soissons in 486 CE, where Clovis defeated the Roman commander Syagrius, effectively ended Roman rule in the region and established Frankish dominance, paving the way for the rise of the Merovingian dynasty and the formation of Francia. Ten years later, his wife Clotilde persuaded her pagan husband to convert to Christianity, and with him the kingdom. She was a Christian of a Burgundian dynasty, and together they founded the Merovingian dynasty in Francia.

So how does Balthild fit in? How does a young woman born in the Anglo-Saxon kingdoms find her way onto the throne of the Merovingians, as bride of Clovis II?

Unearthing details of the life of a woman in the Dark Ages, even a queen, is never an easy task. Most women's stories have been lost completely – evaporating into the ether. Balthild, in contrast, is probably the best-documented woman from seventh-century Francia, and thus the best-documented early Queen of France. Her life was immortalised – creatively no doubt – by a hagiographer shortly after her death in 680, mapping out her journey from a kidnapped and trafficked slave to the queen of the western Frankish kingdom of 'Neustria', and eventually to her retirement at the abbey of Chelles, where her relics were found more than a millennium later. Nine other historical sources attest to her life and reign, albeit somewhat conflictingly, and on top of this, the archaeological record also yields riches. Alongside her relics and the clothes she was buried in, several other artefacts associated with her have survived, including an erotic gold seal-ring, perplexingly found in Norfolk with the name 'Baldehildis' inscribed backwards. Perhaps she had commanded that a part of her was taken back to the country of her birth, but really, the ring presents more mysteries than solutions.

Even with this evidence, Balthild remains a complex figure, and her story is filled with uncertainties, veiled by both excessive praise and excessive slander. It is difficult to tease out the truth of who she was. Nevertheless, the picture of Balthild that emerges from both the written sources and the archaeological evidence points to a tenacious, powerful woman, crowned with beautiful golden hair.

The period from 500 to 1000 in the country now known as France saw the slow and tortured disintegration of the greatness of the Roman Empire, from the ruins of which sallied forth other magnates, kings and emperors who would lay the foundations and draw the frontiers of the Europe and the France we know today.

Following the conquest and consolidation of the region by Clovis and his heirs in the fifth and sixth centuries, the Frankish Empire existed as a concept, but in practice was divided into two distinct parts, Neustria and Austrasia. In both places, there were unionists and separatists, and they were controlled almost always by separate rulers, neither of whom was truly the King of the Franks. Real power and real decisions belonged not to the Merovingian 'kings' but rather to the strongmen known as the 'Mayors of the Palace'.

Austrasia comprised territories in the east and north-east, including parts of what is now Germany and the Low Countries, while Neustria occupied the west and the south – including, a little tenuously, the vastly wealthy regions of Aquitaine and Gascogne.

The Francia into which Balthild was frogmarched was therefore Christian, but deeply divided.

I say frogmarched because the first woman in this book – chosen as a woman who defined the history of France – was, like so many great French women, not born in France at all. Through a variety of channels, whether the importation of slaves, friendly diplomacy, commercial trade or violent invasion and colonisation, throughout history the lands now known as France have played host to immigrants from all corners of the globe, many of whom have risen to great heights. Alongside the name of St Balthild, the names of Marie Antoinette, Marie Curie, Josephine Baker and Gisèle Halimi spring to mind. Some of France's greatest male cultural luminaries were also immigrants – Rousseau, Van Gogh, Camus, Chopin, to name but a few.

Balthild was born in what is now England – the land across the sea – likely in the Anglo-Saxon kingdom of East Anglia. While we cannot know for certain who her parents were, it is likely she was of noble birth and raised in a deeply religious household.

While the Dark Ages were not as devoid of intellectual progress as their name might suggest, in some ways they were certainly unenlightened – notably, in the practice of slavery. These were violent times, and along with the legitimate commercial and cultural traffic that went back and forth across the Channel in the seventh century, so too came raiders. The north coast of England was far from safe, subject to raids, and attacks from other opportunist sailors. While Balthild was still a young girl, her home was invaded by such raiders. She was kidnapped and trafficked to France, where she was sold as a slave.

Slavery in the Frankish kingdoms was pervasive. The economy was fuelled by a steady trade in – and reliance on – involuntary and unpaid labour. Slaves came from a variety of backgrounds: as in the case of Balthild they could simply be kidnapped freemen dragged from their homes during raids; in other circumstances they were prisoners of war, or those who had fallen into deep debt and lost their freedom. Their tasks ranged from domestic work – and sexual slavery – to agricultural labour and even warfare. The Church played a somewhat hypocritical role in this system – while ostensibly promoting the Christian doctrine of spiritual equality, the Church itself often relied on slave labour. This was justified as simply part of the accepted social order of the time.

A pretty young woman with dainty intonation was a valuable prize indeed, and unsurprisingly the captive Balthild did not find herself sold for farm labour – but rather into the royal household. She was bought by none other than the Mayor of the Palace of Neustria, the formidable Erchinoald.

Erchinoald was the chamberlain and puppet-master of a young King Clovis II. Erchinoald, when he first noticed the choice new addition to his household staff, was impressed by her slender beauty and genteel manners – and he swiftly promoted her to the position of cup bearer, a high-ranking slave who waited on the master and his guests.

Her hagiographer emphasises the honour and gentility with which she washed and dried the feet of Erchinoald, casting her in a decidedly biblical role. She also fetched their water, and washed their clothes, never once complaining or bemoaning her fate and reduced status. In fact, the hagiographer is notably silent on the sins of her captors – men who bought a kidnapped Christian woman and enslaved her. Instead he emphasises the dignity, patience and virtue of Balthild.

This virtuous beginning very much set the stage for the next phase of Balthild's career. Erchinoald was so impressed with the beauty and dignity of Balthild that he decided that her position of 'cup bearer' was not exalted enough. He wanted to set her still higher and bring her still closer. He wanted to marry her. That said, this term is open to interpretation. In this context, 'marry' could mean actual monogamous marriage, but it could also mean concubinage, or worse. Balthild was so filled with fear and revulsion at this prospect that she hid to avoid the match. Her hagiographer relates that she concealed herself under a pile of rags, and that Erchinoald – who seemed to be something of an easy quitter – quickly gave up his hopes of marriage with that particular slave girl, and married someone else. After this Balthild felt safe enough to emerge from her hiding place, and continued in her duties for her lord and new mistress.

The next development is perhaps stranger still: the jilted Erchinoald decided to gift his elusive would-be bride to his 'master' – the teenage King Clovis II.

Like Erchinoald, Clovis was smitten by the beauty of Balthild. Unlike Erchinoald, he was impressed as much by her virtue and her faith as by her appearance, and with this in mind he married her with all honour, likely to the consternation of those around. Balthild it seems did not attempt to dodge this match, yielding up her virginity to the king, and – in so doing – became Queen of the Franks.

This peculiar narrative must be viewed with some scepticism. Hagiographers are, by virtue of their chosen genre, intent on extolling the virtue of their subject, and raising them onto a pedestal to set an example for others: more human and sinful attributes downplayed, their more celestial qualities played up. However, what sets this particular hagiography apart somewhat is that it was likely written by someone who actually knew Balthild – it was written within a decade of her death. This gives it a greater stamp of validity than most saints' lives – and it is therefore likely to contain truth at its core, under the layers of gilding.

Balthild was destined to be more than a simple concubine to the King of the Franks, but rather would become the official queen consort. She was likely older than her teenage husband, had seen more of life, and therefore wielded significant influence over the young ruler. Moreover, she cemented her status by bearing him at least three sons – all of whom were destined to rule as kings of the various Frankish kingdoms: Clothar III, Childeric II and Theuderic III. With these much-sought-after male heirs safely born, Balthild was now not only the queen consort but the future queen mother, and this position carried with it a certain amount of real power.

In the Middle Ages, particularly the early Middle Ages (which these were), there was a stark distinction between authority and power, as indeed there remains today. A royal woman's ability to convert authority – the right to power – into actual, hard, progress-making power hinged on two things: the quality of her allies and the strength of her personality. Time would reveal that Balthild had not only high-quality allies, but a will of iron.

Clovis II died young, aged around twenty-four, just five years after the birth of his heir, Clothar III. This left the kingdom in a delicate position. Balthild, aged around twenty-nine, was in an influential position and determined to consolidate it. She was no longer a young girl and had her wits about her.

Five-year-old Clothar III inherited the throne of Neustria despite his age, and Balthild also manoeuvred her still-younger son Childeric onto the throne of Austrasia. In Neustria, she assumed the position of regent, wielding the power of the king on behalf of Clothar. Her role in government is emphasised by multiple sources – but nevertheless she was still under the influence of

Erchinoald for at least one year, until he too died in 657. During her time as regent, Balthild established herself as a force to be reckoned with in Frankish politics. She donated heavily to the Church, both as a sign of faith and out of astute political judgement – the Church was a powerful ally and she would need its support. From her donations, the abbeys of Corbie and Chelles were established, and it seems likely that others, such as Jumièges, Jouarre and Luxeuil, were also founded by the queen. Religious foundations were powerful institutions at a time when men and women were concerned for their immortal souls, and were key physical ways of asserting authority in a particular region. The buildings themselves were impressive, speaking to the power and devotion of the benefactor, for whom prayers were also said. In a time before the printing press, stone inscriptions commemorating founders and benefactors and masses said in one's honour were a powerful form of propaganda. Balthild also supported Claudius of Besançon and his abbey in the Jura Mountains.

Beyond this, she is said to have used her influence to pass several changes to the law, including outlawing simony – the practice of purchasing high-ranking clerical offices and bishoprics – and to condemn the practice of infanticide, which still persisted on a small scale in Francia, particularly in the case of children born with deformities, and also – occasionally – for political reasons. However, what Balthild is best known for – most fittingly – is outlawing the purchase and sale of Christian slaves in France – no doubt in protest of her own ordeal.

Nevertheless, despite Balthild's efforts, slavery continued in the Frankish kingdoms, particularly the enslavement of non-Christians. War captives, especially from pagan tribes, were still taken as slaves, and the distinction between Christian and non-Christian slaves meant the practice shifted rather than ended. The fact slavery was crucial to key industries like agriculture, warfare, domestic service and general trade made it virtually impossible to eradicate, and the impact of Balthild's anti-slavery policies varied regionally. After her death, it seems any momentum to abolish slavery weakened: by the time of the Carolingian Empire there is ample evidence that it had experienced a resurgence on a grand scale.

Balthild was not the first Merovingian monarch to find her voice and make a serious impact on the Frankish kingdoms. The first Queen of the Franks – Clotilde, wife of Clovis I – was famous for bringing Christianity to the Franks, and for likewise ruling as regent for her son after the death of her husband. More powerful still were the rivals Brunhilde and Fredegund who reigned – and fought each other – for decades in the sixth century. While Salic law prevented women from officially taking the role of queen regnant, in practice Frankish queens frequently found ways to take the reins of government.

Balthild followed in this tradition, and her flair for politics was making her enemies in the court. Erchinoald had always been a fan of hers – in more ways than one – but when he died, he was replaced by the Frank Ebroin, who would set himself against Balthild, and preside over a particularly stormy period in Frankish politics, marked by conflicts between Neustria and Austrasia.

Balthild had a complex relationship with Ebroin, now the Mayor of the Palace. Ebroin's ambitions and political manoeuvres often put him at odds with Balthild's policies and vision for the kingdom. Eventually, he was instrumental in ousting her from power and forcing her into a form of retirement in the abbey of Chelles. She had founded it around 657 on the ruins of a chapel built by St Clotilde and provided the first of two substantial endowments for its construction.

As for her children, Balthild's relationships with her sons, Clothar III, Childeric II and Theuderic III, were marked by her strong influence and guidance. She worked diligently to secure their positions and the stability of the kingdom, even after she retired to the abbey of Chelles. Eventually her son Theuderic III would unite the two kingdoms of Neustria and Austrasia, but by this point Ebroin had become so influential as the Mayor of the Palace that Theuderic's personal power was seriously limited. Eventually the Mayors of the Palace would cease to play pretend with puppet kings and would openly usurp the throne. The first to do this was Pepin the Short, who overthrew Childeric III. His son was Charlemagne – the 'Father of Europe' – and crowned emperor in Rome in 800. However, Charlemagne's plans for his succession were at best weak. His son, Louis the Pious, divided the empire among his three sons, which led to its fragmentation and unravelling. Within two centuries the Carolingian dynasty was supplanted by Hugh Capet, who founded the Capetian dynasty of France. His descendants would rule France from the tenth century until the eighteenth, when the head was struck from the shoulders of Louis XVI by the infamous guillotine.

Balthild is now a largely forgotten Frankish queen. She reigned at a time when records were few and far between for any ruler, but female rulers in particular. She is commemorated here and there with statues, stained glass, passing references, but few in France really know her story – despite all knowing St Clotilde. Nevertheless, this queen set the stage for the powerful women who would come later. Among these, none loom quite so large as Eleanor, Queen of France and England and Duchess of Aquitaine.

Queen Eleanor – portrait by Anthony Frederick Sandys.

# 2

# Eleanor of Aquitaine

## c.1124–1 April 1204

> '… by the wrath of God, Queen of England.'
> Eleanor of Aquitaine

Eleanor of Aquitaine was perhaps the most powerful woman of the Middle Ages. She was certainly the richest. Few women had such an influence on French history before the eighteenth century as Eleanor. Queen of France, Queen of England, crusader and mother of Richard the Lionheart and King John as well as eight other healthy children – her biography is almost unrivalled for excitement, power and intrigue in medieval Europe. But it was also marked by periods of powerlessness, fury, frustration and contemplation. Although she spent more decades on the English throne than the French one, her French origins and impact on French history – both as Queen of France and then as Queen of England, the great rival of France – are undeniable.

Eleanor is a gift and an enigma to historians. On the one hand, her career is among the most colourful of any medieval woman. On the other hand, her legacy and memory have been subject to both rampant mythologising and smear campaigns. The picture left to posterity is varied – in texts as diverse as the thirteenth-century *chansons* and the script to the twentieth-century film *The Lion in Winter* she is portrayed as randy, immoral and emasculating. Matthew Paris claimed that her loveliness led to the 'ruin of nations', and Shakespeare presented her as 'the monstrous injurer of heaven and earth'. The reality of who Eleanor was is hard to pin down, despite the many sources we have. What follows is my best effort to piece together the chapters of her life and provide a portrait of her career and impact on French history – but, as we will see, there is still much room for interpretation.

The myth of Eleanor has – since the Middle Ages – superseded the real Eleanor. The truth is that this woman did exist, and she was formidable, powerful and had a profound impact on European history. But who she really was is harder to capture. The nuances of her life are shrouded in mystery.

Eleanor was born Aliénor – the eldest child of Aénor de Châtellerault and William X, Duke of Aquitaine – in c.1124. 'Alia Aenor' in Latin means 'another Aenor'. She had a younger sister, but her parents failed to have the son they needed to secure their dynasty and position. Aquitaine, a vast territory sprawling across Bordeaux and Poitiers and the western coast of France – the land to which Eleanor was heir – was the richest province in that country, and perhaps all of Europe. It was important not only for its size but also for its position in the trade of the valuable commodities of salt and wine, farmed variously from the region's wide Atlantic coasts and rolling vineyards.

Since the time of the Merovingians and Carolingians, control of France had centralised and fractured once again, into different duchies that were laws unto themselves, and often paid little heed to Capetian kings in Paris. The territory of Aquitaine was larger than the northern duchies of Normandy and Anjou combined, and far more significant than the French king's land surrounding the Île-de-France. The duchy was, in principle, held as a fiefdom from the King of France, the dukes' theoretical overlord. However, in practice the Capetian Kings of France had little power over the actions or wealth of the Dukes of

Aquitaine: they rarely even set foot in Aquitanian territory, let alone asserted control or feudal overlordship. The region had its own distinct language and culture, and its people had little love for the northern French.

The Dukes of Aquitaine – given their great wealth and distance from Paris – were the most independent of all the dukes of France. However, the Capetians desperately wanted control over Aquitaine – and in 1137 events took a turn that would allow them to seize the prize they so desperately wanted: Eleanor. Whoever married Eleanor would become the richest man in Europe, absorbing Aquitaine and all of its revenues into their coffers.

Eleanor's father, William X of Aquitaine, died unexpectedly on pilgrimage in 1137, leaving Eleanor and her younger sister Petronilla orphans, and in possession of all Aquitanian territory. Before her father's body was cold in the ground, the French king made his move, and in the blink of an eye Eleanor was betrothed at fourteen to the seventeen-year-old Dauphin of France, Louis VI's eldest son, another Louis. Marrying Eleanor to his son gave Louis VI the chance to bring the Dukes of Aquitaine to heel once and for all, and to break the power of the south – or so he thought. Within three months, the young pair were married in Bordeaux cathedral in south-west France. The Gothic towers that rise from the central square of the city today, carved in weather-beaten white stone, would not have been the ones Eleanor passed under on her way to join Louis at the altar; they are a more recent addition. But the Romanesque nave of the cathedral – the building's heart – is indeed the same structure that surrounded Eleanor as she made the wedding vows that set her on the path to becoming a queen.

The months following her father's death were a whirlwind of sudden changes for Eleanor. Within mere days of the ceremony in Bordeaux cathedral, Louis VI died suddenly of dysentery in Paris – meaning that Eleanor was now married no longer to the

Dauphin of France, but to the new King Louis VII. This in turn made Eleanor not only Duchess of Aquitaine, but Queen of France, and she could not stay in the south – her presence was required in Paris.

She had never left Aquitaine before, and the court of Paris that she travelled to was in many ways the polar opposite of the courts of Poitiers, Bordeaux and Toulouse. She and her sister travelled to Paris together, where they would have found the weather, architecture and – most importantly – the language quite different from what they were used to. Moreover, the position of Queen of France did not necessarily bring power or freedom. She was a child bride in an unfamiliar environment, and a colder and dirtier one than she was accustomed to at that.

Eleanor's main duty as a young queen was to become pregnant as quickly and as often as possible in order to give her husband many sons, an art she would perfect later in life, but which got off to a rocky start. While Eleanor was working on this, her sister was contriving to start a family of her own – and not in the best-advised way.

In 1142, Petronilla hurried into a hasty marriage with Louis VI's cousin, Raoul. He was handsome, and it was an advantageous love match that pleased everybody – except for one rather inconvenient person: Raoul's still-living and well-connected wife, Eleanor of Champagne.

As a favour to Raoul and his determined sister-in-law, Louis VII used his army of biddable bishops to push through a shoddy annulment, which, while a flagrant breach of canon law, was fairly common practice. However, it was not common practice to insult a woman so well connected to such a powerful ally as the Duke of Champagne – the jilted woman's furious brother. The Pope also weighed in, excommunicating both Raoul and Petronilla.

War broke out, and Louis sent soldiers into Champagne. The violence crescendoed in the village of Vitry-en-Perthois in 1142.

Here, petrified residents barricaded themselves in their church to avoid the marauding knights bearing the banner of the King of France. They were right to be afraid, but if they had hoped taking refuge in the church would spare their lives, their optimism was not rewarded. The king's men surrounded the church and set fire to it – burning and choking to death those inside, in a hellish inferno. Contemporary reports stated that thousands died, and while this number is unverifiable, the murder of these civilians sheltering in a church was an inexpungeable stain on the French monarchy, and Louis's and Eleanor's souls. The royal couple were censured across Europe, and it seems Louis at least was truly contrite.

Bernard of Clairvaux, among the most influential churchmen in Europe, led the voices condemning Louis and Eleanor. After publicly censuring them, he agreed to meet them in the Basilica of Saint-Denis on 11 June 1144, ostensibly to discuss a fitting penance. Eleanor also seized the opportunity to broach another matter with him – that of her fertility.

The couple had been trying to conceive for nearly seven years, and fingers were likely being pointed at Eleanor: it was typical in medieval marriages to blame the woman, and Eleanor knew that royal wives who failed to produce babies were often repudiated to make way for more fertile replacements. It seems she struck a deal with Bernard of Clairvaux: in exchange for him praying for her to be blessed with children, she would use her influence with Louis (who adored her) to bring his policies into line with Church teaching. Both parties made good on the pact: within a year Eleanor gave birth to a healthy daughter, and not long after, Bernard called on Louis to take the cross and go on crusade – a call the king heeded, and Eleanor also.

Their lives would never be the same again.

So what exactly was a crusade?

There were several such ventures in the Middle Ages, and Eleanor of Aquitaine's was the Second. The First Crusade took place from 1096 to 1099, in response to a call for help from the Byzantine emperor, who asked the European nobility to come to his aid, to recapture the Holy Land from Islamic rule. The First Crusade, against the odds – and at huge cost – was successful in recapturing Jerusalem and surrounding lands. But that was only the beginning, for in the following centuries more and more crusades were 'required' to protect the lands won in the First Crusade. In 1144 Edessa, a principal Christian stronghold in the south of modern-day Turkey, fell to Zengi, Atabeg of Mosul. This prompted a new call for aid from Europe. Despite the inherent dangers, crusading held many attractions for European royals and nobility: not only was it an opportunity for adventure, and perhaps a chance to gain wealth and new lands, but it was also a sure ticket to salvation. This was a deeply religious society, and the Pope baited the hook of the crusade with the promise of an 'indulgence' – an over-arching forgiveness of all sins, wiping the slate clean once and for all. For Louis and Eleanor, whose consciences bore the weight of the massacre of Vitry, this was perhaps an irresistible prospect.

There was no precedent for kings going on crusade, and there was certainly no precedent for queens taking the cross. Nevertheless, the royal couple did so together in Saint-Denis, and Eleanor, as Queen of France and Duchess of Aquitaine, became the first woman to lead vassals to Jerusalem on crusade.

Many have questioned Louis's decision to bring his wife on crusade, some suggesting that he didn't trust her to stay at home without him, others that he just loved her so much he could not bear to be parted, or simply that she was an important figurehead for the troops – particularly those from Aquitaine – and commanded the loyalty of her own vassals. Perhaps Eleanor herself did not want to be left behind on this adventure of a lifetime.

Their journey to the East marked a pivotal moment, intertwining personal ambitions, religious fervour and political consequences, setting the stage for both tragedy and triumph.

Eleanor's presence on the crusade would prove both blessing and curse, as she navigated the challenges of warfare, diplomacy and personal ambition in the unfamiliar terrain of the East.

Eleanor's journey to the Holy Land would test her faith, her marriage and her understanding of herself and the role she had been born to play. This transformative expedition also left an indelible mark on history, shaping the course of events in Europe and the Middle East for years to come.

Eleanor and Louis's army joined forces with that of the German emperor, Conrad III, who had also been seduced by the call to the East. Their armies travelled to Constantinople, where Eleanor was handsomely entertained at the Byzantine court – the wealth and splendour there surpassed anything she had glimpsed in France. From here, they continued their journey, planning to cross Anatolia and reach the fabled city of Antioch.

This city was rightly famed for its splendour, but Eleanor's journey to Antioch would be anything but simple. They set out from Constantinople riding a wave of naive optimism and cursed by poor information. The result was catastrophe.

Conrad III and the German army had departed before Louis and Eleanor. A little way into their ride, Eleanor found herself confronted by a bedraggled train of wounded and half-starved German soldiers – all that was left of the German army which had been decisively routed by the Seljuk Turks. Instead of heeding this very visual warning and turning back, Eleanor and Louis pressed on – a decision that would prove to be their ruin.

Instead, they continued onwards, and as they neared the area of the coast that today is home to the modern city of Antalya, they were forced to push over a mountain known as Mount Cadmus. It was on these slopes that Eleanor experienced her first true taste of warfare and found herself in very real danger. The French army was ambushed by Seljuk Turks.

For reasons of poor planning and over-confidence, the baggage train – in which the queen and leading clergy travelled – was left to cross the mountain without escort, with contingents of soldiers miles ahead and miles behind. The concealed Turks capitalised on the moment and attacked. Non-combatants like Eleanor – undoubtedly terrified – huddled for protection amid the clash of swords, scimitars and arrows sounding all around. Underneath her fear, she must have been furious that such a mistake had been made – how could they have been left vulnerable like this? The king's chaplain, Odo of Deuil, managed to escape the mêlée and alert the rear-guard who came careening to the rescue – but not before a substantial part of the army, equipment and gold had been lost, along with what was left of Eleanor's good humour. When Louis wrote home to recount the disaster, the list of noblemen killed was too lengthy to include.

The army limped on to Antioch, where Louis's crusade met further challenges, albeit of a very different nature, and pertaining directly to his wife. The city was ruled by Eleanor's uncle, Raymond of Poitiers, the brother of Eleanor's late father. He had travelled east some years ago and married a child bride, the eight-year-old Princess Constance of Antioch. Her mother, Alice, had been promptly exiled, and through his marriage Raymond had taken control of the principality. Relieved to be safe behind the high walls of Antioch, Eleanor tumbled into the arms of her uncle. They began to spend what was perceived as a suspicious amount of time together, and were observed to grow very close, very quickly. Rumours abounded, and it is impossible for historians to say definitively whether their love was filial or sexual. If the latter, it was scandalous indeed – not only as an extramarital affair on the part of the Queen of France, but it was incestuous to boot.

Whatever the exact nature of Raymond's feelings for his niece, he was anxious to win the favour of Louis, who despite the calamities of his journey still brought with him an attractive retinue of armed knights. Antioch was a frontier principality constantly fighting with its neighbours, and woefully short of soldiers and resources. Raymond welcomed them with the lavish hospitality of the Levant, combined with the familiar comforts of southern France.

Eleanor and Louis had marched east with their knights with the purpose of retaking the County of Edessa, but Raymond hoped to convince them to use their army to help him capture Aleppo instead – which posed a very real threat to Antioch's security.

While Eleanor, it seems, was easily convinced by Raymond's arguments for an assault on Aleppo, Louis was not persuaded. For all of Raymond's honeyed words, he remained focused on his initial target of Edessa and his spiritual goals in Jerusalem. To Raymond's dismay, Louis announced his intent to travel on to complete his pilgrimage to Jerusalem.

Together, Eleanor and Raymond began to plot. They had much to unite them: family and cultural ties, but now also a scathing contempt for Louis. Raymond also – arguably – had a stake in the duchy of Aquitaine, so they might also have had domestic matters to discuss. Perhaps this explains the many hours the uncle and niece spent shut away together.

The contemporary chronicler William of Tyre wrote:

> When Raymond found that he could not induce the king to join him, his attitude changed. Frustrated in his ambitious designs, he began to hate the king's ways; he openly plotted against him and took means to do him injury. He resolved also to deprive him of his wife, either by force or by secret intrigue. The queen readily assented to this design … Contrary to her royal dignity, she disregarded her marriage vows and was unfaithful to her husband.

Of course it is not certain what William meant by 'unfaithful'. Perhaps he meant disobedient or disloyal, but to modern readers it certainly reads like an accusation of sexual infidelity. Many other chronicles hint at this affair but few go so far as to explicitly accuse Eleanor of having sex with her uncle. When Louis remonstrated with Eleanor, she hinted that she might have found grounds to annul their marriage. Louis reacted by forcibly separating Eleanor from Raymond, dragging her from Antioch to Jerusalem under the cover of darkness. This action spoke volumes about the deteriorating state of their marriage and Louis's diminishing authority.

Despite the scandal at Antioch, Eleanor, Louis and their armies received a warm welcome when they finally reached Jerusalem. They were fêted at court and prayed at the tomb of Jesus Christ in the Church of the Holy Sepulchre – but Eleanor remained in disgrace. When a war council was convened, presided over by Queen Melisende of Jerusalem, Eleanor was excluded, despite her rank of Queen of France and Duchess of Aquitaine. In her absence, it was decided that the French troops would join the armies of Jerusalem to attack Damascus, a ridiculous idea as the city was so well defended. The plan ended in disaster, the armies were routed, and under the stress and shame of defeat Louis and Eleanor's marriage deteriorated still further. Tellingly, when finally the moment came to leave the Holy Land, Eleanor travelled home in a separate ship to Louis, refusing to be confined in the same small space as him for weeks, if not months, on end.

After the departure of the French crusaders, Antioch had indeed been forced to fight the armies of Aleppo, and without the French reinforcements they had begged for they found themselves outnumbered and were defeated. Raymond, who had led his knights himself, was slaughtered alongside his men. Eleanor learned this news on her arrival in Italy, where the estranged couple broke their journey. Grieving and furious – her marriage a wreck – Eleanor did not take a ship home immediately, but instead made a beeline for Rome, where she and Louis met the Pope to discuss the state of their marriage. It is likely that Eleanor was seeking the annulment she had threatened.

Whatever Eleanor's reasons, the Pope was outraged at the idea of an annulment and refused to grant it. Instead, he forced the couple to reconcile and took steps to renew their marriage contract. This was a humiliation for Eleanor, all the more so because the Pope insisted on supervising as they were literally put into a bed together to 'make up'.

Two years later, Eleanor gave birth to her and Louis's second and final child, a daughter, named Alix. The arrival of a daughter rather than the much sought-after son seemingly defeated Louis, as he clutched at straws to make the marriage work. Now in her late twenties, she had failed to produce a son for thirteen years. It was the final blow to their failing marriage, the breakdown of which had been widely observed and gossiped about across Europe. At this point the Pope could not resist granting Eleanor the divorce she craved, and he gave his blessing to a ruling by four bishops that the marriage should finally be dissolved on the basis of consanguinity. Eleanor lost custody of her daughters, but retained control of Aquitaine, something of a triumph.

Once the annulment had been hurried through the Church courts, and the lands of Aquitaine restored to her, the now thirty-year-old Eleanor was once again the richest and most desired bride in Europe, despite her poor track record in pregnancy. Not only did suitors vie for attention, but she dodged several kidnapping attempts. It would not be the first time a valuable heiress was abducted and raped into marriage, and Eleanor was the most valuable of all. Perhaps because she knew remaining single was no option, she married voluntarily more or less straight away. Her bridegroom of choice? The then nineteen-year-old Henry Plantagenet, Count of Anjou and heir to the throne of England. She wedded him in a clandestine ceremony in the cathedral of Poitiers in 1152. With this move, she shed her title of Queen of

France, burned all remaining bridges with Louis, and started on her path to become Queen of England – and transfer all of Aquitaine to the English Crown. She could have given no greater insult to Louis. She assumed the throne of England, alongside her husband, in 1154.

Her career as Queen of England would continue to be scandalous and glorious in equal measure, and she quickly disproved rumours of infertility. Maybe the greatest slap she delivered to Louis's face was that after divorcing him, she bore Henry eight children, including five sons, four of whom would grow up to rattle France's gates.

For all this, her marriage with Henry was not smooth sailing. The couple spent huge amounts of time apart, and Henry was repeatedly unfaithful to his wife with several well-known mistresses celebrated for their beauty, which led to major rifts. Eleanor was also politically ambitious, and often plotted with her sons against their father. She is credited with a large role in the significant revolt of 1173–4, in which she supported her sons Henry, Richard and Geoffrey in open rebellion against their father. Henry brokered peace with his sons, but captured and imprisoned Eleanor: she had become so dangerous a rival to him that he could not suffer her freedom. She was held under various forms of house arrest until her husband's death in 1189, although they did sometimes celebrate important occasions together.

Following Henry's death, Eleanor's favourite son Richard ascended the English throne. In practice, however, he spent little time in England, concentrating instead on his French lands and joining the Third Crusade. This crusade was launched in response to the loss of Jerusalem to Saladin in 1187. Eleanor ruled England as regent in his absence, and continued to exert significant influence over the politics of France. Eventually she retired to the Royal Abbey of Fontevraud, where she would eventually be entombed alongside her second husband. Before long, Coeur de Lion would join his parents too. The graves of these three rulers lay quiet for centuries before being destroyed in the French Revolution. However, their painted effigies were salvaged, and visitors to the Loire Valley today can stay in the Abbey of Fontevraud, and look upon the sleeping face of Queen Eleanor.

Eleanor's marriage to Henry was a lucrative political union that intensified the existing rivalry between the French and English Crowns, because it had consolidated the greatest rivals to the Capetians into one unit, comprising the English, the Angevins and the Aquitanians. This rivalry between the newly expanded English Crown and the newly hobbled French Crown would shape much of the history of both developing nations for several centuries.

Their marriage further complicated the feudal relationships in France, as Henry II, a vassal of the French king as Duke of Normandy and Aquitaine, was also a powerful monarch in his own right. No longer could he be considered – even officially speaking – a subordinate to the French king. Louis VII faced a formidable adversary in Henry II, whose territories in France often rivalled or surpassed those of the French Crown, and his legacy was continued by his fierce son Richard, Coeur de Lion.

Moreover, the fertility of Eleanor and Henry's marriage also set the stage for further strife down the generations. Eleanor had so many healthy children, who married far and wide into the dynasties and duchies of Europe, that the stage was set for the Hundred Years' War (1337–1453) – a bitter series of conflicts with the possession of Aquitaine at their centre.

As the Hundred Years' War raged, France found itself in a desperate struggle to reclaim its territories and assert its sovereignty. It was into this tumultuous period that a young peasant girl stepped, speaking of visions that would set France on fire, and inspire them to drive the English from French lands once and for all. She was known at the time as the Maid of Orléans, but is better known to English readers as Joan of Arc. This woman, the subject of chapter 5, would become one of the most enduring and iconic figures of French history.

Illustration from medieval manuscript BL Royal 19, entitled 'The Temptation of Lechery', *c.* thirteenth to fourteenth century.

# 3

# Béatrice de Planisolles

## c.1274–c.1322

The year is 1321, and a woman in her late forties stumbles out of an iron gate and into the sunlight in the turreted city of Carcassonne. She has been held in the infamous prison known as 'La Mur' ('The Wall'), built into the city's defensive walls, where she has languished for a little over a year. It is a cold day, although the sun is bright, and she pulls her cape around her for warmth. On the back is stitched a rough-cut, bright yellow cross. It is vibrant, eye-catching, among the sea of brown and grey worn by the peasants milling around. She pushes forward, beginning to attract stares, which grow more intense by the minute, and soon turn to jeers and heckling. A man shouts '*Hérétique!*' and spits on her. With no time to lose, she hurries out of the city, heading for the safety of the mountains. She is lucky to have escaped death but has been sentenced to wear this cross for all of her life.

A little more than a year earlier, Béatrice de Planisolles had been apprehended on the run from the inquisition, in the company of a thirty-year-old priest, who was also her lover. Hauled in for questioning, her possessions ransacked, Béatrice was accused of heresy.

In among her personal effects, which included a rather witchy array of objects, her inquisitors found some morsels of dried bread. These, they believed, were definitive proof of her involvement with the subversive Cathar sect: bread used in the clandestine ritual of *consolamentum*. On the back of this discovery she was subjected to round after round of questioning from perhaps the most meticulous inquisitor of the Middle Ages, Jacques Fournier. Over the course of their interviews, Béatrice's life story unfolded, and the inquisitors wrote it down, unvarnished, unornamented, true. In so doing, and quite unwittingly, these men tasked with rooting out heresy in the Languedoc created one of the most remarkable documents of the Middle Ages. It is now carefully preserved in the Vatican Archive.

Béatrice's testimony, that of an illiterate woman from the Ariège region of southern France, gives us unique insight into the life, beliefs, love affairs and scandals of an ordinary woman in a remote community of medieval France. More than that, it takes us to the heart of one of the most vicious religious campaigns in French history: the Church's opposition to the Cathar heresy.

Béatrice's story is set against the backdrop of the Pyrenees and the Languedoc region of France. Scourged by icy winters and blistering summers, the mountainous region now attracts visitors for hiking, skiing and hearty mountain cuisine. Before ski lifts and snowmobiles, the winter trudges between the villages were not for the fainthearted. Perhaps it is for this reason that the mountain village of Montaillou resisted the fire of Europe's first inquisition for so long.

Like Eleanor of Aquitaine, Béatrice speaks Occitan rather than Middle French. She actually would have called herself Beatriz de Planisola. Toulouse would have been Tolosa; Carcassonne, Caracasonna. The language is closer in sound to Spanish than French. She and her inquisitor, an ambitious priest named Jacques Fournier, have Occitan as a common language – he is also a local boy, from the village of Saverdun – and while their interviews were recorded in Latin by Fournier's amanuenses, the pair would have conversed in their shared mother tongue. Occitan now exists only as a vanishing dialect, in certain corners of southern France. Efforts have been made to protect it, but now only the very old and very remote use it, and more often than not it is used only in weaving odd phrases and vocabulary into sentences in rough-accented French. The region has a long history of independence from northern France. It has changed hands over the centuries – Eleanor of Aquitaine famously bringing her part of the region into the possession of the Kings of England, as we saw in chapter 2. But Eleanor's vast territory did not extend so far as Béatrice's home. Béatrice is, theoretically, under the jurisdiction of the Counts of Toulouse, who often positioned themselves as rivals to the Kings of France. When Béatrice lived, the south had its own rulers, its own laws and its own ways. Both the Pope and the King of France were on a mission to change this.

Jacques Fournier is after Béatrice because he believes her to be one of the last Cathars – the rebel religious minority that (in his view) has plagued south-west France for over a century. The Cathars, or *Bons Chrétiens* ('Good Christians'), as they called themselves, were a breakaway sect of Christianity with roots in Gnosticism, Manichaeism and Bogomilism, teachings that spread on the tongues of travellers from Eastern Europe and the Middle East. They believed in a dualist world, which, simply put, meant they believed that God and the Devil were locked in an eternal struggle – the struggle between light and darkness. Strict followers of Cathar doctrine believed the physical world and physical pleasures were evil, and lived an ascetic lifestyle.

However, perhaps their most 'progressive' belief was that the soul was genderless, incarcerated in the human body. While misogyny was still rife among the Cathars – they could not completely dismantle the framework of feudal medieval society – they did believe in something close to equality between men and women in spiritual matters. They were the first Christian sect in Europe to allow women to become priests. However, they didn't call them priests – they called them '*Parfaits*' ('Perfects').

There were two types of Cathars, the Parfaits and the Credentes: those who lived the perfect life, and those who believed. The difference between them centred on the ritual of the *consolamentum*. Most Cathars were Credentes – indeed it would not have been viable to have a society of Parfaits as they abstained from sex – and would receive the *consolamentum* only on their death beds, after which many would abstain from food and water as a means of purification. Those who undertook the ritual earlier in life would afterwards abjure sex and meat, in theory at least.

The Cathars presented a challenge to the authority of the Catholic Church, and undermined several of its core teachings, not least of which was the belief in the one true God. The Cathars held a 'dualist' view and saw the Devil as an entity equally powerful to the Lord. They also ignored the rule that kept women out of the priesthood. There were many female Parfaits. Fear of challenges to papal authority, and fury at Count Raymond of Toulouse tolerating Cathars in his lands were motivating factors in the launch of the Albigensian Crusade, the religious war that would scourge the Languedoc. It was so named for the city of Albi, which was a Cathar stronghold in the region.

The crusade tore apart southern France. The Languedoc – called thus because of the different language used there, which used '*occ*' for yes instead of '*oïl*', which has eroded to '*oui*' in modern French – was a largely independent region. It had its own language and customs, and the dukes of this region often commanded more real clout than the King of France, although their power waxed and waned. This threatened not only the king in Paris, but also the Pope in Rome. It was for this reason, as much as religion, that the spirit of the south had to be broken. It was for that reason, as much as for concern over doctrinal difference, that they dispatched Simon de Montfort to wipe out the heresy and burn the heretics.

This campaign raged for twenty years, gave rise to the string of Cathar castles across the Pyrenees, and resulted in some of the most infamous massacres of civilians of the Middle Ages. When the armies of the French king burned their way through Béziers in 1209, the soldiers asked their cardinal how to tell the heretics from the innocent. The Pope's representative, Arnaud Amalric, also military leader of the expedition, replied: *'Caedite eos. Novit enim Dominus qui sunt eius'* ('Kill them all. God will know his own'). In Arnaud's own letter to Pope Innocent III describing the atrocity, he wrote: 'within the space of two or three hours they crossed the ditches and the walls and Béziers was taken. Our men spared no one, irrespective of rank, sex or age, and put to the sword almost 20,000 people. After this great slaughter, the whole city was despoiled and burnt.'

And the massacre at Béziers was just one small part of the horrors to be visited upon the resisting Cathars. The crusade officially 'ended' in 1229 when Count Raymond of Toulouse signed the Treaty of Paris, in which he submitted to King Louis's authority and, among other things, gave Louis and the Catholic Church carte blanche in their inquisition to find heretics. It was partly as a result of this treaty that, nearly a century later, Béatrice would find herself obliged to submit to questioning. Interestingly, this treaty was brokered by Queen Blanche – rather than King Louis IX, who was then a minor and still under the regency of his mother. Nevertheless, despite this official surrender of the south, Catharism continued in persecuted pockets across the Languedoc. The believers made a last stand at Montségur. Here, in this hilltop fortress in the low Pyrenees, they suffered their final defeat. Those who would not recant their beliefs were burned at the stake. Dressed in white, they marched singing into the flames, which consumed them.

The mass burning was followed by a series of interrogations that became the first inquisition of Europe. Centuries before the Spanish inquisition attempted to root out heretics in Spain, a similar series of torture-facilitated interviews were conducted in south-west France on the orders of Pope Innocent. This should have been the end of Catharism in the Languedoc. But it wasn't. The movement persisted, but in the shadows.

Béatrice de Planisolles was born in c.1274, thirty years after the defeat at Montségur. Believers survived. The Cathar movement went underground in France, but a network of secret sympathisers and believers kept the old ways alive, smuggling hunted Cathars to Cathar communities in Spain and Italy. In the subsequent decades, they came out of hiding and began to trickle back to France. Among those who returned were members of Béatrice's family. Her father was a known Cathar, and the region in which she was born and spent the first part of her married life was studded with pockets of the heresy.

It isn't known for certain, but all the evidence points to Béatrice's birthplace being the village of Caussou. At the age of seventeen, she was married to Bérenger de Roquefort, lord of the neighbouring village of Montaillou, a remote village steeped in Catharism. Through this marriage she became the chatelaine of Montaillou. She lived in the hilltop château above the rest of the village – but nevertheless her life became closely intertwined with those of the other residents of Montaillou. The village, due to its isolated nature and a somewhat corrupted Cathar influence, had an idiosyncratic set of customs and social hierarchies.

Flash forward twenty-nine years, and Béatrice, forty-six, a grandmother, is sitting in Jacques Fournier's chambers, explaining the bizarre contents of her handbag.

'Those belonged to my grandsons,' she tells him, indicating the dried umbilical cords. 'I kept them because a Jewish woman that I met told me that if I had them with me, I would never lose a lawsuit. But I haven't had a lawsuit brought against me yet, so I haven't been able to see if she was right.'

'Those,' she says, gesturing to the bloody rags, 'are soaked with my daughter Philippa's menstrual blood – from her first period. I was told that if I made a drink for my son-in-law with this blood, then he would never be unfaithful to her. So I saved it.'

## BÉATRICE DE PLANISOLLES

Béatrice's love life was tumultuous, marred by rape, attempted rape, seduction, forced marriage, adultery and elopement. Perhaps she thought her efforts could create a better or simpler future for Philippa. During her interrogation, Béatrice lists the contents of her bag in great detail but deliberately skips over the pieces of old bread. Jacques Fournier notices the omission without surprise. Both of them know what the bread represents: proof of her identity as a Cathar. These sacred remnants of the *consolamentum* are enough to condemn her to the stake.

However, it is Béatrice's connection to Montaillou, more than her affair with a much younger priest or her interest in mystical objects, that has brought her to Fournier's interrogation chair.

Her seven-year marriage to the much older Bérenger resulted in at least two sons and three daughters, making it a practical success. Yet it was far from a love match, and her marriage to the village's most powerful man offered little protection from the unwanted advances of others.

Montaillou was controlled not by Bérenger, but in fact by the Clergue family. It might amuse readers to know that on a research trip to Montaillou I discovered from a printed notice on the door of the town hall that the mayor of Montaillou is still a Monsieur Clergue. Eight centuries later, much has changed in the Languedoc – Jacques Fournier was triumphant in his inquisition – but the Clergues are still running Montaillou. In the thirteenth century, the Clergues became central figures in the life of Béatrice de Planisolles.

Following her marriage, Béatrice's daily life would follow the pattern of any minor noblewoman in Ariège. She organises her household, raises her children, and goes to church. She has a taste for nice clothes, dances at weddings and feast days, and goes for walks. Her husband travels in the course of his duties as chatelain and while he is away, she is protected and minded by their steward, Raymond Roussel. But Béatrice is a beautiful woman, and from a famous Cathar family, and neither of these facts has escaped the notice of Raymond, a convicted Cathar himself. He and Béatrice, in the limited confines of the village, strike up an intimate friendship. They dine tête-à-tête and discuss spiritual matters. Raymond taps into Béatrice's interest in the Cathar movement, which the absent Bérenger had rejected, and uses her sympathy for this belief system to foster intimacy with his master's wife. Even before Béatrice came to Montaillou he had been sentenced in a religious court to wear a yellow cross – the mark of a heretic.

During one of Bérenger's absences, he begins to make advances, both romantically and spiritually, despite the fact that twenty-year-old Béatrice is now carrying her third child. He urges her to abandon her family and travel with him to join a group of Cathars across the mountains. She firmly declines, citing her responsibilities to her sons and the impropriety of leaving with him as a married woman. All her objections are practical rather than spiritual. She seems tempted by the idea, wistful almost, to join the 'Good Christians' on the other side of the mountains.

Despite Béatrice's rejection, the friendship continues – and for Béatrice it is not romantic. For Raymond, however, it seems the true goal has never been saving Béatrice's soul – but rather having sex with her. Frustrated that she won't elope with him, and perhaps misreading her rejections as coyness, he hides under her bed. He waits until she is asleep – then climbs in beside her and tries to rape her. Awaking, she is first confused, then outraged. She describes the incident to Fournier in her own words:

> When I exclaimed 'What does this mean?' he urged me to be quiet. To this I replied, 'How now, you peasant, shall I keep quiet then!' and started to scream and call my maid servants.

This prompts Raymond to flee back to his quarters. In the morning Béatrice admonishes him. She tells him she won't escalate things for fear of being implicated herself in the almost-adultery – but warns him never to touch her again.

Béatrice would experience further sexual assaults from other villagers of Montaillou. In the Middle Ages, sexual assault, both within marriage and without, was a miserable fact of women's lives: queens, noblewomen and peasants were all alike in this. While her husband was still alive, Béatrice would be raped by one of the Clergues, a man nicknamed Pathau. The crime was never reported, or prosecuted, perhaps due to either Bérenger's age or Béatrice's trauma, but Béatrice revealed it to Fournier under questioning. A strange aspect of the story is that, after Bérenger's death in 1298, Béatrice would begin a consensual relationship with Pathau – and it was well known in the village that he kept her as his mistress. To what extent the relationship was truly something Béatrice wanted is hard to glean; as a widow she was in a vulnerable position and may simply have taken the view that it was better to have Pathau's protection, such as it was.

The story takes a stranger turn still on a spring day in 1299 when Béatrice attends the local church to make confession. The priest is Pathau's cousin, Pierre Clergue, a powerful figure in the village. Just as Béatrice is about to confess her sins, up by the altar in the Church of Notre-Dame-de-Carnesses, Pierre lunges forward and takes her in his arms. He kisses her, and tells her how attractive he finds her, and that he wants her. Shocked and mystified, Béatrice leaves quickly, without responding to his proposition, or indeed making confession.

Throughout the spring Béatrice is consistently pursued by Pierre, as he attempts to convince her to leave his cousin for him. He even suggests that they share her. Béatrice rejects this proposition and continues to argue with Pierre that she cannot sleep with him because having sex with a priest is sacrilegious – an objection he smoothly talks her out of, citing some slightly butchered Cathar doctrine. Eventually, she capitulates – ending her relationship with Pathau and taking up with Pierre. They embark on a passionate two-year affair, marked by not only an active sex life but also real intimacy and secret heretical discussions. The affair is filled with tender moments, philosophical discussions and the intricacies of medieval life, including unconventional methods of contraception. When Béatrice asks if she can keep their contraception apparatus between trysts, Pierre declines, pointing out he doesn't want her to use it with other men. He wants to control her sexuality. But for all this, and despite the fact that Clergue is clearly a serial sexual predator, there are tender moments in the relationship. In her starkly frank testimony to Fournier, Béatrice describes combing the lice from Pierre's hair as he sits in a bathtub by a window in her house. She also describes how, on Christmas Eve, he made a bed for them in the church – and they made love there on one of the holiest days of the year.

Eventually she leaves Pierre and remarries; he bounces back, taking the virginity of his teenage niece and having an affair with her, and many other local women. But he sometimes thinks of Béatrice, and does visit her and send her presents, including a fine blouse in the Barcelona style. On one memorable occasion he persuades her to have sex with him in the basement of her marital home, while her long-suffering maidservant stands in the doorway to keep watch.

Béatrice was key to Fournier's project. His main target was not Béatrice herself, but Pierre Clergue, and the other powerful men of Montaillou. Following her eight interrogations, Béatrice would be imprisoned in the infamous Le Mur prison of Carcassonne, where her erstwhile lover Pierre was also incarcerated, as was Barthelemy, her new lover. After one year, however, Béatrice and Barthelemy were both released. Barthelemy escaped further punishment, but Béatrice was sentenced to wear large yellow crosses stitched to her clothes for the rest of her days, branding her a heretic. Pierre Clergue would die in prison. After her release, Béatrice and Barthelemy went their separate ways: both were likely traumatised by their experiences of imprisonment and the inquisition, and sought out separate, quiet lives in Ariège. Béatrice likely returned to live with her daughters – and we can only guess how she filled the latter part of her life.

Had Béatrice lived anywhere else, and slept with any other priest, the intricacies and intrigues of her life would likely have been lost forever to modern historians and readers. But her marriage to Bérenger of Roquefort, who brought her to Montaillou, brought her into the heart of the Cathar heresy and, many years later, would attract the notice of the young and ambitious Jacques Fournier. He was a career Catholic, and most definitely the one to watch in inquisition circles. By the age of thirty-two he was Bishop of Pamiers, and the driving force behind the most fastidious inquisition in European history. By fifty, he was Pope. At the time of his election, the pontiffs sat in Avignon rather than the Vatican – and while the new Pope Benedict XII was happy to continue this tradition (in fact, it was a condition of his election), he insisted on a newer and grander papal residence. It was this man who began the construction of the Palais des Papes which dominates the city of Avignon today. His enduring legacy is one of fastidiousness and attention to detail, but not brutality. For a medieval religious inquisitor, he slaughtered remarkably few people.

Where Béatrice differs from the other heretical women of her day is that she opened her heart with disarming frankness to Jacques Fournier. Her humanity was her defence. She was unabashed and unashamed. She did not cry or make excuses. Nor did she make a political stand or cling like a martyr to her religious convictions. She simply told the story of her life and made it quite clear that she did not want to die for her beliefs. This was a woman who wanted to live, and not just live, but thrive. Her remarkable testimony detailed the abuses and exploitation she suffered at the hands of powerful men, her love for her children and her eventual embrace of sexual freedom. It opens a window onto the distinctly human thoughts and feelings of a medieval woman with little power, but a curious brain and a good deal of courage. Above all, the character of Béatrice that emerges from these records is resilient, impulsive and charismatic. It is a wonder that her words have survived this long, safe in the vaults of the Vatican Archive.

Christine de Pizan in her study with her dog. From 'The Queen's Manuscript', fifteenth century.

# 4

# Christine de Pizan

## September 1364–c.1431

'Why on earth [is it] that so many men, both clerks and others, have said and continue to say and write such awful, damning things about women?'
From *Le Livre de la Cité des Dames* by Christine de Pizan

Christine de Pizan was France's Renaissance woman. The first woman ever to have made a living writing – and primarily writing about and defending women – she has always been an idol of mine. Tenacious, talented and gifted with a euphonic turn of phrase, Christine had a profound impact on literary culture in France, but also on the image of women during the French Renaissance. She pushed boundaries, broke rules, spoke her mind – and did it in such a way that she made her radical ideas palatable to a conservative and male-dominated court. She used her pen to escape poverty, and to secure her own freedom. A trailblazer for women's writing, and female entrepreneurship, she was one of the figures who rose in gold from the banks of the Seine during the opening ceremony of the 2024 Paris Olympics, a heroine of France, wearing one of her iconic two-pronged headdresses.

In the mid-fourteenth century, Venice was a thriving maritime republic, several weeks' ride from Paris. The ideas that would underpin the Renaissance were beginning to stir in educated minds. Petrarch – commonly hailed as the father of humanism, which in turn gave rise to the Renaissance – had settled amid the winding waterways of Venice in 1362, and his ideas and scholarship were already permeating Europe. St Mark's Square bustled with people from every corner of the world, under the watchful gaze of the four horses of the *quadriga* and other treasures looted from Constantinople, along with the ideas and learning of the Greek court.

One day in 1364, a man of middle age hurried through the narrow, labyrinthine streets, over bridges and along the canals. He was rushing home to attend the birth of his child. Perhaps he clutched astrological charts in one hand, and a medical bag in the other. The man was a doctor, and at home in their bed his wife was struggling to bring a daughter into the world, a baby girl born under auspicious stars. The doctor, her father, baptised her Christina.

The proud parents, Tommaso di Pizzano and his wife, were comfortable but not wealthy, and most of their social status hinged on Tommaso's reputation and influential network of connections, rather than coffers of gold or vast properties. Tommaso lived by his wits, and was revered for his knowledge and wisdom as a man of learning. He valued education highly, and despite convention Tommaso would see to it that his daughter was educated. He himself had received a world-class education at the University of Bologna, Europe's oldest university, studying medicine, law, astrology and theology, and had risen to the position of professor himself at that same institution from 1344 to 1356, before moving to Venice to serve the Republic.

Shortly after Christina's birth, Tommaso received an invitation he found hard to refuse, from the King of France no less. This was not the first time royalty had sought out his assistance, but it was the first time he decided to accept. Charles V of France was in the market for a new adviser – on matters both medical and celestial – and invited the learned man to come and assist him at the court of France. He had received an offer as well from the King of Hungary, but the glittering reputation of the French court, and the prestige of the University of Paris, the one institution in Europe that could compete with the University of Bologna, won him over. Indeed, Christina herself would later refer to Paris as the 'second Athens'. More than this, Charles V had a reputation for genuine intellectual curiosity, and was investing heavily in the arts and sciences, developing one of the greatest libraries in Europe, housed in the Louvre Palace. He was attaching real, royal prestige to learning and to writing, and was taking care to establish French as a language of scholarship. This was an ambitious king, and one whom it might be a pleasure to serve. With this in mind, Tommaso set off for Paris for a trial year.

Impressed by the intellectual offerings of the French court, Tommaso – now Thomas – decided to stay. He sent for Christina, her mother and her siblings, and they followed their father to Paris, where they were installed at the French court. This was a journey that would change her life. She grew up amid the luxury of the court of Valois (the house that had succeeded the Capetians), immersed in the treasures of the growing royal library. She would never see her native Italy again, and her name changed permanently to Christine: thoroughly Frenchified, she became staunchly loyal to her adopted country and the Valois monarchs.

In 1368, the year of Christine's arrival, Paris – a bustling city of perhaps 150,000 people – was smarting from recent traumas and bore many scars. The Black Death had swept across Europe not long before in 1348, wiping out one-third of the city's inhabitants. The Hundred Years' War, the generational conflict between England and France that saw Eleanor of Aquitaine's descendants vying ruthlessly for French territories, had been raging for some decades too. Nevertheless, when the family arrived, the capital was enjoying an uncharacteristic period of calm under the young King Charles V, a man in his prime with a thirst for knowledge that would eventually earn him the epithet '*le Sage*' ('the Wise'). Like Venice, the city was beginning to embrace a new way of seeing the world, new ways of thinking, and new respect for literature and scholarship.

Charles V's commitment to learning extended beyond simply hiring erudite advisers, and indeed he invested heavily in the library of the Louvre and other cultural projects. This was the beginning of the Renaissance in France as well.

The lasting legacy of the French Renaissance is profound. It transformed French society, leading to advancements in art, architecture, literature and science. The Renaissance ideals of humanism also had a lasting impact on education and intellectual life, laying the foundations for the Enlightenment in the eighteenth century. The emphasis on individual potential and the value of secular knowledge that emerged during the Renaissance continued to influence Western thought for centuries, shaping modern Western culture and ideas about human rights, democracy and the value of education.

Thomas was much appreciated by Charles V, who always kept him close, eager for medical, astrological, political and legal advice. But when the king died in 1380, his son was less enthusiastic. Charles VI was a problematic monarch, without his father's thirst for intellectual advancement, and with many burdens of his own. He was known as Charles le Fou, or Charles the Mad, and suffered bouts of true insanity, including one instance when he believed himself to be made of glass, and was anxious that he might shatter. He went so far as to have iron rods sewn into his clothes to prevent himself from breaking, and padded the seat of his trousers in case he sat down too hard and shattered himself. That said, these bouts of delirium were not recorded in the first decade of his reign. As a young king, he kept on the ageing Thomas, perhaps out of nostalgia or loyalty to his father, but he did not regard him as indispensable. In keeping with his decrease in status and influence, Thomas's income was reduced. He died less than a decade after his patron, and left his wife burdened with debt.

Readers might wonder why I have written so much of Thomas in a book meant to be about women, but the truth is that, as much as bad men hold women back, good men push them forward. Christine's father pushed her forward; he equipped her with the tools she would need to earn her own living from her mind and from her pen, the greatest gift he was able to give her. She learned to think, to write, to study, to argue at her father's knee, and he was one of the most eminent scholars in Europe. He must also have had progressive ideas about women's education, for he let his daughter learn. More than that, he taught her.

Her love and respect for him and his mind infused her writing. She wrote that he was celebrated everywhere as a scholar, and that she was able to gather 'crumbs falling from the high table'.

When Thomas died, Christine was already a young adult, already a wife, and already a mother. At age fifteen she had been married to a secretary of the French court, Étienne du Castel. The marriage had taken place in 1380, the same year that Charles the Wise died. Reports indicate the marriage was happy – Christine herself singing her husband's praises in her written work. Étienne was older than his teenage bride, but not by much, in his mid-twenties when he married her. She would later describe him as 'handsome', 'faithful' and 'pleasing'. Perhaps Étienne, educated himself, supported his young wife's education and burgeoning literary talent, and they had three children together, one of whom would also forge a career as a writer. But the marriage was not destined to last long. After eleven years, Étienne died of disease while away from home, just a year after her father. The two losses, coming in such quick succession, hit her hard.

These were the trials that unexpectedly set Christine on the path to greatness. This suffering caused her to pick up her quill. She used her writing – something Étienne had clearly encouraged during their marriage – as a way of mourning his loss and processing her grief. In one of her poems, she alluded to the pain and thoughts of self-destruction his death caused her:

> I can never forget this great,
> incomparable suffering which brings my
> heart to such torment, which puts into my
> head such grievous despair, which
> counsels me to kill myself and break my
> heart.[2]

This grief was multifaceted – not only did she miss her partner, but Étienne's death also left her vulnerable: suddenly she found herself alone, with a family to feed, and had no desire to marry again. Hardship can sometimes be the making of people, and so it was for Christine. Now with no father, no husband, and with her brothers returned to Italy, Christine was alone with a young family and a dependent mother in France. For all that her income and status plummeted, Christine was not destitute. She inherited property and was secure enough that she did not have to make a hasty remarriage to the most economically viable option, as was often the case for young widows. With no husband or father, Christine was unprotected. But she also became her own mistress for the first time in her life. She wanted to keep things that way, and to try to make her own living by writing.

This was a courageous goal. No secular woman had ever made a living this way before. Christine was breaking fresh ground in patriarchal and oppressive medieval society. An educated woman, writing for pay, was a new concept, and potentially a threatening one. That said, she was already well integrated and well known at the court, and she played her hand well. She courted aristocratic patrons to protect, fund and legitimise her work, and she did not

---

[2] *The Selected Writings of Christine de Pizan: Norton Critical Edition* (New York: W.W. Norton, 1997), 17, ll.7–12.

start her career with controversial projects. Moreover, her loyalty to the Crown was evident throughout her work, and particularly to the powerful women of the court. She celebrated the former Queen Consort and then Queen Mother Blanche of Castile in her works, and dedicated many of them to the new French Queen Isabeau, wife of Charles VI.

One of Christine's most revealing works is the autobiographical *Le Livre de l'Advision Cristine* (*The Book of Christine's Vision*), written in 1405. She offers analyses of the causes of the civil conflicts embroiling her adopted country in that year. She calls for peace and resolution with a prophet's voice. This work, in addition to offering insights into the Hundred Years' War – for that is what these conflicts would become – also reflects poignantly on the hardships faced by women in medieval society, in particular widows. This poem takes her back to her grief and rudderlessness after the death of her husband.

In another poem she describes a female character, thrown into extremities at sea in a captain-less boat, picked up by fate, manipulated and 'palpitated', and eventually remade as a man. This serves as an allegory for her transformation into the breadwinner for her family. Then – in her new male form – she sets to work. She bails out the water flooding the craft, she plugs the holes, mends the damage and takes the tiller, steering herself to safety.

The scars her widowhood left on her were deep and lasting – this work was published nearly twenty years after Étienne's death. Prior to establishing herself as an author, it is likely Christine worked as a copyist for some years to make ends meet, spending her days in the proliferating manuscript workshops of Paris. But from 1399 she began to draft original works. She started with lyric poetry, designed to appeal to royal princes and attract patronage.

Nine years after the death of Étienne, Christine published her first complete work, and after that there was no stopping her. She wrote both poetry and prose, mostly in the French vernacular – progressive in itself, as most court writers had hitherto favoured Latin. More than simply rebelling with her choice of language, she went a step further and challenged more established writers, established social practices, misogynistic portrayals of women and much more. She was engaged in the political life of her day. She didn't write pretty ditties and banal romances but shrewd and thought-provoking texts, in elegant style. Her writing glittered.

Christine was not only a talented wordsmith, but an artist, producer and businesswoman all at once. Then, as now, simply writing a good book is not enough to earn a living as a writer. Christine had to hustle. She oversaw every step of the production process, building relationships with female artists and book binders, and many of the manuscripts were written in her hand – no untidy twenty-first-century scrawl but works of painstaking calligraphy and illumination. More than this, she worked with other professional women too. In one of her most popular works, she waxed lyrical about the talents of a certain Anastasia, who painted her illuminations for her. Christine wrote:

> I know a woman today, named Anastasia, who is so learned and skilled in painting manuscript borders and miniature backgrounds that one cannot find an artisan in all the city of Paris – where the best in the world are found – who can surpass her, nor who can paint flowers and details as delicately as she does, nor whose work is more highly esteemed, no matter how rich or precious the book is. People cannot stop talking about her. And I know this from experience, for she has executed several things for me, which stand out among the ornamental borders of the great masters.

Not only does this give lasting praise and acknowledgement to Anastasia herself, but it also sheds light on the roles played by women in book making and art at this time, which have otherwise slipped from the historical record.

Together, Christine and Anastasia produced beautiful manuscripts, many of which included illustrations of Christine herself, hard at work at her writing table. Gorgeous flowers in gold leaf and lapis spiral down the edges of the pages and illuminate Christine's words. The texts are luxurious, complex, multifaceted and rich. No wonder the leading aristocrats of the court wished to collect them, and be associated with such art.

Spurred on by successes, she turned her hand to complex works, including *Le Livre de la Mutation de Fortune* (*The Book of the Mutability of Fortune*) – a more contemplative work reflecting on the role Fortune played in the lives of men and women, with the power to raise them up and break them. Before long, she was receiving commissions, the most significant of which was perhaps a biography of Charles the Wise, commissioned for his brother, the Duke of Burgundy. As her reputation grew, she began to attract patrons who sponsored her. There was prestige in being associated with the growing literary movement at the French court, propelled by Charles the Wise's ambitious library project. There were periods of war and periods of peace during her career, so much so that she was even patronised by the English Earl of Salisbury, who took an early interest in her work, and offered her son a position in his household. Aristocratic patronage came in many forms. It could be hard cash, but it could also be as simple as lodging offered in a great house, with food and expenses provided, in exchange for the gift of a prestigious book.

One of the best-known texts circulating in France in the fourteenth century was a poem entitled *Le Roman de la Rose* (*The Romance of the Rose*) by Guillaume de Lorris and later extensively added to by Jean de Meun. This allegorical dream vision presented women in a deeply misogynistic light, chiefly as seductresses and schemers. This text was hugely popular, with over a hundred copies discovered in France, many sumptuously illustrated – demonstrating the reach and importance of this work. One hundred may seem like a very small 'print run' by today's standards, but in a time when every book was created by hand with painstakingly crafted letters and illustrations scratched onto vellum with quill and ink and adorned with precious gold leaf and pigment paints, one hundred copies was a significant literary footprint.

Christine took it upon herself to set the record straight. In 1402 she penned *Le Dit de la Rose* (*The Tale of the Rose*) as an acid-tongued response to the slanders levelled against her gender in de Meun's work – a decision Simone de Beauvoir would later herald as the first time a woman took up her pen to defend her sex. In contrast, Christine's contemporary at the French court, court secretary Jean de Montreuil, published praise of *Le Roman de la Rose*, and subsequently the pair became locked in a heated debate, resulting in Christine publishing *La Querelle du Roman de la Rose* (*The Quarrel of the Romance of the Rose*). This was bold, and this open dispute with a respected *male* scholar cemented her reputation as a force to be reckoned with in the intellectual world of the French court. More than this, given that she had a readership large enough to ensure the circulation of this text, it demonstrates that people wanted to know what she thought, and that her opinion mattered. She was sailing into uncharted territory as a female intellectual.

Christine did not just confront misogyny in this text – rather, proto-feminism became a theme that underpinned her work. After this debate came her two most celebrated prose works. In 1405, *Le Livre de la Cité des Dames* (*The Book of the City of Ladies*) and *Le Trésor de la Cité des Dames* (*The Treasure of the City of Ladies*, also known as *The Book of the Three Virtues*) were completed. In the former, she creates an allegorical city filled with women, guided by Lady Reason, Lady Rectitude and Lady Justice. Christine places herself at the centre of the narrative, studying the writings of the thirteenth-century French cleric Matheolus, who blamed women for men's unhappiness. As she wrestles with this text, Reason, Rectitude and Justice appear personified. They instruct her to challenge misogyny, correct the hateful narratives about women in literature, and build the symbolic city where virtuous women can reside, underpinned by wisdom. The work highlights the achievements of historical and mythological women, including Sappho, Dido, St Catherine of Alexandria, Lucretia, the Amazons, and Queen Blanche of Castile, who ruled France during the Albigensian Crusade. She gives these women voices, arguing for their intellectual and moral equality with men while advocating for women's education and celebrating their contributions to society. Through this work, Christine offers glimpses into the lives of mythological, historical and biblical women, defending their reputations and celebrating their achievements.

In the second of her works from 1405, *Le Trésor de la Cité des Dames*, Christine provides practical advice for women of all social classes, promoting education and moral conduct. Her *Book of Deeds of Arms and of Chivalry* (1410) is a comprehensive treatise on military strategy and the ethics of chivalry, illustrating her diverse interests and knowledge. Christine drew heavily on Boccaccio's work as a source for this, and undoubtedly had access to Boccaccio's writings through the palace library.

Christine emphasises the important contributions made by women to the development of civilisation – across cultural, religious and political arenas. She even claims that women can equal men in leadership, military skill and intelligence, thus elucidating concepts in the fifteenth century that underpin the fundamentals of modern feminism. However, she stops short of actually encouraging her contemporaries to claim such equality, or to forge careers for themselves. She is progressive, but not *that* progressive.

But this is not to undersell the important and radical nature of Christine's works about women. They were radical indeed. It is hard to overstate the misogyny of the day, which was so widely accepted that it did not raise an eyebrow for a medieval doctor to consider a female as little more than a 'defective' or 'secondary' male. It was not shocking for women to be considered to have no rights or free will, and the oppression of women was widely held to be justified on account of Eve's sin of tempting Adam. Of course, the situation was nuanced, and in some cases women – particularly widows – were able to claim some independence, but, for the most part, the lot of women was quite miserable, and entirely dependent on the goodwill of the men in their immediate family circle. The law afforded them few rights or opportunities of their own, and certainly very few recognised women as equal beings with minds and skillsets on a par with men's. Christine's presentation of a lively, loquacious, courageous and bright collection of ladies in *Le Trésor de la Cité des Dames* was ground-breaking.

However, by 1405, the year that saw the publication of these two major works, things were dire in Paris. Charles V's son and successor Charles VI – the mad king – had been suffering from bouts of real insanity that made him less and less fit to rule, leading to civil war as rivals jostled to take his power, pushing into the vacuum his illness created, and the English exploited this.

In 1407 Louis, Duke of Orléans and a member of the House of Valois, was murdered by John the Fearless, a Burgundian, and from this point on Paris itself was not a secure or peaceful environment. A stalwart ally of the Valois monarchy, Christine responded by becoming more political. She veered away from her previous poetry, and into political tracts, commenting on the ongoing events and attempting to guide her readers. Although she enjoyed patronage from English nobles during periods of peace, Christine's life was marred by war and violence, which were recurring themes in her books. The defining socio-political development of Christine's lifetime was the feud between the Burgundians and the Armagnacs that eventually developed into a full-scale civil war. This divide completely polarised French society throughout Christine's career, and weighed heavily on her mind, permeating her work.

## CHRISTINE DE PIZAN

Christine was forced to leave her beloved Paris by Burgundian besiegers in 1418 and took refuge in an abbey in Poissy where she would spend the rest of her life. In the 1420s Joan of Arc burst onto the scene, and raised the Siege of Orléans – bringing a golden blaze of hope into French hearts. Christine was as much captivated and inspired by the Maid of Orléans as anyone else, and she became the subject of Christine's final, completed work.

She wrote 'the sun began to shine again in 1429' – showing the despair that had been before, and the joy that came of her successes. However, Joan's story is far more complicated than Christine's poem would suggest, as we will see. Joan would die at nineteen, burned by the English, an event that, fortunately, Christine did not live to see, as she predeceased Joan, dying just after completing the poem in her honour.

She had lived in a period of upheaval – the mad king, the Hundred Years' War, conflicts with the English. Indeed, she did not know a time when the Hundred Years' War was not going on, but it was more of a backdrop than an active part of her life.

Christine's importance as a proto-feminist writer is profound. Debates are ongoing as to how truly feminist her ideas actually were – and it is certainly true that Christine was defending the reputation of the female sex in literature, rather than making any meaningful strides or campaigning to improve their actual rights and living conditions. Nevertheless, while she was not a social activist campaigning on behalf of others, she led by example. She made a career for herself, and employed other women, and defended the female sex. While tangible change in women's lives was gradual, Christine's writing and life showed that women could be independent, and sowed the seeds of change, and her influence has extended well beyond her own lifetime. However, Christine focused on much more than the lot of women in medieval society. She was a prolific writer across all genres: poetry, letters, political treatises, philosophical tracts and more.

Then, as now, being good at writing isn't enough. Making it commercially as a writer is hard. To sell enough books to make a living, even with the modern infrastructure of printers, publishers, agents and booksellers, writers must be dextrous. They must write things not only that excite them, but that will please their audiences. They must be astute. They have to temper their truth with the pretty phrasing that will make it palatable. They must package new, threatening ideas appealingly. And they must promote them. They must drip honey in the right ears, smile at the right events, flatter the right people. Christine did all of these things with aplomb, and in so doing forged a career for herself as the first professional female writer in Europe. She was a true Renaissance woman, whose work was infused with humanism and proto-feminism, and was deeply in touch with the political, military and philosophical questions of her day. She was astute and, above all, she was talented.

Joan of Arc. Anonymous miniature, late nineteenth-century.

# 5

# Joan of Arc

## c.1412–30 May 1431

Immortalised in Christine de Pizan's final work, Joan of Arc was an inspirational figure, both during her lifetime and after. The version of Joan that Christine celebrates is the triumphant saviour of France, and her poem was composed when Joan was just seventeen years old, and at the height of her achievements, fulfilling prophecies left, right and centre as the virgin leading France to freedom, before her spectacular fall.

Was Joan ever the prophesied saviour? Was she guilty of hubris? Was she a fraud? Was she schizophrenic? Or was she genuinely inspired? These are the questions this chapter aims to answer, giving a glimpse of the extraordinary story of an ordinary young woman, who through sheer force of will and faith in her visions shot to prominence as the leader of the French.

It is 23 February 1429, and a young girl, aged just sixteen or seventeen, rides into the courtyard of the imposing fortress of Chinon. This is the same castle used by Henry II to imprison Eleanor of Aquitaine, following her defeat in the revolt of his sons. The girl is unapologetically dressed in men's clothing, with her dark hair cut curiously short – just like a boy's. She looks up at the imposing white stone walls that had once contained the rebellious Queen of England and Duchess of Aquitaine, and swells with a sense of purpose. She has ridden for days, from the town of Vaucouleurs, in the company of an entirely male armed entourage, who treat her with a mixture of bemusement, scepticism and reverence. She has ridden to Chinon, in the heart of the Loire Valley, on a holy mission that she believes has been entrusted to her by angels. She has come to meet the Dauphin of France, uncrowned heir to the Capetian Crown, with the aim of persuading him to take up the mantle of his inheritance and become King of France, and banish the English from his lands.

The teenage Joan dreamed of uniting the French against the English, driving them out of France, and turning the strength of their nation to a new crusade against the infidels of the East – the *real* enemies of Christ. Her name was Jeanne, and although she hailed from the small village of Domrémy in the north-east of France, in the region of Lorraine, she is known to history as Joan of Arc.

Joan's life, like that of Béatrice de Planisolles, is unusual for the level of detail historical records have bequeathed us about her life, her faith and her mind. Following her downfall, she was put on trial, like Béatrice, for heresy and witchcraft – and, like Béatrice, in the course of her interrogation and cross-examination, the answers she gave revealed much about her life and state of mind. The meticulously kept records of her trial are a gold mine – and while they record Joan's words not quite verbatim, they were about as close to that as one could get in the Middle Ages. Joan defended herself robustly against the accusations, in a dignified tone and with a strength beyond her years. Of course, this is not the only thing that makes her interesting. Joan merits attention not only for what she said at her trial, and what has been written about her, but for what she *did*. Joan achieved remarkable feats in her short life. She *did* raise the Siege of Orléans, as celebrated by Christine. She *did* see the Dauphin crowned at Rheims. She *did* stand a gruelling trial, and she *was* martyred. A patriot and a devout Christian, she dreamed of seeing her countrymen and women united. But, more than this, she was just nineteen years old when she went to the stake to burn before a crowd of baying English and Burgundian onlookers. Joan's story is one of faith, tenacity, doubt and tragedy.

So how did she come to be there? How did the country girl from Domrémy become such an important figure, such a threat to the English, that they burned her?

Joan was born into a brutal world of conflict and persecution. She was born in *c*.1412, 168 years after the mass burning of so-called heretics at Montségur, and nearly a century after the interrogation of Béatrice de Planisolles, but this was far from the end of European inquisition and the burning of heretics. She was not the first young woman to be burned, and she would not be the last – but the impact of her life and death were such that her name and legend have never been forgotten, and she holds a special place in the popular imagination.

Joan's legacy has had far-reaching effects beyond France. In Latin America she is hailed as the original freedom fighter, a female Che Guevara; in 1920, nearly 500 years after her death, the Catholic Church made a saint of her. In England – the home of her executioners – she became a mascot for the suffragettes. She has become an enduring image of female and nationalistic bravery in the face of oppression. This is possibly why her story has resonated so.

Perhaps the most famous woman in French history – certainly in English circles – Joan's life and legacy are often misunderstood. Many English readers' perceptions of Joan are shaped by her appearances in popular culture – in plays and films and books. She has been a popular icon in England for centuries, despite initially being the hammer of the English. George Bernard Shaw wrote *Saint Joan* in her honour, before her beatification. This is how I first encountered her, an accented and chain-mailed Anne-Marie Duff (far too old to play the teenage Joan) marching with wide eyes alongside a host of banners across the stage of the National Theatre in London. It was a moving and impressive performance, which made Joan slightly mad, and deeply vulnerable, but always, always strong – daring to do what no one else did.

Joan was born to a family of farmers in Domrémy, when her country was already three-quarters of the way through what would become known as the Hundred Years' War. Unlike Christine, she did not come of age amid the many truces, but amid the thick of the fighting and, unlike Christine, she did not grow up with access to education and an ivory tower in the protected capital, but in a vulnerable and unwalled village in north-east France, periodically raided by warring soldiers. The family of seven lived in the only stone house in the village, and it was not a prosperous place. Her father, Jacques, lived in fear that his daughter would be taken by soldiers. In time, his fears would prove well founded.

Life in this village, a collection of farms and dwellings with a small church, was hard, not only because of the climate and the toil of agriculture, but because of the threat of violence that hung over the inhabitants' heads for more than a lifetime. The young Joan and her siblings were used to rushing for cover, from English invaders, and from Burgundian and French troops too, all of whom vied for control of Lorraine. In the midst of the Hundred Years' War, little did the villagers know that a young ingenue from among their own ranks was about to change everything.

Unsurprisingly for a village girl in medieval France, Joan received no real education. She was illiterate, but she was possessed of a charisma and confidence well beyond her years. She was a gifted and persuasive orator, and while she had received no lessons in literature, science or literacy, Joan had received a spiritual and religious education through her mother and the Church. From a young age Joan showed the signs of a profound devotion, to the point of being teased for dropping to her knees to pray whenever she heard church bells ring out over the fields.

Growing up against the backdrop of the devastating war, she was no stranger to violence. These conflicts saw the descendants

# JOAN OF ARC

of Eleanor of Aquitaine fighting over French territories. In France, the English, often in league with the Burgundians, fought the Capetians. By the time of Joan's birth, the war had been raging for generations. No one living could remember a time of true peace.

A power vacuum was created when the French King Charles IV died in 1328 without a direct male heir. Edward III of England, a nephew of Charles IV, tried to lay claim to the French Crown. However, the French nobility favoured Philip VI of the Valois dynasty, leading to conflict. Both Edward III and Philip VI were descendants of the French royal house. They reached no agreement, and nor did the next generation, or the next. Edward's great-grandson, Henry V, would invade France repeatedly, and win a mighty victory at Agincourt on the back of his English longbows. Joan was three years old when this historic battle took place.

Joan was born in the reign of the mad king Charles VI, son of Charles the Wise, whose insanity caused political instability, which was compounded by the fact that his son, also baptised Charles, was unpopular and considered weak. There were even rumours that he was illegitimate, the product of an incestuous affair of his mother. In medieval times, weakness was an invitation for the vultures to circle, and in this instance those vultures took the form of Charles VI's cousin, the Duke of Burgundy, and his other (distant) cousin, Henry V of England. Henry V invaded when Joan was three years old, and the Burgundians allied with him against the French king.

The backdrop of Joan's childhood is one of war, survival, scrambling and prayer. The country is full of soldiers. Invaders, occupiers and defenders alike ravage the countryside, stealing, raping, and burning crops and homes. Throughout the 1420s, her village is victim to many violent raids.

Among the demons and likely traumas she fights, angels come too. Joan hears voices. Not just any voices, but those of angels and saints. She hears them like whispers in her ears.

When Joan is thirteen, and walking in her father's garden, she hears the first of these mysterious mutterings, and it frightens her. When it comes again, she is no longer afraid, because she has realised that it is a message from God. The disembodied sound is accompanied by a bright light, and both the light and the voice seem to emanate from the direction of the church. Once she has heard the voice several times, she realises it is that of an angel, whom she would later identify as Archangel Michael.

At first it tells her only to behave well and attend church, but then it commands that she liberate France. Then the voice becomes more and more specific, eventually telling her that she must raise the Siege of Orléans. It then instructs her to first approach the captain in nearby Vaucouleurs and ask him for men and horses.

It seems that Joan did as the voices commanded. And she begins to hear others, the voices of her beloved Saints Catherine and Margaret. She can smell them, is dazzled by their radiance, and grasps their hands. Her saints are as real to her as any normal encounter she has ever had.

In 1428 Joan has reached a point in her struggle with her duty to her saints that she cannot delay any longer. France is in a piteous state, and by now she has had visions for so long that she truly believes she is the virgin destined to save France. She can't wait any longer and decides the only thing she can do is present herself to the Dauphin and make her case. However, there are many barriers and gatekeepers between peasant girls from Domrémy and the French throne. It would be like a teenager who thought she had the key to the immigration crisis deciding to borrow her father's Peugeot and drive to Paris, pull up outside the Elysée Palace and demand a private audience with the president. Joan is smarter than this, and before deciding to borrow a donkey to ride to the court, she picks a more manageable target. At the behest of her voices, she travels to nearby Vaucouleurs to speak to the French military captain there and ask for his help.

Arriving in the fort of Vaucouleurs, she tells the commander, Robert de Baudricourt, that she has been sent by God to drive the English out of France, and she requests an audience with the Dauphin. She is laughed out of the camp, but – determined – a year later returns to press her case again. This time, he acquiesces. It's not clear why, but France's situation has gone from bad to worse. Perhaps he is impressed by Joan's earnestness, or perhaps he simply now believes that anything is worth a shot.

Together they ride to the fortress of Chinon, where the Dauphin is holding court. It seems that it is at this stage that Joan casts off her woman's skirts and assumes male costume. She also hacks off her dark hair, wearing it close-cropped, like a soldier. Her reasons for this are unclear. Maybe it was to put off sexual advances from the soldiers she travelled with (to me that seems unlikely; a pair of trousers or tights never stopped a rapist) or maybe it was purely for practical purposes – trousers are comfier for riding. Maybe men's clothes made her feel powerful. Maybe she was transgender. We will never know. All we know is that it was on this journey that Joan began to outfit herself like a soldier, a decision that would prove her undoing in time, but which would make her a champion of equality and female empowerment for centuries to come.

Who knows what Joan is thinking and feeling as she rides into the courtyard of the imposing fortress of Chinon? A tall, intimidating building, built for battle, not pleasure – this is a fortress, not a palace. Six soldiers accompany her inside. This will be her first taste of royal splendour. Stronghold as it is, this Loire Valley castle is home to the dauphin and would have been furnished accordingly. The closest Joan from Domrémy would have come to this magnificence would have been in churches. But she is not intimidated; if anything, she is emboldened as she sweeps through the stone halls at the head of her entourage. When she enters the great hall, she is met with a mêlée of 300 courtiers, one indistinguishable from another. The throne is empty, and there is nothing to identify the dauphin. Nevertheless, it seems that by gut instinct or divine inspiration she correctly identifies him. Maybe the soldiers briefed her, we will never know, but without faltering she marches up to a group of men, perhaps dressed more sumptuously than the rest. One of them, bejewelled and richly dressed, stands up and studies her. She pushes past him, to kneel at the feet of another, hidden behind. The man protests that he is not the dauphin and attempts to dismiss her. But Joan stays resolute. Her voice rings out, loudly and clearly: 'My noble dauphin.' The crowd is amazed. How did she know the dauphin if she had never seen him? She declares that she has been sent by God to speak with him. In a daze, the young heir rises and leads his peculiar visitor away for a private audience.

Accounts differ as to what exactly occurs between the Dauphin and Joan at their first encounter, but nevertheless this is the beginning of a relationship that will change history. Joan presents herself as the fulfilment of the ancient prophecy that a virgin would lead the French to salvation, the saviour of France in the form of a simple girl from the provinces. But the Dauphin is not reckless. He wants proof. He invites theologians to quiz her, and hands her over to an irreverent group of noble women to 'test' her virginity, through a physical examination – a humiliating experience for anyone, but even more so for someone who rarely strips naked and has never had sex or heard of a gynaecologist.

Invasive as the tests are, Joan passes. Her reward? An army.

Joan learns to ride a war horse, and armour is made for her. She is kitted out like a Renaissance knight and sits astride her horse at the head of an army numbering as many as 5,000. Could this be the battle to liberate France? Together they ride out, Joan and her bannermen at the head of the column. She is going to relieve the Siege of Orléans, emboldened by her angels, and certain she is right. Carried away by her image and her fervour, the men are brimming with new confidence.

Now what exactly was this famous Siege of Orléans that made Joan's name?

In 1428 the English army – numbering around 4,000 men with horses, artillery and mining equipment – was encamped outside Orléans, a fortified city in central France, and the most ambitious target for the English in the whole of the Hundred Years' War. It was strategically significant: Orléans lies on the Loire River and served as a gateway to the central and southern regions of France, and indeed the Loire Valley – the temporary headquarters of the Dauphin of France. It was a strong city with thirty towers surrounding it, five gates and a fortified bridge. While not impregnable, it represented a serious challenge, with guns, a garrison and a horde of civilians ready to defend their city.

Timing too was on the side of the French, as the English arrived after a good harvest. The odds of starving the population out were low, and the people of Orléans had had ample warning of the approaching English army, and they had burned the surrounding countryside, to leave it bare of food for men and horses. If anything, it was the besiegers who would starve before the besieged.

The siege had commenced in October 1428, when English forces under the command of the Earl of Salisbury made the decision to try to take the city as part of a wider strategy to dominate northern France. After a strong start, gaining ground and erecting siege towers and equipment around the city, the English faced a serious setback on 12 October, with the loss of their veteran commander. He had his face blown apart when a cannonball hit the tower he was in, and he was struck by part of a window. He survived a few days, but died in agony, leaving the English scrambling for a new leader, eventually supplied in the form of the less experienced Duke of Suffolk.

Following her successful petitioning of the Dauphin, Joan arrived before the walls of Orléans on 29 April 1429, bringing much-needed supplies and reinforcements. Her appearance galvanised the besieged French troops and the citizens. The belief that Joan was sent by God gave a much-needed morale boost to the French defenders.

The decisive battle occurred on 7 May 1429, when Joan led an assault on Les Tourelles, a heavily fortified bastion guarding the bridge over the Loire River. During the battle, Joan was wounded by an arrow that pierced her shoulder. She was carried from the battlefield, her wound packed with fat and oil and, to the surprise of many, she returned to the fighting the very same day. Her reappearance rallied the troops and was instrumental in the capture of Les Tourelles, a turning point in the siege.

Following the loss of Les Tourelles, the English, demoralised and weakened, began to withdraw. On 8 May 1429, the siege was officially lifted, and the English retreated. Joan's success here demonstrated her ability to inspire and lead, and to turn the tide. This victory significantly altered the course of the conflict: the raising of the siege not only saved Orléans but also marked the beginning of a series of French victories and paved the way for the long-awaited coronation of the dauphin.

Celebrations rang out in the streets, and far and wide Joan was hailed as a hero and the prophesied saviour of the French. Her reputation as a divinely inspired leader grew rapidly and she continued to lead and motivate the soldiers in a series of French victories that seemed to see her go from success to success. The most notable of these was the Battle of Patay, which saw the decisive defeat of the English and the weakening of their control on northern France.

Riding the triumphant wave of these victories, Joan pushed forward with her desire to see the dauphin crowned at last in Rheims cathedral, and in this too she was successful: Charles VII's coronation took place on 17 July 1429. A delighted yet suitably solemn Joan stood by in a place of honour, and her parents looked on from the audience.

But – as noted by Christine de Pizan – the wheel of fortune is a harsh mistress, and no one was destined to feel its rotation more keenly than Joan. Rising from obscurity to glory, she was about to be plunged into darkness once again. Her luck was running out. Military momentum slowed, and political divisions within the French court led to reduced support for her campaigns. She urged the French king to keep fighting, but he refused. He disagreed with some of her strategic ideas and refused to give her more troops when she wanted them. Joan's strong wish was for the French armies to march on Paris after the coronation, to liberate the capital from Anglo-Burgundian control, but Charles VII refused. Joan tried to march on Paris anyway, but without full support from the king and the largest possible army, such an ambitious undertaking was doomed to failure. Joan's credit was beginning to expire. On top of this, Joan was wounded in the leg with a crossbow bolt. She always positioned herself in the thick of the fighting – and she always bounced back from her injuries, with stunning stamina for a teenage girl. Nevertheless, the siege was a failure and a humiliation. Joan's halo was glowing more faintly than before. She was no longer the lucky charm with which they could not fail.

In May 1430, while attempting to defend the town of Compiègne, she was captured by the Burgundians, allies of the English. Joan was eventually handed over to the English, who viewed her as a political threat and a heretic.

What followed next would be not only the trial of the century, but arguably the trial of the millennium.

Joan's trial began on 9 January 1431 and caused an international sensation. It was conducted by a group of clerics, theologians and legal experts, and Joan defended herself from their accusations. The ministers of the English king wanted news of the trial to travel; they dispatched newsletters describing it across Europe, and they ordered sermons to be preached against Joan and her heresy. After much administrative posturing, Joan's first public session – something like a cross-examination – happened on 21 February, followed by many more over the next three months. On the first day that she appeared before her judges, she still wore men's clothes, her hair shorn; she cut a diminutive figure. It was not a quick trial; under the scrutiny of all Europe, her inquisitors wanted it to be irreproachable. They wanted to deliver a solid guilty verdict, not a flimsy one. The records of the trial are extraordinary documents, giving real insight into Joan's life, and medieval theological (in)justice.

The trial of Joan of Arc was a highly politicised process designed to delegitimise her and weaken the French cause. Many of her interrogators and judges were aligned with English interests, and the trial was conducted in an environment where the outcome was largely predetermined. Joan was charged with a range of offences, including heresy, witchcraft and cross-dressing, all of which were used to justify execution.

Joan earnestly answered the judges' questions – respectfully so, sometimes refusing to answer one question but giving great detail in her answer to the next. She told them of the voices she heard, and what they had commanded her, and the great light that accompanied them. What is striking about her answers is the clarity with which she gives detail, and her strength in refusing to answer questions she finds insulting or unhelpful. Beyond this, she reasons well, saying it is the right of any prisoner to try to escape, and she will not perjure herself by promising not to.

However, her answers never have the ring of a heretic. She continues to say above all else that she respects the infallibility of God and the Pope. Eventually, they examine her on the matter of her cross-dressing – something she dismisses as insignificant, but which could, by the standards of canon law, be enough to condemn her.

She stays strong, until the point that it really sinks in that she will burn. On 24 May they take her to the execution ground, a crowd is gathered, and the judge reads the list of her alleged crimes. As she sees the executioner readying his fire, fear – or maybe something else – persuades her that it is better to denounce her visions than stand by them and suffer death. She recants. She proclaims to the crowd and the judges that her visions should not be believed, and she is willing to submit to the Church. She signs a document taking back what she has said about her voices and her saints and agrees to wear women's clothing once again, and never again to wear the attire of a man. The judges confer, and find her repentance and faith genuine. Her sentence is commuted to life imprisonment.

However, three days later, she is found wearing men's clothing once again. She is agitated and upset that she has not been permitted to go to Mass and is being forced to live among men in prison. She tells them that if she is allowed to attend church and live among women, she will dress as a woman once again. They ask her if she can hear the voices of the saints. She nods. She tells the men that the saints have told her that she has damned her soul to save her life. She resolves to tell no more lies, and proclaims that her recanting was false. She would rather burn than suffer prison. Since she has reverted to her original testimony, the Church resolves to regard her as a heretic once again, and she is sent to the stake. She is nineteen years old, and she is burned alive.

What is perhaps most shocking in all of this is that none of her compatriots lift a finger to help her. The King of France, whom she saw crowned at Rheims, does nothing to negotiate her release. He could have ransomed her. However, she is no longer the hero of the hour, but a hallucinatory teenager accused of heresy and witchcraft – he wants only to distance himself. Joan goes to the stake abandoned by her friends, and burns, strong in her beliefs.

After Joan's death, she was commemorated as a martyr by those who had variously abandoned and condemned her, and her visions of French victories came true, if not completely. The wars would continue for another twenty years, but eventually conclude in 1453 – albeit without the finality of a formal peace treaty. The English had lost almost all their French territories, and Charles VII had solidified his rule over a unified France.

In 1456, a retrial ordered by Charles VII exonerated Joan, declaring her trial and execution unjust. This marked the beginning of her transformation into a national symbol of France and the Church. The monarch whom she had raised up, and who had abandoned her, ultimately continued to profit from her legacy after her death.

Joan has endured as a symbol of French nationalism and female empowerment. When the female rider, clad in silver armour and astride a galloping silver destrier, glided down the Seine during the opening ceremony of the Paris Olympics, Joan's spirit once again stirred in Paris.

*Portrait of Caterine de' Medici, Queen of France*, attributed to Germain Le Mannier, *c.* 1547–1559.

# 6

# Catherine de' Medici

## 13 April 1519–5 January 1589

Tucked away in a museum in northern France, a peculiar, mummified leg can be glimpsed in a display case. Not only is this artefact peculiar in itself, but its provenance makes it more striking still. It is more than five centuries old, and once belonged to a queen. How it came to be in the Musée Tavet-Delacour, an hour north-west of Paris, rather than attached to the rest of the body, is an interesting story.

\* \* \*

At the height of the French Revolution, in 1793, a furious, baying mob battered down the doors of the Basilica of Saint-Denis on the north side of Paris. As well as stripping the mighty cathedral of its gold and silver plate, and tearing down the Stations of the Cross and the statues of the Holy Virgin, they set with gusto upon the royal tombs. The vaults of the various dynasties were forced open, and the coffins torn out and opened, under the pretext of requisitioning lead. The bodies, in various states of preservation, putrefaction and decay, were pulled roughly from their rest. Bones and hair were brandished with delight, stolen as souvenirs, or tossed into a pit nearby. One source claimed that a leg was stolen from the body of a dead monarch – torn from the tomb of the woman known as the 'Serpent Queen'.

That leg had once belonged to Catherine de' Medici, a figure who, even centuries after her death, still provokes controversy. Catherine's life was filled with turmoil, violence, political machinations and betrayal, a mirror to the fractured world of sixteenth-century France in which she lived.

Catherine de' Medici is the shadowy Queen of France who presided over the country in the aftermath of the Hundred Years' War and during the infamous French Wars of Religion. She was given the epithet of 'the Serpent Queen' by her detractors, who sought to portray her as a scheming and malicious woman with ruthless tactics, presiding over a court full of Machiavellian political intrigue during her time as Queen Consort and Regent of France. There were even (recently debunked) rumours of a 'flying squadron' of aristocratic ladies who slept around on the queen's behalf, gathering intelligence through pillow talk.

Perceived as a master manipulator, Catherine, while initially not considered important during her early years at the French court, became a key player in the volatile and factionalised environment of the Valois court, as she attempted to maintain a delicate balance between the Catholics and the Huguenots, who grew powerful in France in the wake of the Reformation. For all this, looking back at her reign with the rigour of a modern historian, it becomes questionable how much of this reputation was deserved. As a queen, she has been vilified for generations. The true nature of her character, motivations and reign is more complex – and these shall be the subject of this chapter.

What is particularly striking about Catherine, a woman who to all intents and purposes ruled France for more than a decade during one of the most turbulent periods in its history, is that she was never, *ever*, meant to be a queen.

She was born long after the bitter conclusion of the Hundred Years' War – nearly seventy years after it ended. Nevertheless, her life and actions were shaped by the legacy of that conflict and the subsequent political and social turmoil in France.

Like Christine de Pizan, Catherine de' Medici was born in Italy. She was – famously – a commoner, rather than royalty, born into the powerful and staggeringly wealthy Medici family of Florence, who had made their fortune in banking and their reputation in scheming. But when Catherine was born, on 13 April 1519, their power and chokehold on Florentine politics were under threat. She was the only legitimate child of Lorenzo de' Medici, Duke of Urbino, and the famously beautiful Madeleine de la Tour d'Auvergne, a French noblewoman, but she was orphaned within months of her birth. Madeleine died of childbed fever, perhaps complicated by venereal disease, and her father died of something similarly ambiguous not long after, following injuries sustained in battle fighting for his contested lands in Urbino. The infant Catherine was suddenly alone in the world, and heir to a great fortune but not a stable one. Her guardians failed to secure her inheritance immediately. On top of this, she did not inherit her mother's beauty.

Familial and political instability dogged Catherine's youth. Following the deaths of her parents, the baby girl was passed around various Medici caretakers, who treated her with varying levels of affection and indifference. Her childhood was not an easy one, and she had no stable and lasting parental figures at this time. This situation continued until the family's enemies – this time a republican faction – rose up and ousted the Medici from Florence. Aged just eight, Catherine was taken captive. She was imprisoned in convents – gentle prisons as they were, and suitably safe for a girl of noble birth. However, there were those who were baying for Medici blood, and called for the child to be raped, stripped naked and hung still living from the city walls. Fortunately, she was spared this fate.

Once Florence was retaken, the Medici restored to power and Catherine safely (or dangerously) back in the possession of her family's allies, she was conveyed to the care of her uncle – none other than Pope Clement VII. He welcomed her in Rome with genuine relief. He had been born Giulio de' Medici, the son of Giuliano de' Medici and his mistress, Fioretta, and as such was a great-uncle of Catherine. He began to plan for her future, and sought a great match for her, one that would strengthen the alliance between the Medici and the Valois monarchy in France. A match with the House of Valois would be mutually beneficial: for the French royals, Catherine was an attractive bride, bringing a colossal dowry, and would forge an alliance with the Pope himself. One clear objection, however, was that, as a Medici, she lacked royal pedigree. With this in mind, she could never be considered for the dauphin – heir to the throne – but rather for one of his younger brothers.

At the age of fourteen, Catherine was betrothed to Henri, Duke of Orléans – the King of France's second son. The young Catherine might have hoped this was the beginning of some stability: throughout her entire childhood she had been shunted from pillar to post, from relatives to captors and finally to St Peter's. Could this be her escape, and perhaps a route to happiness? But if she expected a peaceful and fruitful marriage, she was quickly disillusioned.

In many ways, the marriage was a disaster and rendered Catherine deeply unhappy for much of her adolescence and early adulthood. That said, Catherine was genuinely in love with her husband. The problem was that he did not love her back.

Catherine was smitten with her bridegroom, who was handsome, and just a little older than her; Henri had little interest in her. She was no beauty, and her manners and accent seemed strange in the refined French court. Worse than this, Henri was already deeply infatuated with another, older woman, with whom the inexperienced and insecure Catherine could not hope to compete. Her name was Diane de Poitiers.

Diane was to become Henri's official mistress, and she was no ordinary concubine. Nineteen years older than her teenage lover, and already a widow when their affair began, she was renowned for her beauty, grace and influence. Diane held extraordinary sway over Henri and remained his closest confidante throughout his life, and for a long time ruled at the Valois court as queen in all but name. She took on the roles of both lover and mother for Henri; she had seduced him for the first time in his mid-teens while she was in her mid-thirties, and she had been meant to be teaching him. She was experienced, sophisticated and irreverent. Catherine, on the other hand, was naive, plain, in an unfamiliar court with an unfamiliar language, and deferential. She could not prevail upon her husband to love her, and found herself in a precarious position, side-lined not only in her marriage but also at court, where her status as a foreigner and an upstart Italian was viewed with suspicion. That said, to her great advantage, she managed to build a close relationship with Henri's father, King François I.

To make matters worse, in the early years of their marriage Henri rarely visited her bed, preferring Diane's, and Catherine failed to produce the expected heir. At a court where the production of a male heir was paramount, this failure placed Catherine in a still more vulnerable position, with whispers of annulment circulating.

Diane, understanding that her own influence was tied to Henri's status and the presence of a passive, biddable wife, sought to protect herself by ensuring Catherine remained in place as queen. She encouraged Henri to fulfil his royal duty by sleeping with his wife and even offered Catherine sexual advice in an effort to help her conceive. This came not out of concern for the French succession but rather out of self-preservation. If Catherine were put aside, another queen might take her place – someone who would be far less tolerant of Diane's position of power. Furthermore, it was imperative that Catherine have children to ensure the succession: in 1536 Henri's elder brother François had died of infection, leaving Henri and Catherine as the unexpected dauphin and dauphine – heirs to the throne of France.

Catherine's desperation to conceive drove her to extreme measures, from drinking mule urine to smearing herself with cow dung on the advice of healers and wisewomen. There were even reports of her watching Henri and Diane having intercourse through secret peepholes carved in the woodwork, hoping to glean what she might be doing wrong in the marital bed. Both doctors and Diane counselled her on sexual technique, and there were reports that Diane participated in their efforts to conceive – 'preparing' her lover for his wife. Finally, after more than a decade of prayer and somewhat degrading efforts, Catherine gave birth to her first son, François, in 1544. This pregnancy was the first of many that would eventually give her ten children, seven of whom survived to adulthood. Of these seven, five would become monarchs.

However, even the birth of children, which often secured a husband's affection, did little to improve Catherine's romantic situation. Henri's love for Diane never wavered, and Diane drank gold to preserve her youth and beauty. While Catherine had provided the necessary heirs, she had not managed to win the love of her husband. Her position remained one of duty, not affection, but this cannot be considered unusual for the time period. Marriages were strategic and pragmatic diplomatic and business arrangements, rather than love affairs. In many cases – particularly for royals – they were about land, gold and getting heirs. Romantic love was an afterthought, if it entered the equation at all. Following the birth of twins, who died in infancy after a difficult labour, Catherine was advised to have no more children for health reasons, and it seems Henri abandoned their bed altogether. It was Diane who still held Henri's heart.

In 1547, following the death of his father François I, Henri ascended the throne as Henri II, elevating Catherine to the position of Queen Consort of France. Yet this brought her little relief. Diane's influence remained unshaken, and she continued to act as the dominant female presence at court. Henri constantly side-lined his wife in favour of his mistress, giving her the best of everything: jewels, property, and even giving her a place on the privy council. Throughout Henri's reign, Diane even took on many of the ceremonial duties typically reserved for the queen and held control over royal finances and patronage. Catherine, though queen consort in name, was effectively shut out. Her humiliation was acute, but she was pragmatic. She maintained her dignity, observed the political landscape and waited for her moment.

It was in 1559, during a jousting tournament, that Catherine's chance finally arrived. The joust celebrated the marriage of Catherine's daughter Elisabeth of Valois to the Spanish King Philip II. Henri, wearing Diane's colours rather than his wife's, participated in the tournament despite Catherine's warnings. She had reportedly begged him not to compete, having experienced a premonition of disaster, and read prophecies by the celebrated astrologer and occultist Nostradamus that predicted his death in a duel. Her fears were realised when a splintered lance struck Henri in the face, piercing his eye. Despite the best efforts of the court's doctors, Henri's condition worsened. In vain they even experimented on prisoners from the Bastille, forcing splinters into their eyes and trying to find ways to remove them, but they were unsuccessful.

As he lay dying, Henri called out for Diane, but Catherine, now holding the reins of power, refused her entry. Diane's entire status had been built on Henri's favour, and with him incapacitated and unable to assert his authority, Catherine was finally in control. The line between authority and power is a fine one, and Catherine was finally on the right side of it. Diane was shut out in the cold. For all that, when Catherine sent men to retrieve the royal jewels her husband had given to his mistress, she reportedly refused to part with them until the king was dead. Diane had controlled the king in life, but at last, in death, Catherine was able to take control.

Once the king had breathed his last, Catherine exiled Diane, albeit to a fine château in the Loire Valley. While this was certainly still luxurious as exiles go, it was not the magnificent Château de Chenonceau which Diane had made her own during Henri's reign. Catherine had coveted it for herself, but her husband had given it to Diane who had lavished much attention and expense on its beautification, building the famous bridge across the River Cher and planting elaborate gardens. It was with grim satisfaction that Catherine now seized Chenonceau for herself. She was lenient with Diane, but the turn of the tables was definitive.

Chenonceau remains perhaps the most beautiful château of the Loire Valley, standing astride the River Cher in stately white glory – a testament to the two rival women who clashed for its ownership, and lavished their passion for design upon it. Diane enlarged the castle her lover bestowed upon her, but Catherine made it grander still, building up the section bridging the Cher into a celebration hall to house parties for her children, resembling the Ponte Vecchio in her native Florence. There is something still quite stunning about this black and white gallery bathed in light, and it is curious that Catherine chose to decorate it in black and white tiling – the colours of her rival.

Inside, the bedroom of Diane de Poitiers abuts the chapel, elegant, with a small bed, and a portrait of Catherine above the fireplace. In Catherine de' Medici's bedchamber, the ceiling is decorated with Hs and Cs, for Henri and Catherine – but occasionally these intertwined letters overlap, to give the impression of Ds as well, a strange testament to the intertwined fates and relationships between this *ménage à trois* of a king and two noble cousins.

Following Henri's death and Diane's fall from grace, all eyes turned to the succession. Catherine's eldest son François II – then aged fifteen – ascended the throne. The removal of Diane marked the beginning of Catherine's own political ascendancy. That said, she was not without rivals. François II, despite his youth, was already married to the headstrong and devout Mary Stuart – better known in English circles as Mary, Queen of Scots. She was a year older, was more mature, and hated the Huguenots, a group who had already begun to proliferate in France. She was powerful too; now the Queen Consort of France, she already had strong connections within the court, having spent much of her childhood there in preparation for her marriage. She also commanded the loyalty of the powerful and fervently Catholic Guise faction, relatives on her mother's side. This family would become one of the most powerful and unruly families in France over the next decades and would eventually prove the undoing of Catherine and her heirs. The period of their supremacy would become known as the *Tyrannie Guisienne*.

Catherine came to power in the midst of an age of great upheaval in Europe – the height of the Reformation. The European Reformation had started in earnest in 1517 when Martin Luther nailed his Ninety-Five Theses to the door of the Castle church in Wittenberg, criticising corruption, double standards and the selling of indulgences within the Catholic Church. It became a continent-wide revolution against the perceived corruption and chokehold of the Church and called for a return to the fundamentals of Christianity, a purer and simpler form of worship rooted more firmly in the Bible.

As Lutheranism spread throughout Europe, spurring the English Reformation too, another form of Protestantism began to take hold in France, aligned with the teachings of French theologian John Calvin. His ideas differed from Luther's, with Calvin placing much greater emphasis on predestination, but both rejected the Pope and much of the doctrine of the Catholic Church. The term that arose for French Protestants – mainly Calvinists – was Huguenots. During Catherine's reign there was a wealthy, vocal and well-placed Huguenot minority in the upper echelons of French society, pushing their claims to power. The warring nobility, already rivalrous, leaned into the religious conflict as a way of bolstering their claims against each other and throwing off the often suffocating authority of the Catholic Church. But despite these politics, the Reformation and the wars that followed it were really about ideas, salvation, Church structure and the Eucharist. France was caught in the middle, between northern Europe which was embracing Protestantism, and southern Europe which rejected it. France became a battleground, with real bloodshed starting in 1560. Moreover, the power of the monarchy was rooted in Catholic rituals and beliefs, so the spread of Protestantism was seen as a substantial threat to the Valois monarchy.

Mary Stuart's maternal uncles, the Guise brothers, Charles and François, had been raised to powerful positions during the reign of Henri II, becoming respectively the Cardinal of Lorraine and the Duke of Guise. They loathed the Huguenot faction, the most prominent of which were the 'Princes of the Blood', Louis de Bourbon, Prince of Condé, and Antoine de Bourbon, direct descendants of the Capetian royal house who had nevertheless embraced Calvinism. In the event of the extinction of the Valois dynasty, they were considered the next heirs to the throne of France. The Guise brothers saw these two, and another Huguenot leader, Admiral Gaspard de Coligny, as their direct rivals at the court. Seizing power immediately after Henri's death, they moved into the Louvre Palace alongside the young royal couple. Catherine had little choice but to tolerate their presence as they surged into the power vacuum formed by her husband's unexpected death.

However, any jostling for power that may have occurred between Mary and Catherine after the accession of François II was strictly limited. François II would last just one year on the throne; he died of infection at the age of sixteen. His death gave his mother even more power than his father's had done, and extinguished Mary Stuart's power in France. Catherine's second son, the ten-year-old Charles IX, was crowned, and Catherine became his official regent – effectively ruling as king on his behalf until the boy was of legal age. Charles was not much luckier than his brother, however, dying at twenty-three years old, after thirteen years of rule, during which time he had struggled to claw back control from his mother, who had by this time found power to her taste. It was then that her third son, Henri III, took the throne, and Catherine would continue to rule through him for most of his reign.

For all that she managed to hold onto power, this period of Catherine's life was fraught with challenges. The tensions between the Protestant and Catholic factions were threatening to engulf the country. France was teetering on the edge of civil war, and Catherine, as regent, was tasked with finding a way to maintain peace while preserving the power of the monarchy.

Ostensibly, she pursued a policy of religious tolerance, issuing the Edict of Saint-Germain in 1562, which granted limited freedom of worship to Protestants. The edict was half-boiled, however, and irritated all the concerned groups – not conceding enough to placate the Huguenots and seeming too lenient and potentially dangerous for the Catholics. The grumbling 'peace' the edict brought was shattered within months when François, Duke of Guise, arbitrarily massacred a group of Huguenots at Vassy. The duke referred to this slaughter as 'a regrettable accident'. This 'accident' was the catalyst for the outbreak of protracted religious violence that would dominate the politics of Catherine's life. She presided over one of France's bloodiest periods in the early modern era, known to history as the French Wars of Religion, a protracted series of conflicts that lasted thirty years between the Catholics (supported by Catherine) and the growing Huguenot faction.

Over the next decade chaos reigned. Catherine shifted constantly between the two sides, her priority being to maintain control, while attempting to broker peace and ensure the survival of the Valois dynasty. Throughout, she used her children as pawns, arranging marriages for them to some of the greatest royal houses in Europe. These alliances were meant to bolster Catholic support in France, but they did little to stem the tide of violence. François, Duke of Guise, the elder of the Guise brothers, was assassinated at the Siege of Orléans in 1563, and the Admiral de Coligny was implicated. The Guise family never passed up an opportunity for revenge, and this revenge would be served cold but most bloodily by the murdered man's son Henri – the new Duke of Guise – nearly a decade later.

Throughout this period, Catherine relied on a small group of trusted advisers who supported her policy of guarded religious tolerance. Yet her efforts were consistently undermined by the conflicting ambitions of the Guises and the Bourbons. These families saw the religious conflict as an opportunity to increase their own power, often at the expense of the Crown. Forced to navigate this volatile political landscape, Catherine's position was never stable.

In 1572 came an event that would thoroughly eclipse the delicate balancing act Catherine had been seeking to maintain, supplanting her reputation as a diplomat with that of a genocidal zealot. This event, after which the Seine 'ran red with blood', is one of the most infamous in French history: the St Bartholomew's Day Massacre. It was the culmination of years of religious tensions, rivalry, political manoeuvring and half-hearted attempts at peace-making.

The massacre took place in the immediate aftermath of an unexpected and politically fraught wedding – between none other than Catherine's daughter, the Catholic Princess Margaret, and Henri, the Huguenot Protestant King of Navarre. This wedding, celebrated in summer on 18 August 1572, in the cathedral of Notre-Dame, was intended to unite Catholic and Protestant factions and bring an end to the religious conflict that had plagued the country for years. Peace had been reluctantly brokered two years previously with Catherine's Peace of Saint-Germain – but it was flimsy, and this marriage was intended to strengthen it.

Instead, it became a bloodbath.

Paris was hot, stiflingly so, and all the religious tensions of the previous decades were simmering dangerously close to the surface, as the city bustled with members of the rival religious factions who had descended on the capital for the celebrations, which Catherine herself had spent months planning. Many prominent Huguenots, including their leader Admiral de Coligny, were in the capital. The Catholics, particularly the remaining Guise brothers and their sons and allies, viewed the presence of so many Protestant leaders in the capital as a threat. More than this, as we have seen, they wanted revenge for the death of Francois, Duke of Guise, killed by a Huguenot assassin in 1563.

The wedding went off without a hitch. Protestants danced with Catholics at the feast. Catherine's plans for pageantry were a triumph. The court collectively breathed a sigh of relief.

But it was just the calm before the storm. Just four days later, on 22 August 1572, an assassination attempt was made on Admiral Coligny. He was shot in the arm, but survived, and, seemingly initially unfazed by the wound, raised his good arm and pointed to a window, still with plumes of smoke around it, identifying where the gunman must have been hiding. While the assailant escaped – just – his smoking musket was discovered where Coligny had pointed. When word reached Charles IX he reacted with genuine surprise, furious at the news. While the royal family ordered an investigation (although most believed it to be the work of the Guises, with whom Coligny had a long-standing bitter feud), the Huguenots rallied around Coligny's house to protect their leader, and Catherine and Charles attended his bedside, offering the services of the royal doctor.

Nevertheless, in the days that followed, the tide turned against Coligny – even in his wounded state. It seems that over the course of three emergency councils called by Charles IX and attended by his mother and the Guise brothers, the royal family and their advisers and allies decided to assassinate the leading Huguenots in Paris. They were anxious that the fury of the Huguenots at the attack on Coligny was about to boil over into open rebellion and civil war, and with thousands of Huguenot soldiers within close proximity of the capital, this was considered too dangerous a threat to ignore. Together, the councils drew up kill lists and assembled assassination squads to this effect. Coligny's name topped the list. Henri de Guise got his wish and was permitted to lead the execution of his rival, the man he also believed to have been behind his father's assassination. He and a posse of assassins forced their way into Coligny's lodgings. Guise waited downstairs while a young man entered Coligny's room. He found the admiral composed, ready for death, having heard the commotion below and gleaned what was happening. The assassin addressed the lord roughly, for which Coligny admonished him that he was too young to address him thus, at which point the younger man stabbed him, quipping that he was old enough to kill him. The still-breathing Coligny was then hurled from the upper window, and Guise inspected his broken corpse below.

This was just the beginning of the horrors. All through the early hours of 24 August 1572, on the feast day of St Bartholomew, Catholic forces, led by the Duke of Guise, began systematically murdering Huguenot leaders across Paris in an unprecedented bloodbath. What started as a targeted assassination of prominent Protestants quickly spiralled out of control, to the dismay of Catherine who had never envisaged this escalation and had instead intended the assassinations to avoid wider war. Catholic mobs, fuelled by religious fervour and encouraged by the violence of the royal guards, swept through the streets of Paris, slaughtering thousands of Huguenots. In desperation, Catherine opened her palace doors to shelter Huguenots seeking refuge, including the English spymaster and ambassador Francis Walsingham, who did not feel safe in his bed. The violence spread to other cities across France, leading to the deaths of an estimated 30,000 people in the days and weeks that followed. Henri of Navarre – Catherine's new son-in-law – was spared, along with the Prince of Condé, on the condition that they pledged to convert to Catholicism.

The St Bartholomew's Day Massacre remains one of the most controversial and debated events of Catherine's reign. Historians have long argued over her role in the massacre. Some contemporaries and later writers, particularly Protestant ones, portrayed her as the mastermind behind the bloodshed, casting her as a Machiavellian figure who had orchestrated the massacre to eliminate her political enemies and secure the future of the Catholic monarchy. This interpretation of events contributed to her enduring reputation as the 'Serpent Queen'. Yet it seems she did do her best to protect those Protestants she could as the slaughter spiralled out of control. Walsingham made a point of thanking both François and Catherine for 'the particular care' they gave to the English Protestants at this time.

However, other historians have suggested that Catherine's involvement was more nuanced, and even that she was not involved at all. While it seems that she was aware of the decision to target Protestant leaders, and potentially even participated in the planning, it is highly unlikely that she foresaw the scale of the violence that would follow. Even the Duke of Guise did not predict that. Catherine had spent much of her regency attempting to broker peace between Catholics and Protestants, and the massacre was a catastrophic failure of that policy. It is possible that, in the days leading up to the massacre, she believed that eliminating a few key Protestant figures would prevent a larger conflict and preserve the fragile peace. Instead, the massacre plunged France into even deeper chaos.

After the massacre, Catherine set to work to attempt to reconcile the fractured kingdom. Just weeks later, she was already working towards peace, going so far as to bar the nuncio of Pope

Gregory XIII from court, following the Pope's letter expressing joy over the massacre. By Christmas of 1572, she was actively negotiating peace between the Catholic and Protestant factions.

When Catherine's son Charles IX died in 1574, she was named regent as his successor, Catherine's next son Henri, was still in Poland, serving as King of the Polish-Lithuanian Commonwealth. Henri abandoned his Polish throne, becoming Henri III of France. Needless to say, Catherine maintained a prominent position at court and continued to wield a good deal of influence, despite Henri defying her in his choice of wife. Indeed the next years of Catherine's life were marked by filial conflicts and disappointments. Her slightly wild youngest son, François, Duke of Alençon, who styled himself as simply 'Monsieur', was a particular source of angst. In 1576, he allied with Protestant princes, leveraging the civil wars for his own advantage, and moving against the Crown. Catherine and Henri were forced to capitulate to many of the Huguenots' demands in the Edict of Beaulieu, a treaty that became known as the 'Peace of Monsieur' due to François's influence.

In 1578, Catherine attempted to rehabilitate her reputation among the Huguenots by embarking on an eighteen-month tour of southern France to meet their leaders directly. This effort earned the queen mother new respect, and upon her return to Paris she was greeted by cheering crowds. But this period was not without personal challenges. Her daughter Margaret, whose marriage to Henri of Navarre had not brought peace, returned to court in 1582 without her husband and under a cloud of scandal. It was common knowledge that she had multiple lovers, something Catherine publicly berated her daughter for. Enraged by her daughter's indiscretions, she had sent an envoy to bring Margaret back under control. This was only one of the many familial dramas that would plague Catherine's later years as her unruly children caused chaos around Europe.

In 1584, François 'Monsieur' died from consumption. His death drastically altered the political landscape, leaving the Protestant Henri of Navarre as heir presumptive to the throne. This development horrified many Catholics, especially the Duke of Guise, who – spurred on – formed the Catholic League to prevent a Protestant succession. Tensions escalated, and by 1585 Henri III was forced to go to war against the League. He lost and was forced to capitulate to their demands with the Treaty of Nemours – even being forced to pay the wages of the soldiers that defeated him. Catherine was left to clean up the mess.

Catherine's troubles went from bad to worse in 1587, when her erstwhile daughter-in-law and rival Mary Queen of Scots was executed in England, after decades of house arrest, by the Protestant Queen Elizabeth. The perceived martyrdom of this woman, executed for treason for plotting to take Elizabeth's throne, sent shockwaves through Catholic Europe. The Catholic League, with support from the Spanish Crown, seized much of northern France, preparing for an invasion of England. Paris erupted in rebellion, and on 12 May 1588 Parisians set up barricades, refusing to obey anyone but the Duke of Guise – ignoring Catherine's authority completely. Catherine herself was blocked from attending Mass and, according to chroniclers, spent the day weeping. Despite her advice to compromise, Henri III continued to lose control.

That December, Catherine found herself further side-lined. Henri III finally had enough of the vaulting ambition of the Duke of Guise and ordered his assassination. On 23 December, Guise was summoned to the royal apartments under false pretences and was murdered there on the king's command. On Christmas Day, Catherine lamented to a friar, 'Oh, wretched man! What has he done?'

Not long after, on 5 January 1589, Catherine de' Medici died at the age of sixty-nine, likely from pleurisy. She had spent her final days visiting her old friend, Cardinal de Bourbon, as if trying to hold on to the remnants of her political influence. Despite her power and prominence, her death came quietly, and she was initially buried at Blois rather than in Paris, which was held by her enemies. Her remains were eventually reinterred in the Basilica of Saint-Denis, but her tumultuous life and the legacy she left behind continued to cast a long shadow over France for centuries to come. Her final son, Henri III, died just months after his mother, assassinated by a fanatical friar at his military camp in Saint-Cloud, where he had assembled troops to march on Paris and reclaim it from the Catholic League. He was succeeded by Henri of Navarre, the Protestant prince whose wedding to Margaret of Valois had triggered the St Bartholomew's Day Massacre, and who had allied with him against the Catholic League.

Despite his controversial Protestant origins, Henri IV was a judicious ruler of predominantly Catholic France, who had more success balancing the interests of the Catholic and Protestant factions at his court. Indeed, he converted to the Catholic faith – reportedly acknowledging that *'Paris vaut bien une messe'* ('Paris is well worth a Mass'). He ushered in a calmer period, until he too was assassinated by a Catholic zealot in 1610, after a twenty-one-year reign.

Émilie du Châtelet, engraving, 1751.

# 7

# Émilie du Châtelet

## 17 December 1706–10 September 1749

'Minerva dictated, and I wrote.'

Voltaire

The year is 1740, and a woman in her mid-thirties, wearing a dress with a plunging, fur-trimmed neckline, is alone in a room, down on her hands and knees and clutching a metal ruler. She is meticulously measuring a curved indent in a piece of soft, dark clay. Around her, on the floor, a series of balls are rolling incoherently as she notes down the measurement shown on her ruler.

She straightens and snatches up one of the rolling balls. Taking a longer piece of measuring tape, she holds the ball exactly one metre above the clay, and then releases it. It strikes the surface with a loud slap. She kneels once again and carefully measures the imprint. She repeats this process many more times, dropping the balls from various, meticulously recorded heights, each time checking the depth of the crater. Every result is carefully noted. She is methodical and precise, but clearly also excited – she is onto something, and she knows it.

This woman, preoccupied with her measurements, is named Émilie. She is married to a military officer called Marquis Florent-Claude du Chastellet-Lomont – making her the Marquise of

Châtelet. She is known to history as Émilie du Châtelet, although throughout this chapter I will call her simply Émilie, as that is how she referred to herself. Her close friends and familiars even referred to themselves '*Émiliens*'.

She is carrying out these experiments in the sprawling Château de Cirey, owned by her husband, but in which she presently lives with her lover – a man significantly more famous than she, although it is Émilie who has the faster grasp on scientific principles. Elsewhere in the château, lounging in a luxurious feather bed, sleeps the bad boy of the French Enlightenment: Voltaire. The oft-imprisoned and still more oft-exiled poet was a man so controversial he might even give Lord Byron a run for his money. Tiredness begins to creep over Émilie, but she dips her fingers in ice water to stir herself and continues with her work.

Believe it or not, with her balls and her clay and her ruler, Émilie has just laid some crucial groundwork for Einstein's theory of relativity. She was using the balls and clay to investigate the relationship between velocity and energy, aiming to test a controversial theory put forward by Gottfried Leibniz. Unlike Newton, who claimed that an object's kinetic energy was proportional to its velocity, Leibniz argued that it was proportional to the *square* of the velocity. By dropping the balls on to the clay from a height, Émilie found that when a ball's velocity was doubled, the indentation in the clay was four times as deep, confirming Leibniz's theory. This challenged the Newtonian idea widely prevalent at the time, and by carrying out these experiments Émilie was wading into the fierce rivalry between supporters of Newton and Leibniz – a particularly awkward move, given that her lover, Voltaire, was an ardent Newtonian.

The Enlightenment was a time of ideas. A time of challenging old ideas, and meticulously crafting new ones. It was a movement that turned the way we see the world upside down – and at its heart stood Émilie.

\* \* \*

# ÉMILIE DU CHÂTELET

According to Voltaire, Émilie du Châtelet 'was a great man whose only fault was being a woman' – although it must be said that, for many years, he didn't seem too put off by this.

The progress and ideas of the Enlightenment paved the way for the modern world. Yet, among its many luminaries, few women shone as brightly or made as profound an impact as Émilie du Châtelet. She was France's first celebrated female scientist and mathematician, she pioneered female participation in scientific and mathematical discourse, and she became the first woman unanimously elected to the Academy of Sciences at the Institute of Bologna, one of the oldest and most prestigious scientific institutions in Europe.

Émilie was a thinker, but also a fighter. In a deeply misogynistic society and an age still far from enlightened, any woman who wanted to be taken seriously, not only as a writer or an artist but as a philosopher, mathematician or scientist, had the odds set against them. Any woman wanting to establish herself as a challenger – a force to be reckoned with – in rapidly evolving intellectual circles had to fight hard. In her youth, Émilie's father lamented, 'My youngest flaunts her mind, and frightens away the suitors.' She had been expected to become a wife, mother and society hostess – all of which she did indeed become – but she wanted more. She had a brilliant mind, and she wanted to use it.

Émilie was born into the upper echelons of French society, during the reign of the Sun King, Louis XIV. It was a glorious time to be an aristocrat in France. The Wars of Religion were past, the Revolution had not yet come, and France prospered. Ideas proliferated, education blossomed, and the king radiated grace. Émilie did not have to fight poverty, penury, squalor or disease – challenges that would have prevented the vast majority of French women from even grasping at the opportunity for education that Émilie had. She had the privileges of class, and of access.

She was the daughter of Louis Nicolas le Tonnelier de Breteuil, a high-ranking official in the court of King Louis XIV. Her father's position as the king's principal secretary afforded early exposure to the aristocratic and intellectual elites of France. From a young age, she exhibited a keen intellect and a voracious appetite for learning, traits recognised and nurtured by those around her. She was the only daughter of the family, alongside five brothers – however, only three of these boys survived infancy. She had two older brothers and one younger – this meant that there were tutors around the family home, seeing to the boys' education. It seems Émilie managed to sneak into some lessons too. That said, her traditional female education was not neglected: she learned court manners, how to laugh daintily, and how to function as a lady ought in high society.

Her youngest brother, somewhat surprisingly named Elisabeth-Théodore, was closest to her in age. He was destined for a career in the Church, a traditional route for younger sons who were unlikely to inherit; what the younger boys lacked in funds, they were often compensated for with education. It is likely that Émilie's precocity and thirst for knowledge encouraged her parents to allow her to join him for his lessons. Although she never wrote of this directly, her presence in these classes is implied by the fact that by her twenties and before her marriage, she already had a more than competent grasp of Latin, Euclidean geometry and mathematics. In this way, against the odds, Émilie had unprecedented access to an aristocratic education, in the aftermath of the Renaissance and on the brink of the Enlightenment.

She would grow to become a woman of extraordinary intellect and determination, who defied the conventions of her time to become a trailblazing mathematician, physicist and philosopher. Through her work, she not only illuminated the scientific landscape of the eighteenth century but also challenged the limitations imposed on women by society.

Despite her unique advantages, university was never on the cards. This would have been a step too far in eighteenth-century

French society; France did not award its first degree to a woman until 1861. Instead, in 1725, at age eighteen, Émilie entered into an arranged marriage with Florent-Claude du Chastellet-Lomont. It was not a love match, nor was it a hateful or abusive union. It was a respectful marriage of convenience, and the Marquis turned a blind eye to both Émilie's studies and her affairs, for which she would become almost as well known as for her contributions to science. In fact, her academic and romantic affairs often intertwined. Émilie frequently mixed business with pleasure, becoming romantically involved with some of her teachers and mentors, before forming the great romantic and intellectual partnership of her life, with Voltaire.

However, before these affairs began, and Émilie truly embarked on her career as a scientist and general lover of life, she had to fulfil her wifely duties. Soon after her marriage, she moved with her husband to Burgundy, dividing time between the Marquis's family estate in the province of Haute-Marne, the Château de Cirey – where we met her at this chapter's opening, conducting experiments with balls and clay – and the garrison town of Semur-en-Auxois. She gave birth to the couple's three children in quick succession: a son, Louis-Marie Florent, and two daughters, Françoise-Gabrielle Pauline and Victor-Esprit. After this, she was able to enjoy greater freedom. Perhaps surprisingly, the Burgundian town of Semur hosted a scientific salon, which Émilie quickly began to participate in. It was there that she met a Parisian mathematician, Charles-Émile-Auguste Camus de Mezieres, who, it seemed, reawakened her interest in mathematical thinking, and perhaps recognised her gift.

Eventually, Émilie returned to Paris. Her husband was often absent for long periods, and on this occasion he was commanding troops in the War of the Polish Succession, a conflict that saw France, alongside Spain and Sardinia, supporting Stanisław Leszczyński, the former King of Poland and father-in-law of King Louis XV of France, against Augustus III, who was backed by Austria, Russia and Saxony. In a bizarre twist of fate, the man whom her husband was defending would later shelter Émilie in the last months of her life, and she would name her final – illegitimate – child after him. But that was still decades away, and it was in her husband's absence during this period that her intellectual life and reputation began to truly flourish. It was also at this time that she began to take many lovers, and revel in her new sexual freedom. Indeed, despite her quite public affairs, her relationship with her husband continued to be mutually supportive, and they remained engaged in each other's lives.

Émilie's first two extramarital relationships were both with men who encouraged her learning.

In 1729, she met the Duke of Richelieu, and they ended up having an affair in the 1730s. This reveals much about her attitude towards love and her social position. Richelieu was the most sought-after man in Paris; two noblewomen – both beautiful and wealthy – had recently fought a duel over him with pistols, in which one was shot in the shoulder. Richelieu had quipped that he refused to choose between them, as both had demonstrated bravery in the fight. Eventually, both came to their senses and left him. This was the social scene that Émilie launched herself into. Her brilliant mind, coupled with genuine attractiveness, made her sought after too. She and Richelieu were sexually involved, but when that cooled – as it was always bound to, given Richelieu's attention span – the two maintained an intellectual friendship for years, continuing to correspond regularly.

Richelieu introduced her across Parisian society. Shortly after her arrival in Paris, she met Pierre Louis Moreau de Maupertuis, a mathematician, philosopher and member of the Academy of Sciences, prominent for his contributions to physics and astronomy, and for his role in the early development of the principle of least action. Alongside his scholarly pursuits, Maupertuis made a hobby of giving mathematics lessons to high-society ladies. The two began an affair, and he also asked Alexis Claude Clairaut, another scholar, to give her dedicated lessons. Émilie's letters to Maupertuis are flirtatious but not passionate and shed light on the casual nature of their sexual relationship. While the affair with Maupertuis burned out, and he would become involved in a prominent academic spat with her future lover – Voltaire – Clairaut remained her principal tutor and friend for the rest of her life.

When Émilie and Voltaire began their relationship in 1733, he was already famous as France's greatest poet, perhaps even Europe's. He had transformed the epic genre with *La Henriade*, the first major epic written in French, and gained acclaim as a playwright and historian. He was also a radical free thinker, opposed to compulsory religion and political despotism, and had been in exile and passed spells in the Bastille. To Émilie, he cut a dashing and romantic figure, with a mind that could keep pace with hers in conversation. To Voltaire, Émilie – aged just twenty-seven – was sparky, vivacious and keenly intelligent. Soon, they were enthralled with each other, and she would become the love of his life.

The affair that erupted between them was emblematic of the Enlightenment: the marriage and explosion of science, mathematics, literature and philosophy. The breaking of social boundaries and dusty patterns. The two met in Paris at a literary salon hosted by Madame Claudine Guérin de Tencin, a lynchpin of the Paris salon scene. The pair were immediately struck by each other's intellect, and Voltaire was also in something of a tight spot. He had recently published a work praising the British constitutional monarchy, lauding it above the absolute monarchy of France, an act which amounted to treason and had left the king and his retinue incensed. He was attempting to lie low and looking to escape Paris – ideally to some kind of safe house where the king's men would not drag him away. Charmed, and doubtless amused by his predicament, Émilie offered him Cirey as a temporary refuge. Together, they set up house, and periodically entertained Émilie's husband when he returned from his wars.

Their relationship blossomed against the backdrop of a crumbling old-world order and the waves of change brought about by the Enlightenment.

Despite their privileges, the world Émilie and Voltaire were born into was a harsh one. Although fashions had changed, fundamental inequalities had not. Although she lived in what we think of as the end of the early modern period – during the Enlightenment and at the start of the age of revolutions – much of the social structure was shocking by today's standards. This was, after all, the era that allowed the wealthy nobility to escape virtually all taxes, while the poor travailed in virtual serfdom. In many ways, society had not advanced much beyond the Middle Ages. Wives could be raped and beaten by their husbands (practices that continued well into the twentieth century, indeed) and gay people could be executed. Religious freedom was virtually non-existent, and France was ruled by an autocratic king who claimed to be a divinely consecrated, benign dictator – but was often anything but benign. It was an age of public executions and book burnings, and one without female education or emancipation. Émilie du Châtelet and Voltaire sought to change this and envisioned a different world.

Together, the lovers restored the crumbling Château de Cirey, at Voltaire's expense, and there they created an intellectual haven. There, they worked together, encouraged each other's research, and entertained the great thinkers of the age – and, as discussed, occasionally Émilie's husband. They explored radical ideas about the monarchy, the nature of free will, the subordination of women, and the separation of Church and state. Their letters to each other were sparkling, passionate and intricate.

Their first task was building their library – soon surpassing the collections of most European universities by amassing more than 20,000 volumes. They also made laboratories for their scientific experiments. Émilie requisitioned the main hall for testing Newtonian theories, with her spheres suspended and swinging from ceiling beams, and commanded specialist objects and tools from the estate's iron works.

In 1738, Voltaire published *Elements of the Philosophy of Newton*, a book met with monumental acclaim. He acknowledged openly that he could never have produced it without Émilie's help: she had coached him through the science and helped him find his way through the abstract ideas of Newtonian physics. The book presented to the French public for the first time an accessible explanation of Newtonian ideas. Newton was Voltaire's intellectual hero, but he knew that Émilie understood his work better than he ever would. Following the publication of this work, he wrote to Émilie, 'I used to teach myself with you, but now you have flown up where I can no longer follow.'

Work would flow thick and fast from the hands of the pair. They were prolific in their writing, inspiring one another to reach still-greater heights. It was in this period that Émilie would produce the three pieces of work for which she is most widely known.

In 1737, Émilie produced her first major scientific work, which she kept secret from Voltaire. This was her *Dissertation on the Nature and Propagation of Fire*. This work was submitted to a competition at the French Academy of Sciences, and although it did not win the prize it was highly regarded. Voltaire, too, entered an essay into the competition – on which he received feedback from Émilie, who concealed that she too planned to submit an entry. Voltaire was obsessed with proving that fire had weight; Émilie believed the opposite. It was not until Voltaire was lamenting that his entry was not awarded the top prize that Émilie's commiserations rang a little too sincere, and she confessed that she, too, had entered and lost. Although her thesis was at odds with his own, Voltaire set about promoting Émilie's work in an effort to get it published, which, in due course, it was. Émilie was the first woman published by the Academy. She was also, following this essay, elected to the

Academy of Sciences at the Institute of Bologna, an honour never before bestowed upon a woman.

Next, in 1740, came the publication of *Foundations of Physics*. This book was written to explain Newtonian physics, including both classical mechanics and theories of motion, to her son. It was also intended as a critique of some of the contemporary interpretations of physics, particularly those of Leibniz. She attempted to synthesise both Newtonian physics and Leibnizian metaphysics, blending their ideas to explain the nature of matter, motion and energy. She also explained the principles of kinetic energy (as she saw them), building on Leibniz's ideas.

Finally, in 1744, after the couple returned to Paris, Émilie began work on what would be her most famous publication: her translation and commentary on Newton's *Principia*, a foundational text of the Enlightenment; Émilie's translation is still in use today. Not only did Émilie translate this work from Latin into vernacular French, but she also interpreted and explained its complex ideas. This was more than a linguistic feat – it was testament to deep philosophical understanding. Émilie transformed geometric proofs into the more widely understood language of calculus, making Newton's ground-breaking concepts, such as his contributions to gravity and energy, accessible to a broader audience. Her work required translation, interpretation, annotation and clear expression of complex theories – an extraordinary achievement that underscored her intellectual prowess. Einstein's most famous equation, $E=mc^2$, relies on the use of the square of the speed of light, $c^2$ – this is traceable to Émilie's work.

However, while her intellectual life and output climbed to still-loftier heights, her personal life was less lucky. The romantic relationship between Émilie and Voltaire broke down, something she mourned, and she became frustrated with herself for how much she missed him, and how his leaving her had such a great effect. Voltaire fell out of love with her first, and it seems she was devastated, but forged ahead. Despite this, they remained deeply intertwined in one another's lives, continuing to collaborate, travel and live together while both pursuing other romantic liaisons. During the winter of 1747–8, Émilie, Voltaire and their entourage settled in Lunéville at the 'court' of Stanisław Leszczyński, the former King of Poland and now duke of the semi-autonomous duchy of Lorraine. In his sprawling estate, he hosted many intellectuals of the Enlightenment, and it was only natural that Voltaire and Émilie would find their way there.

It was during their sojourn here – at which point the exact status of her relationship with Voltaire is hard to glean – that Émilie fell passionately in love with a much younger man, the soldier and poet Jean-François de Saint-Lambert. However, the consequences of this reciprocated love were disastrous. Now in her mid-forties, Émilie became pregnant. This was extremely dangerous for a woman of her age, and there was no safe option of an abortion. Voltaire – despite not being the father – stood by her and encouraged her to tell her husband the truth and return home, but she refused. But she felt her days were numbered, working feverishly on her translation of the *Principia* throughout her pregnancy, anxious that they might be her last chance to finish what would be her magnum opus. On 4 September 1749, Émilie gave birth to Saint-Lambert's daughter, whom she christened Stanislas-Adélaïde du Châtelet. Just days after giving birth, Émilie died of a pulmonary embolism. Both Voltaire and Saint-Lambert were with her in her last days, and her loss struck a profound blow to them both.

Voltaire seemed to bounce back. It appeared that for some time he had been having an affair with his niece – although this was never definitively confirmed – and following Émilie's death he swiftly moved this still-younger woman into her apartments in Paris. Whatever immediate steps he took in his household, he mourned her for years in his writing at least, and saw to it that her last work, the *Principia*, was published and received the respect and attention it deserved. Moreover, Saint-Lambert, it seems, mourned her too, but likewise recovered fairly swiftly.

Émilie was a mathematical genius. She had a gift, and she bemoaned the few opportunities women in society had for independent action and self-sufficiency. As she saw it, it was almost impossible for women to achieve both passion and independence, and thus she concluded that the safest way to achieve happiness for a woman of her social class was to devote herself to study and passion for learning. Nevertheless, her life and her contributions to science were consistently overlooked and dismissed for centuries, much like the work of Christine de Pizan. Immanuel Kant famously wrote that to consider Émilie a great thinker was as preposterous as to imagine a bearded woman, consigning her to the status of mere circus freak. For centuries, critics preferred to imagine her merely as Voltaire's conquest or, at best, his sidekick, rather than recognising her as a brilliant mind in her own right.

Émilie was a flame who burned brightly. She loved life, she loved knowledge, she loved love. Her legacy has been too long overshadowed by Voltaire, who was her inferior at least in so far as science and mathematics are concerned. He may have been a trailblazer, and a genius, but so was she – and the odds were stacked against her.

Olympe de Gouges, watercolour, 1793.

# 8

# Olympe de Gouges

## 7 May 1748–3 November 1793

> 'Man, are you capable of being fair? Tell me? What gave you the sovereign right to oppress my sex?'
> Olympe de Gouges, *Declaration of the Rights of Woman and of the Female Citizen*, 1791

It is a grey Sunday evening in Paris, 1793. A middle-aged woman – still of remarkable beauty – with white hair pulled loose in the wind, ascends a flight of wooden steps. Mounted on a platform, in the centre of the Place de la Révolution, is the guillotine.

The woman contemplates the grisly instrument, which claimed the life of the former queen, Marie Antoinette, just one month before, and of revolutionary Charlotte Corday four months earlier – and countless more in between. It was designed by a medical man to put an end to messy, torturous, drawn-out deaths on the wheel, or being torn apart by horses, or strangulation by hanging. Swiftly, it has evolved into a symbol of brutality and the Terror – for this is the bloodiest period of the French Revolution – of which this woman is about to become yet another victim.

She turns to the crowd, the tears on her cheeks dry at last, and cries out: '*Enfants de la Patrie, vous vengerez ma mort!*' ('Children of the Fatherland, you will avenge my death!')

# A HISTORY OF FRANCE IN 21 WOMEN

Her voice is strong but is snatched by the wind. Then, she is strapped to a wooden board, face down, prostrate and horizontal, raised a metre from the ground. Her hands bound behind her back, rough hands push her hair from her neck, and the executioner places her throat on the bloodstained, stinking butcher's block. If animal panic set in, it would be now. There is a whoosh, a creak, the blade falls, two thuds in quick succession, the crowd bays, and the life of a woman who for a short time was France's greatest champion of liberty, equality and fraternity is extinguished.

\* \* \*

The execution of Olympe de Gouges was a farce, a symptom of the disorder and disregard for life that characterised the Terror. This series of executions without fair trial, numbering in their thousands between 1793 and 1794, culminated in the deaths of many of the period's architects. Robespierre and his cronies found themselves strapped to that very same board that bore the bodies of Olympe de Gouges, Marie Antoinette and Charlotte Corday as they suffered execution. Other members of the so-called 'Committee of Public Safety' died earlier – Danton killed on Robespierre's orders, and Marat famously murdered in his bath by Charlotte Corday.

Olympe had been a revolutionary – she was not a beneficiary of the *Ancien Régime* – and came from humble origins. Initially fervently supporting the revolutionary cause, she had dared to ask questions about the gratuitous bloodshed, and to demand that the 'equality' pursued by the revolutionary French should be afforded to everyone under French jurisdiction – she called for the emancipation of slaves and the empowerment of women. Even during a period of great change and new ideas, she was ahead of her time and that was something dangerous.

Olympe de Gouges was a prolific proto-feminist and abolitionist. She was fearless, determined and brilliant. Almost entirely self-taught, and subjected to a forced marriage in rural France, she managed to raise herself to become a woman of letters – and a militant one at that – in revolutionary Paris.

I grew up with the name of Olympe de Gouges all around. My summers have always been spent around La Garonne, and – after D'Artagnan, Armagnac and foie gras – Olympe de Gouges is probably the region's most famous product. However, during her adolescence in Montauban, near Toulouse, no one would have known the name Olympe de Gouges. She was born Marie Gouze in the small city in the south of France, officially the daughter of a butcher and a laundress, named Anne-Olympe, the name from which she would eventually fashion her own. In keeping with the practices of the time, she was not sent to school – but nevertheless scraped an education, stealing snatches of teaching from whoever would give it to her, and teaching herself as best she could.

Her relationship with her parents was complicated. It is highly likely that she was an illegitimate daughter born from an extramarital affair her mother had with the Marquis de Pompignan, a local lord. Her mother's family had long worked for his, the two grew up together, and it seems she was the love of his life. But rigid social structures separated the pair, and saw the young man sent away for his studies, and Anne-Olympe married off. Her legal father did not attend her baptism and died two years after her birth. At this point, her mother could have yielded Marie to her biological father to educate, but she refused, choosing instead to keep the young Marie with her, and eventually remarrying. Whether this was better or worse for the child is hard to say, and it certainly meant she missed out educationally, but it also meant she developed a close relationship with her mother, which lasted all of her life.

This is perhaps surprising, given that she was forced to marry against her will, aged just seventeen. She was violently opposed to the match. The man in question was Louis-Yves Aubry, a local tradesman. He brought her little joy, but the couple did have a son, Pierre. Much to Olympe's relief, he died two years after their marriage when the Tarn burst its banks and a catastrophic flood swept through the area, claiming many lives.

The marriage had been a disaster – not only because of his death. In Marie's eyes, it was a bitter cruelty and the utmost injustice. Not only did she detest the man she was forced to chain herself to legally, and submit to sexual intercourse with, but on top of that he was her social and financial inferior. It is unknown why her parents forced the match, but in any case, the death of Aubry heralded the rebirth of Marie, in the form of the formidable Olympe de Gouges.

Widowed, she found freedom for the first time in her life. She took a new lover, Jacques Biétrix de Rozières, and travelled to Paris, where, using her dower portion and with aid from her new man, she managed to establish herself in the fashionable literary circles of Paris, living with her son and her sister. She crafted herself a new name, Olympe – from her mother – and *de Gouges*, as an aristocratic reimagining of her birth name. She wanted a new life, and to put the traumas of her past behind her.

It was a new chapter not only for Olympe, but also for France. These were the decades of free thought, economic challenge and social change that laid the groundwork for the hurricane of revolution.

Olympe arrived in Paris possibly as early as 1768, and few details are known about her early years there, except that she received significant financial support from the lover who had funded her move. It is likely they did not have an exclusive relationship, and the newly liberated Olympe, now in her twenties and thriving in Paris, was determined to live a free life. She was known for her beauty, one chronicler referring to her as the 'perfection of southern beauty: her eye sparkled with the fire of thought and passion, her superb black hair fell in bountiful curls'. Paris was a city of pleasure, frivolity was fashionable, and a beautiful and only slightly educated woman brimming with ideas was certain to be popular. She became a kind of intellectual courtesan, and by all accounts relished it.

The mostly uneducated Olympe, hungry for knowledge, managed to scrounge an education by frequenting the literary and cultural salons of Paris in the 1770s and 1780s. She wrote of her lack of access to formal education: 'Fate has deprived me of deep knowledge; I have sought the truth by feeling my way.' It was a time of free-flowing ideas, and revolutionary talk, and Olympe delighted in the diversion and the intellectual freedom. She had much to learn before she could truly invent herself as an author, and it was fifteen years before any works of note were published. She may not even have been fully literate upon her arrival in Paris. On top of this, her first language had not been French at all; her mother tongue was Occitan, still commonly spoken in the south at this time. This put her at a still-greater disadvantage when it came to launching a literary career in classic French. Indeed, traces of Occitan phrasing are detectable in her writings.

Once confident in her skills, she wrote extensively, although still often employing scribes when needed. She made a name for herself as a prolific writer. Her first novel, entitled *Mémoire de Madame de Valmont*, published in 1788, was largely autobiographical and epistolary in format, and in it she reproduced – it seems almost word for word – letters exchanged between her and her biological father, the Marquis de Pompignan. Its value lies primarily in the light shed on Olympe's early life. After that, she turned her hand to writing plays.

However, Olympe's time in Paris was far from a pleasure trip, and her writing quickly took on a distinctly political and angry edge. Even in her first novel she railed against the injustice of the female condition. She came up against hostility and prejudice due to her origins and outspoken views, and she was not financially independent. Her looks gave her an edge, but social and literary acceptance were still an uphill struggle.

Olympe's years in Paris coincided with a critical time for the nation, one marked by hardship and unrest. Her arrival there occurred during the last years of the reign of Louis XV (known as 'Louis the Beloved' – not for the esteem in which his citizens held him, but rather for his impressive succession of mistresses and lovers); he was succeeded by France's last Capetian monarch, Louis XVI, who ascended the throne in 1774 with Marie Antoinette at his side.

The social and political background of Paris in the 1770s was characterised by a rigid class structure, economic hardship and the influence of Enlightenment ideas. Against this backdrop, Olympe de Gouges and other thinkers began to challenge traditional norms and advocate for reform, setting the stage for the revolutionary changes that would soon sweep France.

Louis XVI lived a famously lavish, decadent and totally immoderate life with Marie Antoinette. They had little detectable regard for their public image, and the monarchy was beginning to show signs of weakness in the late 1770s and 1780s. The country was in debt. France's recent loss in the Seven Years' War – a global conflict often referred to as the real First World War, due to the fact that battles were fought everywhere from the Caribbean to India, including Europe, North America and Africa – had been devastating. The primary conflict had been between French and British colonial interests, and France had borrowed heavily to finance their operations, but ultimately lost territory, and emerged no richer for it. These debts were compounded by those incurred when France had lent to revolutionaries during the American War of Independence. France had naturally sided with the United States against their old rival, England.

Furthermore, the ideas and progress of the Enlightenment were reaching their zenith and Paris was a hub of intellectual activity. Thinkers like Voltaire, Rousseau and Diderot questioned traditional authority and promoted ideas of liberty, equality and fraternity. Their writings inspired many, including Olympe de

Gouges, to advocate for social and political reform. Such writers and philosophers – the influencers of their day – were vocally critical of the Church and the monarchy. Denis Diderot had famously declared that 'Man will never be free until the last king is strangled with the entrails of the last priest.'

These were pivotal years in French history, and with the benefit of hindsight, we can clearly discern the first sparks that would ignite the Revolution.

The French class system – the *Ancien Régime* – had reached such extremes of inequality that the population was mutinous. On top of this, they had greater access to education, meaning they could better give voice to their discontent. France divided society into three classes – clergy, nobility and commoners. Commoners had the least power but worked the hardest and bore the brunt of taxation. In the 1770s and 1780s taxation rose to compensate for debt – as did the cost of food, leading to Marie Antoinette's alleged response to the news that the people had no bread: 'Let them eat cake.'

Although there is no evidence that Marie Antoinette ever uttered this sentence – and if she did, she said 'brioche' rather than 'cake' – it is unquestionable that Louis XVI would have understood the dangers of the food shortages that were prevalent in France in the 1780s, and yet the monarchy did little to address the problem. Unsurprisingly, the monarchy's poorly received PR campaign, which saw Marie Antoinette depicted in simple 'rustic' clothing in portraits, did little to soothe the fury of a hungry population. Not only were resources mismanaged, but drought and storms also led to a bad harvest, adding insult to injury.

Meanwhile, Olympe's writing career blossomed. The masterpiece for which she is best known was an anti-slavery play, *L'Esclavage des Noirs* or *Zamore et Mirza*, which was performed at the Comédie-Française in 1785. This play was an overt condemnation of the practice of slavery and told the story of a slave pardoned for the murder of an overseer, who was accused of rape. The titular characters, Zamore and Mirza, are enslaved Africans on an Indian island. They are on the run, following a crime committed by Zamore against an overseer. During their escape, they rescue a liberal-minded French couple from a shipwreck, who then proceed to advocate for the death sentence against Zamore and Mirza to be overturned. The play provoked outrage from the colonialist lobby and led to it being shut down after only three performances; indeed, it had taken her some years to persuade the Comédie-Française to stage the play at all.

In the late eighteenth century, slavery played an integral part in France's colonial economy, particularly in Saint-Domingue (present-day Haiti), the world's largest producer of sugar. The Code Noir, enacted in 1685, legally sanctioned the brutal treatment of slaves, granting their owners near-total control over their lives. While the Enlightenment had sparked discussions on human rights, the question of slavery remained contentious, with the economic interests of plantation owners often taking precedence over moral considerations. By the 1780s, however, the abolitionist movement in France began gaining traction, influenced by the writings of philosophers like Denis Diderot and the activities of societies such as the Société des Amis des Noirs, founded in 1788. Olympe de Gouges's work was part of this broader movement that sought to challenge the moral legitimacy of slavery.

The Bastille was stormed on 14 July 1789. This dramatic moment was a powerful visual symbol of the power of the revolutionaries and the overthrowing of the tyranny of the *Ancien Régime*. Only seven prisoners were found inside, which was something of an anti-climax, given the infamy of the fortress. One month before this event, Olympe had written her famous speech, 'The Address to the French by One Who Is Blind'. For Olympe de Gouges, the Bastille's collapse was a transformative moment that heightened her revolutionary zeal and galvanised her political writing. In the words of the nineteenth-century writer Charles Monselet: 'the Bastille is collapsing. The blazing dust of this old monument, similar to that of a great fire, is moving across Europe ... Olympe de Gouges received its baptism; it opened her eyes and ears to listen to the people's cries.'

In the immediate aftermath of the sacking, Olympe herself travelled to Versailles armed with 3,000 copies of a text she had written urging the king to abdicate – but was of course barred from seeing the king. It was titled *Séance Royale*. A few months later came the Women's March on Versailles. Market women – incensed by the sky-rocketing prices of bread – merged with agitators to ransack Paris in search of weapons and, thus armed, marched on the king and queen at Versailles. Besieging the palace, they were successful in forcing Louis to acquiesce to their demands and the family to decamp back to Paris with them. This would be the last journey the French royal family ever made.

In the following years Olympe de Gouges contributed to revolutionary activity through her writing. She produced dozens of pamphlets, declarations, plays and speeches. She was against the execution of the monarchy, instead supporting a constitutional monarchy. She wrote extensively on various social issues, advocating for divorce, gender equality in civil partnerships, maternity hospitals, and homes for the elderly, while also speaking out against slavery. Her significant works include *The Philosopher Prince*, published in 1792, and her voluntary tax initiative, where she encouraged women to pay taxes and led by example.

Her most famous and best-remembered work is her *Declaration of the Rights of Woman and of the Female Citizen*. Written as a pamphlet, this was a pioneering and passionately written demand for equality between the sexes and a pivotal document in the history of feminism. It was written in reaction to the *Declaration of the Rights of Man and of the Citizen* of 1789 – drafted by the Marquis de Lafayette, Thomas Jefferson and Abbé Sieyès – which conspicuously excluded women from its pages, alongside children, the poor, the enslaved and foreigners living in France. It inspired Mary Wollstonecraft's similarly titled *A*

*Vindication of the Rights of Woman*, which was printed in Britain the following year. In this manifesto, Olympe articulated fundamental rights that she believed should be extended to all individuals, regardless of gender. These included equality before the law, the right to participate in government, the right to education and freedom of speech. She also advocated for women's right to own property, divorce and challenge unjust power structures that upheld male dominance. It was a radical call for gender equality and justice, dedicated (somewhat ironically) to *La Reine* Marie Antoinette.

Meanwhile, events in the Revolution moved quickly, and internal conflict arose between the newly installed republican government and the Girondin party, aligned with federalism, with whom Olympe de Gouges sympathised. On 10 August 1792, the Tuileries Palace, where King Louis, Marie Antoinette and their close family had been living as prisoners since the Women's March, was stormed and the monarchy effectively overthrown. Louis was arrested, and in September the institution of the monarchy was officially abolished, and the National Convention declared France a republic. That same summer, the guillotine was erected in the Place de la Révolution. Louis was put on trial without his titles, known only as *Citoyen* Louis Capet. He was found guilty of multiple broad-reaching crimes against the public and the state and sentenced to death. He was executed on 21 January 1793, his severed head brandished before the crowds. From this time, the writing was on the wall for Olympe de Gouges, who was so zealous for the revolutionary cause that she either believed her own life worth sacrificing or failed to read the room.

In the months leading up to the execution of the queen, Olympe had published her most incendiary offering to date, a poster and pamphlet entitled *Les Trois Urnes* (*The Three Urns*). Previously, the leaders of the Revolution had been able to turn a blind eye to Olympe's writings – they were not unpatriotic, and her progressive writing on women and emancipation was dismissible. *Les Trois Urnes* was different. In this work, she challenged the concept of the Republic as 'one and indivisible' by proposing a democratic vote across the country to choose a truly representative form of government. Each urn represented a ballot box: one for monarchy, one for federalist/Girondist government and one for republican government.

Such promotion of democratic voting had been declared treasonous and punishable by death in March 1793. De Gouges's assertion that the current system was driving France towards bloodshed and civil war, in addition to its struggles with foreign powers, was too direct for the authorities to overlook.

She published this during the Terror, while Robespierre was running the Committee of Public Safety, and heads were falling left, right and centre. Olympe was arrested, and the administrator of the Committee of Public Safety interrogated her himself. He had her quietly incarcerated in the *hôtel de ville* in a tiny attic room, under constant surveillance. Conditions there were worse than the Bastille had been, and Olympe was appalled at the squalor. When they searched her papers for something incriminating, they found nothing – Olympe was a revolutionary and a patriot.

The summer that followed, during which time Olympe remained a prisoner (now in the Prison de l'Abbaye Saint-Germain), was atrocious. The Terror continued to rage, as did civil war, and other conflicts. The economic crisis worsened, and so too did Robespierre's mental health. More and more people, including his close allies, were sent to the guillotine. With the executions continuing at such a pace, a previously mild middle-class woman from Normandy decided to commit an extreme act of violence in protest. In July 1793, Charlotte Corday talked her way into the home of Jean Marat, one of the instigators of the violence, and stabbed him to death while he bathed. Speaking in her own defence at her trial she declared, 'I killed one man to save one hundred thousand.' For all this, she was not able to save herself.

Olympe continued to fight from prison, somehow managing to erect posters pleading her case in the capital. She was desperate, conditions were foul, and she had a leg wound that would not heal. Eventually she was transferred to a nursing facility, which was a little better, but expensive, and she had to fund herself through selling her jewellery.

Next came the September Massacres – a wave of mob violence and summary executions marked for their brutality and scale – whose victims included the close friend of the queen, the Princess de Lamballe, who was murdered by the mob, her remains mutilated and paraded through Paris. Misogyny was rife at this time, and the republican government decided to crack down heavily on the activities and freedoms of women. The National Convention banned all women's clubs, including the Society of Revolutionary Republican Women, viewing them as threats to stability.

On 16 October, Marie Antoinette – whom de Gouges had defended – was sent to the guillotine. She likewise stood trial, but by this point the process had become a farce; she was accused of many false charges, including the molestation of her son, a crime of which she was certainly innocent.

Two weeks after this execution, Olympe was transferred to a new prison, the Conciergerie. On 2 November she was brought before the revolutionary court, in little state to give her own defence. To top things off, her lawyer was not present.

She attempted to defend herself. She was accused of calling for a vote, which was twisted into inciting civil war, and of criticising members of the republican government. She said she had not changed her mind on these matters. But this was irrelevant. Like so many trials during the Terror, this was a kangaroo court, and the verdict a foregone conclusion. Olympe did not want to die, and at the last minute claimed to be pregnant, in the hope of stalling her execution – but to no avail.

Back in her cell, she drafted what would be her last letter, addressed to her son, Pierre, born all those years ago in Montauban:

## OLYMPE DE GOUGES

> My dear son, I am dying, a victim of my idolatry for my country and our people. Our enemies ... have driven me, remorseless, to the scaffold ... I am dying an innocent woman.

Olympe took one last look in the mirror to compose herself, before making her way to the scaffold. With her died one of France's greatest, and fairest, revolutionaries, a woman who had fought her whole life for liberty and equality, and arguably fraternity too.

The death of Olympe de Gouges makes clear that the French Revolution, while perhaps based on heroic ideas, was neither heroic nor glorious. Nor was it permanent. Many of the real heroes of the Revolution were women, like Charlotte Corday and Olympe de Gouges, who found their heads in the basket of the guillotine, put there by the misogynistic men who used the spirit of revolution for their own ends, and wanted to put down those who genuinely sought equality. Many of the noble ideals outlined in the *Declaration of the Rights of Man and of the Citizen*, issued shortly after the storming of the Bastille in July 1789, were significantly undermined by radicals who seized control and initiated the Reign of Terror.

The Terror would be brought to an end with Robespierre's dramatic fall from grace, which culminated in his head being struck off by the same blade he had turned against so many. The coup that saw a new government take control in the power vacuum that formed after his dispatch was known as the Thermidorian Reaction – named after the month of Thermidor in the French revolutionary calendar. By revolutionary dating, this event took place on 9 Thermidor, Year II, but by traditional dating it was 27 July 1794. It was a political movement, a backlash against the atrocities of the Terror.

A young Corsican officer, who had distinguished himself in command of artillery during the siege of Toulon and subsequently come to the attention of Robespierre, found himself tarnished by association and placed under house arrest. Likewise, in another part of Paris a newly widowed young woman from Martinique was languishing in prison – although the death of Robespierre brought her freedom. The two were destined to meet in the aftermath of the Thermidorian Reaction and become the Emperor and Empress of France.

The Revolution concluded with a further coup in 1799, led by this very officer – none other than Napoleon Bonaparte. The Creole woman who was to become his wife was the much talked-about Josephine de Beauharnais.

Detail from *Joséphine in Coronation Costume* by Baron François Gérard, *c.* 1807–8.

# 9

# Empress Josephine

## 23 June 1763–29 May 1814

'I don't love you anymore; on the contrary, I detest you. You are a vile, mean, beastly slut. You don't write to me at all; you don't love your husband; you know how happy your letters make him, and you don't write him six lines of nonsense ...

'Soon, I hope, I will be holding you in my arms; then I will cover you with a million hot kisses, burning like the equator.'

Napoleon Bonaparte, November 1796

It is 6 August 1794. Robespierre has been dead for nine days, and the Terror raging for over a year. The smack of heavy boots can be heard striding down a first-floor corridor in the now infamous Prison des Carmes; which until a few years before had been a silent place, home to a community of Parisian priests and monks, hundreds of whom were slaughtered in the September Massacres. Now it is the most feared gaol in Paris, where aristocrats and troublemakers are held in foetid conditions prior to arbitrary execution. For some weeks now, lawyers, cross-examination, evidence and a defence have not been permitted at trials. The accused are tried in batches of as many as fifty and condemned to death.

The people in the cells of this prison exist in a sorry state. The women have shaved their hair, their clothes are filthy, and they are crammed like sardines. They shaved their hair for two reasons: to avoid lice and to be ready for the guillotine. They have become used to men coming each day to take more of them for the chop, and they know that, any day, they might be next. Goodbyes are no longer tearful and demonstrative, but matter-of-fact.

In one of these cells, trembling lest the guard in his thudding boots is coming for her, is a woman named Marie-Joseph Rose de Beauharnais – known as Rose to her friends. She has good reason to think today is the day she will be executed, as her husband Alexandre de Beauharnais was guillotined just two weeks earlier, and ever since he was sentenced, she has been waiting for her turn. When husbands are axed, the wives usually follow.

Rose has been suffering in the Prison des Carmes for over three months. Her health has been ruined by the conditions. Food has been scarce, hygiene terrible and the guards cruel – taking sexual advantage of the desperate women in the cells. She has seen countless friends go to their deaths and lived in fear for her life every day. She has managed to smuggle letters to her children, and saw her husband most days before his death, but all this has been scant comfort. The only way for women to escape execution is to become pregnant. She has been having an affair with a higher-status prisoner, perhaps in the hope her fertility will save her, but so far, no joy.

Nevertheless she has been lucky and is about to become luckier still. She has not been killed, and this is rumoured to be because a young man – a B-list actor who somehow curried favour with the Committee of Public Safety – had taken a shine to her. The story goes that each day he tactically loses the files of the condemned that he knows personally and as such they evade execution. There is no direct evidence of this; does her gift of a thousand francs, sent to him after her release, support the tale?

Every day not selected for execution is a good day for Rose, but today will be on a different scale. The bolt scrapes in the lock and the guard who usually calls out the names of the dead calls her name. Her heart plummets, and she freezes. She scarcely hears the words he utters. He has to repeat them several times before they sink in. He is not summoning her to the block at all, but rather telling her she is a free woman. She blinks, and shakily stands, pulling a threadbare shawl about the flimsy nightdress that now serves as her best dress. Hesitantly, she staggers from the prison, stepping blinking into the light of Rue de Vaugirard, just next to the Jardin du Luxembourg. Still reeling in shock, she stumbles through the chaotic streets to the address where she knew her children to be staying with trusted servants. Finally Rose is safe: the Terror is over, and a brave new world dawning in France.

Just months later, Rose, the hollow-cheeked waif from the Prison des Carmes, can be seen gallivanting around Paris. Her hair has grown out a little to a chic pixie-cut, a style now referred to as '*à la victime*', and she wears a red ribbon tied around her neck to mock the cut of the guillotine. Her dress is still white, flimsy and diaphanous, more revealing than anything she might have worn before the Revolution, but now she sports this prison-esque garb with debonair pride. Now, it is the latest fashion. These dresses are a reaction to the highly intricate, formal corseted style of the *Ancien Régime*, but they are also highly sensual: the women walk around in a state of *déshabillé*, as they might in their bedroom, in front of a lover. The aristocratic ladies who stumbled out into freedom from the Prison des Carmes – missing death by inches – are now the toast of Paris, swanning around 'Survivors' Balls' and dancing on Robespierre's grave. French society is rebounding from the horrors of the Terror with a manic glee. The trend of *bals des victimes* is sweeping Paris.

Rose embraces this new world order – so much more favourable to her than the one just past. But, as before, she is dancing on a knife edge. Nothing is certain, and she is anything but secure. Rose is a widow in her early thirties, with two children, and no income. Her only path to survival is to reinvent herself as a fashionable lady of society, and hope that she catches the eye of rich and powerful men who might make her their mistress or marry her. Once again, in October 1795, luck is on her side. Rose is introduced, through one of her less jealous lovers, to a rising brigadier general named Napoleon Bonaparte. Something about her piques his interest. This encounter changes not only her life, but his as well, and will come to shape the fate of France.

Napoleon Bonaparte is perhaps the most famous Frenchman of them all, and Josephine de Beauharnais drove him crazy.

Josephine, rightly or wrongly, is not a woman I necessarily 'look up' to. She was not a self-made woman in the vein of others in this book. She is not a moral role model either. Josephine de Beauharnais was clearly intoxicating, stylish, sophisticated, intelligent and beautiful, but her fame and importance in French history comes not – I reluctantly admit – from these, but from her passionate and often toxic relationship with the man who would forge a new French Empire out of the ruins of the Revolution. She fascinated him, and looking at her life, the obstacles she overcame, and what she achieved, it is easy to see why.

The Napoleonic era was a defining period in the history of France. Not only for the decades-long wars which saw the burgeoning French Empire undo many of the reforms of the Revolution, expanding its territories across Europe and further afield by pitching itself against various coalitions of European countries, before a crushing defeat at the Battle of Waterloo, but also for the cultural and legal strides made at this time. Many of the legal, administrative and cultural reforms implemented under Napoleon Bonaparte are still in place today, and many of Napoleon's territorial gains have stood the test of time. Napoleon is regarded by many still as history's greatest military tactician, and history's greatest Frenchman. Paris reverberates with his legacy, whether in the neighbourhoods named after his great victories, or in the gilded Egyptian art brought back by him from his campaigns. The golden *Dôme des Invalides*, glinting in sunlight, dominates the skyline, and inside this church his porphyry marble tomb rests in honour, surrounded by self-aggrandising artworks inspired by imperial Rome. His legacy is that of a giant. But in life, he was always humbled by his love for Josephine. This is not a book about the deeds of great men, but the lives of great women and Josephine – so often eclipsed by the shadow of her husband – deserves some attention of her own.

While Napoleon was away on his various campaigns, back home the centre of his glittering court was the great love of his life – the Empress Josephine. A woman of humble, Creole origins, whose first husband sneered at her for her rotten teeth and provincial manners, she rose to become the richest and most influential woman in France. She redefined fashion, and the social mores of the French court, and moulded the role of empress for herself, haunted by the ghost of Marie Antoinette, in whose bed she came to sleep. Above all Josephine was a survivor, and a player who knew the game.

Josephine is not an enigma in the same sense as Christine de Pizan or St Balthild. She lived in a post-Renaissance, post-Enlightenment, revolutionary age of letter writing, education and documentation, and is one of the most written-about women of French history. A library could be filled with all the pages written about Empress Josephine and her still-more famous second husband, Napoleon Bonaparte, first Emperor of the French.

Nevertheless, despite all these reams and reams of paper, only glimpses of her personality filter through – and much is lost in the cracks between the tesserae that make up the mosaic. We have hundreds of letters that Napoleon wrote to her, but precious few of her replies. Napoleon, it seems, was more careful with her privacy than she was with his. And, more than this, because of her connection to one of the most powerful men in European history, and the huge influence she held over him, she has been mythologised, and slandered, by writers and historians for centuries. Josephine's true legacy has been muddied by misinformation. There exists no *good* portrayal of her in mainstream popular culture: most recently Ridley Scott's film *Napoleon* – which critics quipped would have been better titled *Josephine* – among its other failures failed to depict Josephine accurately. The characterisation was off, not least because Josephine was portrayed as decades younger than her husband, when in fact she was a widow in her thirties when she first captured the heart of the awkward Corsican brigadier general in his mid-twenties.

So, despite the plentiful sources, she has been mythologised as an unfaithful temptress who never loved her husband, and who was put aside because of her infertility. How much of this is true is open to speculation – in part because, as discussed, where the historical record has access to Napoleon's passionate and intense letters to his wife, her letters to him were burned, adding to her mystique. We have half of their relationship, leaving the rest open to interpretation to at least some degree.

Visiting Fontainebleau, I stopped short in front of a portrait of Josephine. Her gaze is surprisingly tranquil and sweet for such a flinty woman.

Her skin creamy and soft, she is wearing the empire-line gowns I've grown up seeing on Austen heroines in the period dramas set against the backdrop of the Napoleonic Wars. Josephine is a grander version of these beauties. Looking at the portrait, you see a woman whose bosom threatens to spill out of the cream and golden gown. Delicate, almost translucent white skin, small lips fixed in a tepid smile, and lovely – truly lovely – dark eyes.

At the same time, the portrait is slightly unsettling. Josephine is perched uncomfortably on her throne, and she looks a little bored, like she is indulging a whim of her husband by posing for this slightly stuffy, imperial portrait. She is adorned with jewels, a monumental diadem of pearls and diamonds and large dark emeralds. From her ears cascade long, bright earrings. Her neck is long, her shoulders sloping, and a magnificent necklace – also dripping with emeralds and pearls – adorns her décolleté. She looks imperious, but not imperial.

And the truth is, Josephine was not imperial.

She grew up running barefoot around a sugar plantation in Martinique, and sucking sugar cane, which was apparently to blame for her darkened teeth.

She was born Marie-Joseph Rose Tascher de la Pagerie on 23 June 1763, in Les Trois-Îlets in Martinique, a French Caribbean island, half a world away from Paris and the court of Louis XV. She was raised away from educated society, amid the verdant landscape of the Caribbean, and surrounded by black slaves and crashing waves. It was an isolating upbringing, and she had little early exposure to fashion, learning or high culture. She was not reared on Enlightenment thinkers. She was sent to the Dames-de-la-Providence convent at Fort-Royal from 1773 to 1777 to receive an education, but this education, such as it was, did not give her any sophistication.

The family, while plantation owners and far better off than the slaves they exploited, were not rich. A hurricane destroyed much of their property in 1766 when Josephine was a small child, and her father did not have a good head for management. He had been born in France and was not raised to run a business like a plantation. He made mistakes, and the family fortune suffered.

The marriage of his three daughters was therefore very important for securing their futures, and it seemed most likely that the girls would find good husbands in France. A suitor – Alexandre de Beauharnais – was proposed to the family by Josephine's aunt. He was aged seventeen and decided the then fifteen-year-old Josephine was too old for him, and thus Josephine's younger sister Catherine-Désirée (then thirteen years old) was selected as the bride. Any jealousy Josephine may have felt at this was swiftly stifled when Catherine-Désirée took ill and died before the wedding could take place. With the arrangements already made,

Josephine was substituted for her sister at the eleventh hour and put on board a ship bound for France to meet her dead sister's betrothed, who was now hers instead.

The marriage was not a happy one. Despite Josephine's later reputation for beauty and sophistication, when she arrived in France Alexandre de Beauharnais was horrified. To his eyes, she was plump and lacked refinement, and had a grating accent, an empty head and a slouching posture. She was nothing compared to his elegant Parisian mistresses. Nevertheless, he still managed to pinch his nose and impregnate her twice. She gave birth to two children: Eugène, born in 1781, and Hortense, born in 1783, whom she would keep close to her even in their adult life.

Off to a bad start, the marriage deteriorated rapidly. Alexandre was ostentatiously unfaithful, but still sought to slander her, writing filthy and baseless accusations. The ensuing legal battle found in Josephine's favour: she was awarded custody of the children, and the eighteenth-century equivalent of alimony, not that Alexandre always paid. Following this settlement, she spent some time in Paris before returning to Martinique for a while.

Beyond these personal struggles, the Revolution was looming, and Alexandre was involved from the start. When revolutionary slave-riots broke out in Martinique, inspired by the fervour in France, Josephine decided to return to France again; her reasons are slightly unclear, but maybe she thought she would be safer in the comparatively vaster country, with more exit routes than the island. While initially profiting from the tumult, Alexandre experienced a rapid fall from grace and brought Josephine down with him.

When Josephine arrived back in France, Alexandre de Beauharnais was gaining influence in revolutionary politics. He supported reforms and held prominent positions, including President of the Constituent Assembly, before becoming commander-in-chief of the Army of the Rhine, which during the years of the Revolution still had the job of keeping the Prussians and their allies at bay. In

1793, Alexandre's military career was derailed when the Prussians succeeded in taking Mainz after a short siege, and Alexandre was blamed for the city's fall. For his part in this failure, Alexandre was arrested.

As we have seen, the tide of Revolution was fickle, and those who one day rode the wave could quickly find themselves dashed against the rocks or drowned under it. Following the loss of Mainz, Josephine and Alexandre both found themselves thrown into prison in 1794. Both held in the Prison des Carmes during the height of the Terror, roughly five months after the executions of Marie Antoinette and Olympe de Gouges, they were subjected to the terrible conditions and abuses already described. They were kept apart, but managed to meet for a few hours each day, and their children would smuggle messages to them and weep at the prison gates. After several months' imprisonment Alexandre was executed in July. The Terror ended with Robespierre's death, just five days later. While news of her husband's death made Josephine mentally prepare for her own execution, fate had other adventures in store for her. Against the odds, she was freed in the aftermath of Robespierre's fall, along with many other prisoners, marking the end of the Terror.

This seemingly miraculous survival was certainly a cause for celebration for Josephine, but she was still by no means secure. In fact, she had nothing. Alexandre's property had all been confiscated, and she was left penniless, with no means to support herself or her children. She relied on the charity of friends and struggled to maintain a basic standard of living.

However, a new world was emerging in the wake of the Terror.

Josephine suddenly, after being the unwanted wife of an unfaithful man, was now an object of interest, and single. It was *most fashionable* to have lost a husband to the guillotine, and to have narrowly escaped it oneself. It also seems she had acquired some refinement and society airs: no longer a bumpkin but rather a society darling. The fashion for chemise dresses suited her, as testified to by the many portraits of her dressed in this style. Sexual liaisons became freer still than they had been before the war, and Josephine took many lovers, perhaps to embrace living in the moment but also to ensure her own survival and that of her children. One of her lovers was Paul Barras, a member of the new government; through him Josephine first met the young Corsican general, the hero of the Siege of Toulon, named Napoleon Bonaparte, in 1795.

It must be remembered that Josephine was a widow six years older than Napoleon, thirty-two to his twenty-six, which raised eyebrows at the time. For all this, Napoleon's first impression of Josephine could not have been more different to Alexandre's. Josephine had changed a lot from her first days in mainland France, and the young officer was intoxicated by her.

After an intense courtship, during which Josephine seemed somewhat aloof and dismissive of her suitor, they married in 1796, taking many by surprise. Napoleon's family were furious. They had not consented to the wedding, which was a hasty and small-scale civil ceremony rather than a grand affair. Napoleon left Paris almost immediately afterwards, departing on his successful Italian campaign against the Austrian Empire, but he wrote passionately to his new bride all the while. Despite the continued assurances of her husband's affections, Josephine nevertheless began an affair with a younger and good deal more handsome French officer named Hippolyte Charles. At first, Napoleon had no idea. Then, after concluding the Italian expedition and moving onto his Egyptian campaign, word of her infidelity reached his ears.

He was distraught. Contrary to how it was portrayed by Ridley Scott, he did not abandon the campaign to rush home and throw Josephine out of the house. Nevertheless, Napoleon's Egyptian campaign was a fiasco, despite the many artefacts he looted, cities he sacked, and the several pretty paintings that he commissioned of himself looking powerful in front of the pyramids. The many failures of the campaign included the routing of the French fleet by Nelson at the Battle of the Nile, the failure to capture Acre, and the loss of vast swathes of the army to the bubonic plague.

While Napoleon was beset by calamity after calamity in North Africa and the Levant, Josephine was busy not only entertaining Hippolyte but also purchasing the Château de Malmaison in his absence. This estate, an imposing manor house located on the banks of the Seine just outside Paris, would become her haven. She expected her husband to return triumphant from Egypt, laden with gold that would pay for the house and the extensive renovations she had in mind. Unfortunately, he returned having lost money, and furious with her.

Having learned of the affair, an incensed Napoleon had instructed his brother to begin gathering the necessary proofs and materials for a divorce case. Desperate not to appear to the world as a cuckold, Napoleon further retaliated by taking the wife of one of his officers as a lover and parading her around Cairo, returning to France with her on his arm.

When Josephine received news of her husband's arrival, she rushed to him and threw herself at his feet begging for forgiveness. After blazing rows and many tears, they patched things up, apparently in quite steamy fashion. She even persuaded him against divorce, to the stupefaction of his brother and wider family. Nevertheless the extent of infidelity enraged Napoleon: when Josephine had visited him during his Italian campaign, she had even had the audacity to bring Hippolyte with her as her escort. He insisted that she give up Hippolyte – which it seems she duly did.

Recovering from these setbacks and the banishment of her lover, Josephine put her energy into transforming her new house at Malmaison into her own miniature Eden. She cultivated English roses, alongside exotic plants from her native Martinique, including pineapples – developing a true passion for botany. The house is still famous for the rose gardens she planted. The interiors showcase her exquisite and original taste in design as well, which differed from Napoleon's. While the château's interiors are grand, they are much less lavish than those favoured by Napoleon. Visitors to the château today are often surprised to find something more akin to a smaller English manor house than a palace or a true château. Rooms are relatively small, ceilings surprisingly low. It feels much more like a home than their other estates, the palace of Fontainebleau or the Tuileries.

Josephine filled the house with art looted from Europe, Napoleon's rather grandiose equivalent of souvenirs sent back from his campaigns. Even his failures enriched her collection, with Egyptian antiquities being some of the first art pieces to decorate the château's halls. Her personal taste, and indeed her and her husband's vanity, can be read in the art collection that adorns the walls of Malmaison to this day. The house is filled with paintings acquired and commissioned by Josephine herself, and indeed portraits of the pair. Likenesses of Josephine, rendered in oil paint, watercolour, plaster, marble, even tapestry, hang in almost every room.

She collected not only art and plants, but also animals. Kangaroos were soon hopping around the grounds, as were zebras, ostriches, antelope. And, beyond her collecting, she made the house an intellectual and social hub. Walking in the gardens today, it is not difficult to imagine Josephine strolling in her diaphanous gowns, wafting from room to room, from rose garden to rose garden. The couple's bedrooms and personal furniture are preserved. Napoleon's bedchamber is decorated like a military tent, Josephine's with softer, light furniture. Family portraits adorn the walls.

While Josephine was enjoying carefully curating her personal paradise, her husband took centre stage in a *coup d'état* in 1799 that would become known as the coup of 18 Brumaire – Brumaire being a month in the French revolutionary calendar, still used at this time, that coincided roughly with November. The French Directory, the five-man executive government that ruled France from 1795 to 1799 (marked by corruption, political instability and reliance on the military), was overturned, and Napoleon, still popular for his victories despite his defeat in Egypt, was made First Consul – de facto leader of France. This marked a turning point in French history by bringing an end to the Directory and setting the stage for Napoleon Bonaparte's rise to power as First Consul. This made Josephine into something like the First Lady of France. She was about to take up her role at the centre of French politics, presiding over the salons of Paris during the height of the eponymous Napoleonic era. She was a great asset to Napoleon during the early years of his supremacy. Although his family loathed her, she was popular with the French people and softened his public image. She also used her position to help smooth the way for the Concordat of 1801, which saw Napoleon make peace with the Pope and the Catholic Church. However, her affair with Hippolyte Charles had almost cost her this position of influence.

This affair and the public humiliation for Napoleon that it had brought with it had been the first of many great stains on their relationship, which would prove to be stormy, and vacillate between intoxicating love and plain toxicity. But Napoleon's passion for Josephine cannot be overstated: she was the great love of his life, and when he died it was her name on his lips. But one problem plagued him that would prove their undoing as a couple: she had not given him a child. The world may have changed a lot since the reign of Louis VII and Eleanor of Aquitaine, but for a man with dynastic ambitions, an heir remained of pivotal importance.

Josephine's family played a crucial role in Napoleon's political plans, and her daughter, Hortense, stood at the centre of this strategy. Given Josephine's now apparent infertility, Napoleon adopted Josephine's children as his own, and in 1802 forced the marriage of Hortense, Josephine's nineteen-year-old daughter, to his highly objectionable brother, Louis Bonaparte. The marriage was intended to secure ties between the two families, and, if it resulted in children, these could be declared Napoleon's heirs, vessels of Bonaparte blood. Hortense protested as best she could, but ultimately went through with it, only to be made desperately unhappy by her erratic and STD-riddled husband. Louis was known for being cold, possessive and jealous – famously on their wedding night, he bullied and disparaged her, mocking her by reading out a list of her mother's lovers, before presumably raping her. He also told her that if the rumours were true, and she was already pregnant with his brother's child, he would see her shamed and banished from society.

Hortense did give birth, but more than nine months after the wedding, which bought her more time in her unhappy marriage. She and Louis, despite their unhappiness, had three children together. That said, rumours persisted that their firstborn, christened Napoleon-Charles and born in 1802, was in fact not Louis's son at all, but rather Napoleon's – born of a semi-incestuous affair with his sister-in-law-stepdaughter. While there was no proof of these claims, the emperor seemed to dote on the baby boy. Although Napoleon never officially designated the boy his heir, everything pointed to this being the imperial intention. The birth of this child, strengthening the link between the Bonaparte and de Beauharnais families, seemed to grant Josephine a stay of execution, but the cost was her daughter's happiness.

For all this, as her husband's power solidified, Josephine was frightened and living under the threat of divorce. While Hortense's son was celebrated, he was an insurance policy, a back-up plan, and Napoleon still craved a true heir. At forty, and after eight years of marriage, it was doubtful she would suddenly succeed in this endeavour. Her in-laws always hated her, and many were whispering in her husband's ear – with growing volume – that he would be better served by putting Josephine aside and marrying a young, fecund, European princess. On top of this, because they had been married in a civil ceremony rather than a religious one, her status as his wife was particularly vulnerable. But Josephine was a survivor – she had survived the Terror; she would survive this too.

## EMPRESS JOSEPHINE

Napoleon made the error of coming clean with his wife about his train of thought. He was deeply torn and wanted to be honest with her about his view of their situation. He loved her, but he needed a wife who could give him an heir, and he was becoming more and more convinced that this could not be her. Josephine, publicly at least, managed to contain her distress, acting the part of a long-suffering woman willing to make sacrifices for the good of her country.

Napoleon, in his enthusiasm to be associated with the great emperors of the past, not least Charlemagne, had decided to have the Pope crown him emperor. When Pope Pius VII arrived, Josephine was asked to entertain him – she was after all a famous hostess, and a great asset to her husband. The night before the coronation, when stakes were at their highest, Josephine seized her moment. Begging a private audience, she revealed to the Pope that her marriage with Napoleon had not been blessed by God. The pontiff was horrified. Immediately, he informed Napoleon that he would crown no man emperor who was living in sin with a concubine. If Napoleon wanted the ceremony to go ahead, he would reaffirm his vows to his wife in a religious ceremony. Backed against the wall, with no time for games or negotiations, Napoleon was cornered. Reluctantly, he led his wife to the altar.

The next day the newly religiously married couple set out in a splendid carriage drawn by four pairs of white horses from the palace of the Tuileries to the cathedral of Notre-Dame. They were decked in gold and diamonds, sumptuous beyond measure. Napoleon's mother was not in attendance. She refused to watch 'the whore' be crowned. Napoleon's sisters were there, begrudgingly conscripted to carry their sister-in-law's train by petty bribery. There were a thousand diamonds in Josephine's diadem.

Before the assembled audience, Napoleon was crowned the first Emperor of the French. But actually, he not so much was crowned as crowned himself. When the Pope had finished anointing him and reached to place the crown atop Napoleon's head, the irreverent First Consul plucked it from his grip, raised it to the ceiling, and then placed it atop his own head, to the shock of those assembled. Then, he turned to watch his wife, resplendent in satin, rubies, diamonds and pearls, gleaming with gold, advancing towards him. She kneeled, and, in a moment immortalised in art, he raised the second, lesser coronet – touching it to his own head, and then settling it affectionately on hers, taking care to make sure it sat just right. Marie-Joseph Rose Tascher de la Pagerie was now Josephine, Empress of the French – the most illustrious woman in all the world. She beamed joyously up at her husband, tears flowing down her cheeks. For once her smile was so genuine, so wide, that her blackened teeth were visible.

One of the most famous paintings of French history – *The Coronation of Napoleon* by Jacques-Louis David – was commissioned to commemorate this event. Today, it hangs in the Louvre. Massive, measuring ten metres by six, it depicts the moment of the ceremony when Napoleon placed the gilded coronet upon Josephine's head, raising it heavenwards while she kneels in demure grace. Somehow, while it was unlikely to be Napoleon's intention, she is undeniably the focal point of the painting. The painting is misleading. Napoleon wanted to give an impression of imperial unity, and thus commanded the artist to paint his mother into the picture, presiding from a central balcony, and his two spoiled sisters simper over Josephine's train. It suggests a strong, unified royal family, but in truth it was anything but.

After her coronation as empress, Josephine's life became more complex, marked by political engagements, family responsibilities and the increasing strain of Napoleon's dynastic ambitions. Still with no heir in sight, in 1805 Josephine accompanied Napoleon to Italy, where he was crowned King of Italy, though she was not crowned and anointed as she had been in Notre-Dame. Festivities followed the coronation, including a spectacle where flowers were scattered over the imperial couple from a hot-air balloon. Soon after, Napoleon left to tour northern Italy, while Josephine explored the Italian lakes, and they reunited in Genoa before racing back to Paris due to new threats from a European coalition. It seems that in this period the power dynamic in their relationship shifted. Josephine lamented her husband's long military absences, and his replies to her became curter. She ran up huge jewellery bills.

Back in Paris in 1806, Josephine focused on securing advantageous marriages for her children, including a marriage for her son, Eugène, to Augusta Amalia of Bavaria. This strengthened the Beauharnais family's position and further integrated them into Napoleon's imperial plans. That same year, Louis was made King of Holland, while Hortense remained in Paris, under Napoleon's protection but far from her husband, who grew increasingly resentful. This arrangement provided Hortense with some relief from Louis's possessiveness but fuelled his suspicions about her loyalty and contributed to their marital discord.

Amid these family struggles, Josephine herself faced challenges in her role as empress, especially as Napoleon seemed if anything to become more obsessed with the idea of securing an heir, rather than letting the matter rest. In 1806, a son was born to Eléonore Denuelle de La Plaigne, a young noblewoman and an erstwhile mistress of Napoleon. This boy, Charles Léon, would be Napoleon's first acknowledged child. His birth, along with several other rumoured illegitimate children, seemed to act as evidence that the reproductive issues between Josephine and Napoleon were on her side, rather than his. On top of this, in 1807, Hortense's adored son, Josephine's grandson and Napoleon's nephew, Napoleon-Charles, died of illness, wiping out that potential plan for succession. By 1809, with pressure mounting, ministers began advising Napoleon that a divorce might be essential for France's stability. Though initially resistant, Napoleon ultimately decided in late November that they must separate. In a private meeting on 30 November, he broke the news to Josephine, who, devastated, collapsed and had to be carried back to her room.

In December, the couple formally announced their divorce in a ceremony at the Tuileries. Napoleon emphasised that he was sacrificing their marriage for the good of the state, while Josephine, though heartbroken, read a statement supporting his decision. The marriage was formally dissolved, but Napoleon insisted that Josephine retain her imperial title and ensured her financial security. Josephine retreated to Malmaison. She continued to see Napoleon regularly, but they would not live together again.

In 1810, Napoleon married Marie Louise of Austria – gifting her a sumptuous emerald necklace and earrings, recently looted from the Louvre – and the following year secured the heir he so desired. His son, Napoleon, was born on 20 March 1811 at the Tuileries Palace. Josephine spent these years at Malmaison, focusing on her gardens and art collection, and maintaining an influential social circle. When Napoleon's power began to falter in 1813 following his catastrophic Russian campaign, she prepared for potential exile, and she and Napoleon were destined to see very little of each other, as he scrambled to hold together his fracturing empire and repel allied forces.

The Russian campaign of 1812 was one of the most disastrous military ventures in history, leading to a near-total collapse of Napoleon's army. Starting with over 450,000 troops (the exact number is debated), the battered remnant of the army that limped back to France scarcely numbered 100,000. The campaign was intended to secure Russian submission through a quick, decisive strike. However, the Russian forces employed scorched-earth tactics, systematically destroying crops, supplies and villages as they retreated, leaving Napoleon's army stranded in barren territory with no resources. As the French advanced to Moscow, they found it deserted and partially burned, forcing them to retreat just as the brutal Russian winter set in. With temperatures dropping below −30°C, thousands died from exposure, starvation and Russian attacks on the retreating forces.

The impact back in France was profound. News of the catastrophic losses shattered the illusion of imperial invincibility, sent shockwaves through French society and unsettled his allies. Napoleon had suffered losses before, at the Nile and Trafalgar, but none like this. Critics grew bolder, questioning his judgement and his seemingly insatiable ambition. This campaign also weakened Napoleon's alliances across Europe, emboldening opposition forces to unite and challenge his dominance.

For Josephine, the collapse of the Russian campaign marked a turning point. Although they were divorced, she remained emotionally tied to Napoleon's fate and was anxious for the future. As rumours of defeat spread, she prepared for a possible shift in power by quietly moving to her estate at Navarre and securing her valuables, anticipating potential exile. The campaign's failure also revived Josephine's status in the eyes of many French citizens and European dignitaries, who saw her as a stabilising, sympathetic figure compared to the increasingly embattled emperor. Napoleon's diminishing power inadvertently elevated her, and she emerged as a beloved symbol of a more prosperous, peaceful time.

In 1814 she returned quietly to Malmaison. She arrived just months before Paris was surrendered by Napoleon's brother Joseph on 30 March 1814. Russian and Prussian troops marched through the streets in a victory procession, and within a month Napoleon was forced to abdicate. Josephine, a famed beauty and hostess, was an object of delight and not scorn to the invaders, and Tsar Alexander I even visited her at Malmaison, and walked with her in the rose gardens. She played her hand well and survived the transition of power in the French capital far better than her estranged husband, exiled to Elba following his abdication. She continued her sumptuous lifestyle, entertaining – in addition to the Russian tsar – the King of Prussia, the Grand Duke of Baden, the Prince of Bavaria, the Prince of Mecklenburg, visitors from England and Russian grand dukes.

That spring, after contracting an illness following a visit to her daughter Hortense's estate, Josephine's health declined. Despite medical attention, she died on 29 May 1814, at Malmaison, her children by her side. Her death sparked widespread mourning, with thousands paying their respects. She was remembered as '*la bonne Joséphine*' – a woman who, despite her complex life and tumultuous marriage, left a lasting legacy of grace and kindness in the hearts of the French people. After her death, her body lay in state for three days, and nearly 20,000 French mourners turned out to pay their respects to their erstwhile empress. Napoleon received word of her death while in exile on Elba, and took the news badly, shutting himself away and refusing to see anyone for several days. He carried her memory with him for the rest of his life, with his last words when he died on St Helena reported to be '*France, l'armée, tête d'armée, Joséphine*' ('France, the army, the head of the army, Josephine').

Forty-two years after her death, a statue of white marble would be erected in her native Martinique. In 1992 the statue would be beheaded, never to be mended, and in 2022 toppled for good by protestors as part of the Black Lives Matter protests that reverberated around the world. Local authorities gave the police instructions not to interfere.

Josephine's legacy is a complicated one. She wielded no hard power, but a tremendous amount of soft power during her lifetime, and was a highly influential figure during a pivotal and turbulent point in French history. She was the right-hand woman of the most famous Frenchman of all time, and it was her descendants, not his, who would populate the thrones of Europe even to this day. Hortense's and Eugène's children would marry into European royalty, and the legacy of the de Beauharnais family is far-reaching indeed. Above all else, Josephine was a survivor, and a trendsetter. There is some irony, therefore, that the illness that killed her was attributed to her choice of a flimsy and revealing dress '*à la victime*' on a cold day, to walk with the Tsar of Russia in the gardens of her daughter Hortense.

*Portrait of George Sand* by Auguste Charpentier, *c.* 1837–1839.

# 10

# George Sand

## 1 July 1804–8 June 1876

> 'Man dominates, woman submits: such is the natural order of things, say the men who insist on taking charge of the government of the world. But from submission, there is only a step to slavery, and from slavery to revolt.'
>
> From *Indiana*, by George Sand

In September 1866, a large crate – weighing as much as a small person – was delivered to the door of Gustav Flaubert, then a rising star of literary Paris. It contained in the region of seventy novels, all by the same author: George Sand. The author had instructed *her* publisher to send her complete works to this new friend, whom she had met at a dinner party thrown by Mathilde Bonaparte – a novelist herself and niece of the former emperor. Sand was sixty-two, Flaubert forty-four, and both were among the most celebrated writers of their day, although their styles contrasted radically, as did their intentions as writers: Sand wrote for her contemporaries, to entertain and influence, whereas Flaubert wrote in pursuit of creating the 'perfect novel'. Sand's gift of seventy novels in one go amused Flaubert, who had so far published just two – *Salammbô* and *Madame Bovary*.

A prolific writer, Sand was also an early 'influencer' – and slightly more sophisticated than today's variety. In addition to her massive output of fiction, she wrote essays, was politically active, staged plays, and was celebrated as a hostess and icon of her day. She was a famous beauty, dark-haired with eyes that seemed to hold the night. Nevertheless, outside France at least, she has been more or less forgotten – certainly in comparison to her male contemporaries.

Her friendship with Flaubert was profound, and lasted until the end of her life, with him hailing her as the only woman he could call his friend. While they had significant creative and political differences, Sand belonging to the Romantic movement and Flaubert breaking away into Realism, they held each other in high esteem and had a deep respect for each other's work. When Sand died, Flaubert said of attending her funeral, 'It seemed to me that I was burying my mother a second time.' Flaubert was not the only great man who grieved the loss of Sand's mind and heart. Among her lovers, admirers and friends were some of the great creatives and thinkers of the age: Victor Hugo, Balzac, Delacroix, Liszt, Chopin, Dostoevsky and many, many more. Balzac described her to his future wife in exultant terms after their first meeting: 'She is a boy ... she is an artist ... she is great, generous, devout, chaste; she has all the great traits of a man; ergo, she is not a woman ... I was talking to an ally.' Her eyes were remarked upon by nearly all who met her, Balzac stating, '*Toute la physionomie est dans l'œil*' ('The whole physiognomy is in the eye').

Aurore Dupin – or George Sand as she became – was a figure of fascination and controversy in Parisian society and her legacy is profound, both in literature and in the wider cultural consciousness of Paris. Indeed, her influence spread far beyond France, and she was celebrated across Europe. Romanticism, which had begun in the late eighteenth century, reached its zenith in the early nineteenth, and George Sand was a lynchpin of the movement in Paris. She brazenly flouted gender norms, wearing men's clothing, smoking cigars, and strolling through Paris with a proprietorial air. At a time when women were confined to restrictive, high-maintenance corsets and crinolines, Sand donned tailored trousers, frock coats, cravats and top hats. Some speculated that her decision to dress in men's clothing was for comfort and convenience: women's fashion was expensive and impractical, after all. But Sand was never one to shy away from a spectacle. Her choice of dress, combined with her striking beauty – dark hair carefully coiffed, and those famous black eyes so deep and expressive – was a deliberate challenge to society's expectations of women.

Of meeting her aged twenty-five, poet Alfred de Vigny wrote in a mixture of admiration and affront:

> She looks like the famous Judith from the museum. Her black, curly hair falls onto her neck, like the angels in Raphael's paintings. Her eyes are large and dark, shaped like the model eyes of mystics and the most magnificent Italian heads ... She lacks grace in her bearing, is rough in speech. Manlike in manner, language, the sound of her voice, and the boldness of her remarks.

Her ancestry and social class were complicated too. Born on 1 July 1804, on her father's side, she was deeply aristocratic – with direct (if illegitimate) links to the monarchy – and her great-grandmother and grandmother were celebrated salonists and intellectuals who entertained and exchanged ideas with leading Enlightenment thinkers. They inhabited the same world as Émilie du Châtelet and Voltaire, and it is highly likely Sand's great-grandmother would have entertained the couple.

As Romanticism replaced the rigidity of the Enlightenment and neoclassicism with passion, emotion and the sublime, George Sand thrived. Individualism and imagination were set above reason and order. Salon culture persisted, remaining vital as a means of fostering progress and exchanging ideas. It was in this context that Sand developed deep friendships and relationships with the other celebrated writers of her day. Among the great minds she surrounded herself with was Victor Hugo, author of *Les Misérables* and one of the most famous proponents of Romanticism.

While Sand's father's family was well respected and socially established, her mother's was not. Sand's mother, Sophie, had been a courtesan prior to her marriage, and had been imprisoned during the Revolution. She fell in love with Maurice Dupin, accompanying him as his mistress on a military campaign in Italy. She already had a young and illegitimate daughter when she became pregnant with Maurice's – prompting their marriage. At first, until after Sand's birth, Maurice concealed the marriage and child from his mother. Although he eventually came clean, Sophie was never truly accepted by her new mother-in-law, the formidable Marie-Aurore de Saxe, who lamented the marriage as a grotesque misalliance for her only son and railed against it, before settling for grim acceptance.

Indeed, much of Sand's early life was marked by trauma and tumult, and the family was unconventional in structure.

She had half-siblings from both her parents' previous relationships. Her mother brought a daughter, Caroline, from a previous affair, and her father likewise had an illegitimate son, Hippolyte, but despite these unusual elements, the family was cohesive and Aurore was, in her early years at least, close with both her half-siblings. However, tragedy struck. A baby brother was born blind, and in moments of rage Maurice would blame Sophie for the malformation. Despite this, the child was loved, making it all the more tragic when he died suddenly of a fever. The couple were mad with grief for the lost child, and Sand remembered that her mother's agony was so intense that she sent Maurice to dig up the body of the buried child, afraid that a mistake had been made and wracked with panic that he had been buried alive. The child was very much dead, however, and his parents reburied him secretly with all due devotion in their garden, watched by an uncomprehending Sand. To compound the black cloud, Sand's father Maurice also died within weeks of reburying his baby son, killed in a riding accident. Sand recalled that she was thoroughly shielded from the trauma of what had happened, so much so that she asked her horrified mother if her father would still be dead the next day.

Following these events she was taken to her grandmother's château at Nohant, an oasis of peace in the heart of rural France. It seems that there she enjoyed a stable and happy childhood. Her world was dominated by her mother, her grandmother and a servant's daughter who became her closest playmate and confidante, and she remained deeply attached to the estate and the countryside around it. There was also an 'irreproachable' donkey, who had free run of the garden, town and house – often straying into the dining room and her grandmother's apartments, never to be scolded, but instead given treats. She described him as having 'a philosophical air' about him.

But the carefree days were not to last. Sand's grandmother Marie-Aurore eventually succeeded in turfing Sophie out of her daughter's life in 1811. Once Sophie was widowed, Marie-Aurore began to doubt her daughter-in-law's 'respectability' once again, and did not see her as a healthy influence in Sand's life. She paid her off in return for sole custody of Sand and set about making a lady of the wilful child. Sand was taught to shed the Berrichon dialect she had picked up running among the fields with local children, to wear gloves, stop rolling on the floor and stand poker straight. She was not yet eight. Strict as this upbringing was, it was stable and marked by a good education and plenty. And Sand was still permitted to visit her mother in Paris. There was a cast of servants and tutors who guided, scolded and adored the young Sand, not least her misanthropic tutor Deschartres, a relic of the *Ancien Régime* who doted on the girl and taught her well.

As a teenager, Sand demanded again and again to be allowed to go and live with her mother in Paris, at which point her grandmother, painfully, divulged the secret from which she had shielded her granddaughter – her mother was not a 'respectable' woman. She had not been 'respectable' before her marriage, and she was not 'respectable' now, and it was for that reason that her grandmother had separated them. This revelation – told so damningly and shamefully by her grandmother – precipitated something of a crisis for the teenage Sand and struck her confidence deeply. She started to go off the rails, and eventually her grandmother decided there was nothing for it but hard routine and strict discipline, and the teenage Sand was dispatched to a convent in Paris, run by an order of English nuns who some centuries ago had fled Henry VIII's dissolution of the monasteries. At sixteen she returned to Nohant, and a year later her grandmother died. Sand mourned the loss bitterly, and although she inherited Nohant, she was now rudderless and lost in a world that was constantly remaking itself.

Without her grandmother to supervise her and separate them, Sand got what she had wished for and finally returned to live with her mother in Paris. But the experience was not what she had hoped. Instead, she found her mother's sphere unsettling. Sophie's chaotic lifestyle, marked by emotional unpredictability, which today reads like symptoms of borderline personality or bipolar disorder, deeply troubled Sand, who had become accustomed to her grandmother's order and discipline. It was a rude awakening after the structured, secluded worlds of Nohant and of the convent, and soon Sand found herself once again longing to escape.

It was perhaps in pursuit of this elusive independence that, in 1822, Sand made what would prove to be an ill-fated marriage to a military officer nine years her senior: François Casimir Dudevant. At first Casimir seemed to offer the companionship and security Sand craved. He was calm, practical and, in some ways, a sensible choice for a young woman who felt a bit lost. He told her bluntly that he did not find her beautiful, but he felt a connection with her and had envisioned them building a life together from their very first encounter. Despite the hysterical objections of Sophie, who conjured several unhinged narratives to derail the match – including that Casimir had worked as a waiter in Paris and as such was beneath her – the marriage contract was brokered, and the two were wed.

The couple moved to Nohant and, for a time, Sand – or Madame Dudevant as she was now known – seemed to settle into the role of wife and mother. She gave birth to two children, Maurice in 1823 and Solange five years later.[3] But her marriage soon began to fray. Casimir was not the steady, supportive husband Sand had hoped for. He turned to alcohol, hunting and infidelity, and Sand, with her intellect and her passionate and rebellious spirit, quickly grew disillusioned with the constraints of a domestic life in which she was side-lined. We can read the dissatisfaction with her marriage in the pages of *Indiana*, the novel she would pen some ten years after. By her mid-twenties, the eponymous heroine also found herself trapped in an unhappy marriage, surrounded by the stifling conditions of nineteenth-century bourgeois domesticity.

Books became Sand's escape, and before long reading turned to writing, which served as her catharsis. She poured her soul into the characters she created, the landscapes they populated, the trials they faced. Though she adored her children, their care could not provide the intellectual stimulation she desperately needed. In 1830, she was introduced to a young man named Jules Sandeau at a friend's house. Sandeau, seven years younger than Sand, was only nineteen at the time, but he was an aspiring writer, and the two quickly struck up a connection both romantic and literary.

---

[3] There has been doubt cast on Solange's paternity, with some asserting she was the result of a brief affair Sand had with Stéphane Ajasson de Grandsagne in 1827.

Their affair provided Sand with the excitement and intellectual engagement she craved and, together, they began to write. After much negotiation with Casimir, the couple reached an arrangement that allowed Sand to leave for Paris with Sandeau, taking her eight-year-old son Maurice with her, while leaving Solange behind.

In Paris, Sand and Sandeau took their partnership to the next level and co-authored a novel, *Rose et Blanche*, under the pen name 'J. Sand'. This experience gave Sand the confidence to attempt her solo debut, and to fashion a new identity for herself as an independent author in Paris. The result was *Indiana*.

*Indiana* catapulted Sand to fame. Published in 1832, it shocked and captivated French society. The author was listed only as the mysterious G. Sand. The themes were radical for their time, fiercely critical of the institution of marriage and patriarchal French society. Set between mainland France and Bourbon Island (now Réunion), it also touched on issues of colonialism and racial inequality. The heroine's loveless marriage was presented as domestic slavery, and the young woman yearned for social, economic and even *sexual* freedom. Sand's descriptions of Indiana are lyrical, introspective, incisive. Literary critics were vocal in their praise, clamouring over the work's emotional depth and revolutionary tone, but it sparked outrage in more conservative circles. It was provocative, and the irreverent treatment of marriage and portrayal of the heroine's thirst for freedom struck a chord with contemporary readership. It was a bold, unapologetic book, and everyone wanted to know who had written it. But none could immediately identify G. Sand, leaving literary Paris in a swirl of speculation about this mysterious author.

As gossip and curiosity grew, clues began to surface. The pseudonym 'G. Sand' recalled the sometime nom de plume of Jules Sandeau, who some remembered had recently co-authored a novel with his lover under the pen name 'J. Sand'. Soon enough, it was revealed that this radical new writer 'George Sand' was none other than Amantine Lucile Aurore Dudevant, *née* Dupin, known to her friends as Aurore, who had recently left her husband and moved to Paris with Sandeau. This discovery shifted the public's focus from the book itself to the woman who had written it. Suddenly, all eyes were on Sand, who was now living her life as unconventionally as she wrote. The conservative moralists who had already been offended by her novel were now still more scandalised by George Sand's lifestyle.

Aurore Dudevant, unhappy wife of Casimir, stepped into the identity of George Sand, and never stepped out of it. In September 1832 she wrote to a close friend, '*À Paris Mme Dudevant est morte. Mais Georges Sand est connu pour un vigoureux gaillard*' ('In Paris, Mme Dudevant is dead. But Georges Sand is known as a vigorous fellow'). She broke off her affair with Sandeau and moved to her own apartments on the banks of the Seine, fetching the little Solange to live with her, finally embracing an independent life, and determined to flourish. George Sand was twenty-eight.

Until this point, she had lived quietly, drawing some attention for her unconventional lifestyle but not yet famous in any significant way. A year before the publication of *Indiana*, while living in Paris with Sandeau, Sand had applied for and been granted a permit to wear men's clothes – as was necessary at the time for women under French law. Despite her peculiar style of dress, she had not attracted too many strange looks in a city with more eccentrics than most. However, with the sudden sensation caused by *Indiana*, all that was about to change. On top of this, three months after the novel's publication, France seemed ready to tear at the seams.

For all that Sand was enjoying striding around Paris in men's clothing and smoking cigars, and even referring to herself using masculine grammar on occasion, she was still a mother. She described an afternoon in June 1832, watching her daughter Solange play in the Jardin du Luxembourg, and fearing for her safety because of the cholera epidemic that had swept Paris that year, killing in the region of 18,000 Parisians. While her daughter played, riots broke out in Paris. Sand snatched Solange up in her arms and rushed through the panicked crowds to her apartment, carrying the little girl upstairs and spreading a mattress across the window to protect against stray bullets from the gunfire she heard in the streets.

The June Rebellion of 1832 – for that was what these riots were – was a pivotal moment in post-revolutionary France, and it had a lasting impact on Sand. It was not her first taste of violence or tragedy, but it was the first time she was caught up in it and felt in real danger. The experience was rattling. The popular military leader, General Lamarque, had died during the epidemic, and it was his death at a time of simmering tensions that triggered this uprising, and indeed inspired the most famous literary work of this period, *Les Misérables*, by Victor Hugo. While Sand panicked and snatched up Solange in the Jardin du Luxembourg, in another part of the city, Victor Hugo was strolling in the Tuileries Garden when he too heard gunshots, and dodged bullets as he ran for cover.

Sand and Hugo occupied the same literary and political landscape; they were often referred to as 'Mama' and 'Papa' by their contemporaries, a testament to their influence on nineteenth-century French fiction, and they were both inspired by this episode and the political turmoil of their time. Despite this, Sand's legacy has often been overshadowed by Hugo's, even though he held her in such esteem that he delivered the eulogy at her funeral.

The rebellion lasted only two days before being swiftly crushed by government forces, but nevertheless symbolised the unresolved conflict between the supporters of the Bourbon monarchy and republicanism in post-revolutionary France. France, in the years following the fall of Napoleon, was a nation in turmoil, caught between the old monarchies and the new revolutionary spirit that had not yet fully and lastingly asserted itself. The July Revolution of 1830 had placed Louis-Philippe on the throne as the 'Citizen King', but many republicans and working-class citizens were disillusioned with the monarchy. This, compounded by economic strife and political repression, highlighted the violent divisions within French society, which would only worsen in the decades to come, resulting in still more uprisings and revolutions.

The aftermath of the rebellion, and the slaughter of the revolutionaries, affected Sand more lastingly than the danger of the moment. She wrote in a letter to her intimate friend Laure Decerfz:

> For the partisan men there are only assassins and victims. They don't understand that they are all victims and assassins in their turn. And yet it is a horrible thing to see blood shed! To discover a red furrow in the Seine beneath the morgue, to see them spread the straw that barely covers a heavy cart, and to glimpse beneath this crude packaging twenty or thirty bodies, some in black coats, others in corduroy jackets, all torn, mutilated, blackened by powder, filthy with mud and dried blood. To hear the cries of the women who recognise their husbands there, their children, this is all horrible; but more horrible still is to see the end that awaits the fugitive who escapes half-dead while asking for mercy, to hear under your window the groans of the wounded man whom it is forbidden to save and who is condemned by thirty bayonets ... My poor Solange was on the balcony, watching all that, listening to the gunfire and not understanding.

Indeed, the world George Sand lived in was in political disarray. As mentioned, it was the setting of *Les Misérables*, the epic novel of injustice and oppression. It was the environment that gave us the stories of Fantine and Jean Valjean. And this was something Sand had become aware of as a child. She had begged and begged her mother to steal her away from her grandmother, and forfeit their allowances, and make it on their own. Sophie was momentarily moved by her daughter's pleas. Together they came up with a pipedream plan to open a hat shop in Orléans and scrimp and save and live over the shop. But Sophie's common sense prevailed. She explained to her daughter that while she might always be forgiven by her grandmother, and not permitted to perish in the street – and thus the risk was slight – the same was not true for her or her older daughter Caroline. She told Sand, as gently as she could, what happened to penniless girls without protectors. It was a cruel world, and she wouldn't put either her or Caroline in that position. She was referring of course to the threats of prostitution, exploitation and ruin and a life of serfdom and sexual slavery. This fear, this knowledge her mother had of the dark underbelly of nineteenth-century French society, was something that as a child, and sheltered adult, Sand did not fully understand, but as she grew older, more worldly, and saw more, she increasingly spoke out against it, in not only novels but political treatises, for the rights of women, and the need for social safety nets.

Following her debut with *Indiana*, Sand's career moved quickly, and she swiftly demonstrated not only her literary skill but her speed. Within a year of *Indiana*'s launch, she had published two short stories and a second novel, *Valentine*.

Together, these works solidified her literary reputation and significantly improved her finances, making her truly independent at last. She moved from her modest but scenic fifth-floor apartment on Quai Saint-Michel to more spacious rooms at No. 19 Quai Malaquais.

She was now a well-known figure in Paris. She also ignited what is likely to have been a romantic relationship with the celebrated actress Marie Dorval. Apparently, this began when Sand sent Dorval fan mail, to which Marie replied, and the relationship went from there. Sand already had acquired a reputation as a lesbian (rightly or wrongly) and Dorval was warned to stay away from Sand, but the pair were not deterred. Sand wrote extensively about how in thrall she was to the older woman, whom she remained close to until the end of her life. That said, if the relationship was romantic, it was not exclusive. Sand was still involved with Sandeau when they met, and she continued to have affairs with men throughout their relationship.

In early 1833, Sand broke things off with Jules Sandeau. She then had a much mythologised one-night stand with Prosper Mérimée, author of *Carmen* and a lynchpin of the Paris literati – an encounter that did not quite live up to her expectations. She wrote to Marie Dorval, 'I had Mérimée last night, and it wasn't much.' Dorval apparently repeated the story to Alexandre Dumas *père*,[4] who gleefully spread it all over Paris. Their night together also left Mérimée cold, and he likewise smeared her.

In the autumn following this sexual fiasco she met Alfred de Musset, a budding writer, and almost instantly became his mistress. Their letters are one of the great literary correspondences of the nineteenth century, testament to both the strength of their feelings and their literary skill, and their affair was emblematic of the Romantic movement. Musset wrote to Sand: 'Posterity will repeat our names like those of those immortal lovers who have only one left of their own, like Romeo and Juliet, like Héloïse and Abélard.' This relationship ended in tears, however, when while travelling in Venice Sand fell ill, during which time Musset frequented prostitutes. In turn, when Musset became sick himself, Sand began a relationship with the Italian doctor called to tend him, before absconding to the Alps with the same doctor.

Although the relationship failed, and ended with bitterness, it had a major impact on both: both Sand and de Musset wrote novels that explored the downfall of their love. De Musset penned *La Confession d'un Enfant du Siècle* (*The Confession of a Child of the Century*) in 1836 and Sand *Elle et Lui* (*She and He*) in 1859. When Sand returned to Paris with her Italian lover, de Musset begged to see her and the two began exchanging passionate letters again.

---

4 Alexandre Dumas *père* had a son, Alexandre Dumas *fils*, who was, like him, a well-known author and playwright.

Although they agreed they could not be together, they relapsed many times. The doctor went back to Italy. When eventually Musset broke off contact, she cut off her abundant black hair and sent it to him.

Sand's affairs and relationships are inseparable from her work and her legacy. To focus solely on her literary achievements without acknowledging the influence of her personal connections would be an oversight, just as it would be reductive to discuss only her lovers and not her books. Her impact on French society and culture was shaped by both – by the men and women she loved, the friendships she fostered, and her complicated relationships with her children.

In 1837, her domestic matters came to a head when her all but estranged husband, Casimir Dudevant, abducted their daughter Solange in defiance of their legal separation. Sand rushed to Nérac, where the child was being held, and sought help from the young sub-prefect – one Georges-Eugène Haussmann, who would later find enduring fame as the master architect of the new imperial Paris. Haussmann acted swiftly, accompanying Sand and local officials to the Dudevant estate, where Solange was peacefully returned. His intervention not only ensured the safe recovery of her daughter but also marked a decisive end to Sand's turbulent marriage. The following year, Sand formalised a settlement with Dudevant that secured full custody of both her children, in exchange for a significant payment to Casimir. At last she was fully free and in control of herself and her children, and it was at this point that she embarked on her most celebrated and significant love affair.

Sand met the Polish virtuoso Frédéric Chopin in 1838. They were introduced by mutual friends in artistic circles, and although at first Chopin was apparently put off by Sand's unconventional appearance, a deep and lasting bond soon kindled. Their relationship would last nearly a decade, and was perhaps the defining romance of both their lives. Although it was not always happy, the early days of their relationship were bliss. Sand wrote to Delacroix: 'There is not the tiniest cloud in this pure sky, not a grain of sand in our lake. I'm beginning to believe that there are angels disguised as men who pass themselves off as such and who inhabit the earth for a while.' They lived together for long periods, often spending summers at Nohant and a long stretch in Majorca, in an attempt to improve the composer's poor health. Sand provided Chopin with the emotional support he needed during periods of ill health, and Chopin composed some of his most famous works during their time together.

Chopin would spend seven summers at Nohant and each year a new grand piano was sent to him there from Paris, courtesy of Camille Pleyel, son of the composer Ignaz Pleyel. Chopin preferred Pleyel's pianos above all others, and the pair had a strong relationship. Pleyel sent not only instruments for Chopin, but also a small upright for George Sand and her daughter Solange. In those long summers spent at Nohant, which they often stretched out from May to November, Chopin and Sand inspired each other. Chopin composed his music in the room adjoining Sand's library, and one imagines her writing away to the floating notes of the Pleyel next door.

While they argued and had their creative differences, it was a collaborative and supportive relationship. Sand wrote: 'His genius was full of mysterious harmonies of nature, translated by means of sublime equivalents in his musical thinking.' She was devoted to him in his periods of illness, and he was amazed by her ceaseless diligence and energy, not only as his nurse, but also as mother to her children, and still finding time to write. However, their love would fray and after seven years, they grew apart. Their relationship was particularly strained by Sand's son Maurice's great dislike of Chopin and Chopin's decision to support Sand's daughter Solange in a marriage Sand was opposed to. They ended their relationship after nearly a decade together, during which time they had been the centre of each other's lives. Chopin died shortly after they parted ways, and Sand was conspicuously absent from his funeral. He is buried in a tomb in Père Lachaise cemetery in Paris; nowadays it is almost always covered in fresh roses. Nevertheless, she carried no bitterness forward to her description of their relationship in her autobiography, and there can be no doubt that their love and mutual respect were sincere.

George Sand must be remembered not only for her love affairs, and the romance and feminism of her novels and writings, but also for her political contributions. Sand wrote extensively on political and social issues, especially during the Revolution of 1848, publishing essays and articles calling for workers' rights and social reform. Throughout her life, she used her platform as a celebrated writer to challenge the inequalities of nineteenth-century French society, addressing themes of class struggle, individual liberty and the emancipation of women. Her involvement in the Revolution of 1848, which overthrew King Louis-Philippe and established the Second Republic, marked a high point in her political engagement. Sand actively supported the Second Republic and called for sweeping social reforms, including workers' rights and universal suffrage, advocating for social democracy, and she was particularly focused on empowering the poor and women. While she did not campaign for women's voting rights, she did advocate for greater education. She believed deeply in republican ideals and worked alongside socialist thinkers, contributing essays and writings that promoted democratic governance and social justice.

Although disillusioned by the brutal suppression of the June Days Uprising of 1848, Sand continued to push for a more egalitarian society through her novels, political essays and personal lifestyle.

Her early support for Louis-Napoléon Bonaparte, elected President of the Second Republic, soon shifted to disappointment when he staged a coup in 1851 and declared himself Emperor Napoleon III, establishing the Second Empire. Disillusioned by his authoritarian rule, Sand distanced herself from political engagement during this period, though she continued to write and advocate for social causes.

In her later years, Sand witnessed the collapse of the Second Empire after the Franco-Prussian War and the brief rise of the Paris Commune in 1871, which shall be explored more fully in the next chapters through a look at the remarkable life of Sand's sort-of-protégé, the actress Sarah Bernhardt, and of the socialist teacher, revolutionary leader and mother of anarchy, Louise Michel. The last great romantic relationship of Sand's life was with the engraver Alexandre Manceau, which lasted fifteen years until his death in 1865. During their time together Sand continued with her prolific literary output as well as managing the estate at Nohant, where she lived with her son, daughter-in-law and grandchildren.

Throughout her life, Sand consistently worked towards a more equal and just society, even as political turmoil surrounded her; this is a clear theme throughout her literary output, not only in her political texts but also in her novels and plays. She was a luminary and a rule breaker, and was recognised in her lifetime as among the greatest writers of her generation, male or female. Her legacy and writing deserve far greater recognition than they find today.

Sand lived during what we retrospectively call the Romantic period, a cultural and artistic movement that spanned roughly from the late eighteenth century to the mid-nineteenth century. Writers and artists of this time emphasised emotion, individualism and nature, reacting against the rationalism and formality of the Enlightenment and the Industrial Revolution's impact on society, and these themes underpinned Sand's life and literary legacy. Like the other writers, artists and musicians of her social circle, she explored personal expression, the sublime in nature and the complexities of the human psyche and sexual passion. Her life and works exemplified Romantic ideals, and her relationship with other Romantic artists, like Chopin, placed her at the centre of the movement in France.

She died and was buried at Nohant. Flaubert, along with dozens of other illustrious friends, attended her funeral. He wrote that he broke down in tears twice, once when seeing her granddaughter Aurore – named after her – for the first time; her eyes 'so resembled her grandmother's they were like a resurrection ... and the second time on seeing her coffin pass by ... The good country folk cried a good deal around the open grave ... The rain was falling softly. Her funeral was like a scene from one of her novels.'

The family seat of Nohant still stands, almost as Sand left it, complete with the furniture she bought during her lifetime. It is in the middle of '*France profonde*' – that vast central region east of the Loire Valley that tourists rarely visit, if they do only passing through on their way from north to south. It is a splendid part of the country – feeling remote even today, three hours' drive from Paris. On my visit, on a brisk February morning, it is bathed in sunlight, and the gardens filled with snowdrops. The first thing I notice are the Lebanese cedars, planted for each of Sand's children. She died in the blue bedroom of the house, which commands a view of these trees. In the drawing room, family portraits adorn the walls: her father cuts an intense, vigorous figure in his cavalry uniform while her grandmother, then in her prime, glances enigmatically over her shoulder, wrapped in a low-cut leopard-print gown, her powdered wig piled high. Sand herself – with those gleaming dark eyes – takes pride of place, flanked by portraits of her children. On the far wall are her granddaughters – beautiful like her. Conspicuously absent is a likeness of her mother, Sophie Dupin.

Having read a selection of Sand's letters, and many of those written by her close circle of literary friends as well, it was impossible for me to tour Nohant without visions of Sand appearing, nonchalant and decadent, in almost every room. In a letter to his mistress, Balzac described arriving at Nohant:

# GEORGE SAND

I reached the Château of Nohant on the Saturday before Shrove Tuesday, towards half past seven in the evening, and I found comrade George Sand in her dressing gown, smoking an after-dinner cigar by the fireside, in a vast lonely room. She had very pretty yellow slippers, decorated with little fringes, stylish hose and red trousers.

This is the vision I imagine as we enter her drawing room.

Colour infuses the house, the walls of the grand staircase stained pink and blue like a mottled sunset. The house is full of books and portraits, and there is a puppet theatre designed and made by the mother for her son. Everywhere shadows of Sand's personality, and traces of her august guests, are discernible. The dining room in Nohant is still set to receive, with place settings around the table, including some of the illustrious names Sand would come to entertain at her family home. Above the table is an elaborate Murano glass chandelier that she chose herself. The coloured wine glasses, the guide assures me, were a gift to Sand from Chopin.

Louise Michel during her exile in New Caledonia.
Anonymous engraving, *c.* 1873–1880.

# 11

# Louise Michel

## 29 May 1830–9 January 1905

'Yes, barbarian that I am, I love the cannon, the smell of gunpowder, the grapeshot in the air, but above all I am in love with the Revolution.'

Louise Michel, *Memoirs*, 1886

On a cold morning in 1870 a messenger brought news to the Empress of France. Reading the missive, which told of the French defeat at the Battle of Sedan and the capture of her husband Emperor Napoleon III, blood drained from Empress Eugénie's face. She cried out in fury that the news must be false. Her husband could not be captured, the shame would be too great, he must be dead instead. She snatched up her jewels and her most precious papers and possessions, and slipped out. In disguise, she went to the home of her American dentist and implored him to smuggle her out of Paris. First, she went to Deauville, then by yacht to England. She did not leave a moment too soon. The Second Empire of France was over, and the Siege of Paris was about to begin.

\* \* \*

Montmartre is one of Paris's most iconic districts. The white domes of the Basilica of Sacré-Coeur rise serenely over the mount of the martyrs, which is named for the first Bishop of Paris, St Denis, who was martyred atop it during the persecutions of the Christians in the third century AD. Its winding streets climb the steep hill and retain their historic cobbles and charm. Today, tourists pose for innumerable Instagram posts along the steps, and affix padlocks with lovers' initials to railings. It is one of the most atmospheric parts of Paris – in the far north of the city, commanding panoramic views over the other districts and landmarks. It was Picasso's neighbourhood while he lived in Paris, Dalí's and Van Gogh's too; artists have always flocked to the area with its narrow streets and sweeping views, presided over by the Sacré-Coeur, celestially perched above the city, domes nestling amid clouds.

But these serene white domes and what they symbolise are not popular with all Parisians. The Sacré-Coeur is a symbol of the crushing of the Paris Commune, built over the butchery and bloodbath and mass graves of the martyrs of the Commune. The basilica was conceived as an act of penance, and a monument to a perceived moral and religious renewal following the trauma of the violent socialist uprising, and the broader societal upheavals of the nineteenth century.

On 18 March 1871, the forces of the new French government that had taken power following the capture of Napoleon III and the collapse of his Second Empire – based in Versailles rather than the capital – sent troops to Paris to seize a set of 400 cannons placed defensively around the city, many in Montmartre.

These cannons had been purchased with the blood, sweat and tears of the French working classes during the gruelling siege that the city had endured the previous year, following the Battle of Sedan. Parisians had gone hungry, diseases had spread, and many had died. The National Guard, a largely working-class militia, had raised the funds and distributed them across Paris to defend the city, including working-class neighbourhoods, and this had meant a lot to the people. The guns became a symbol of the strength of the city, a city that belonged to her people. So, when the soldiers came to seize them, the Parisians had had enough.

The Siege of Paris had finally been raised with the signing of an armistice between France and Prussia on 28 January 1871. Conditions in the aftermath were marked by continued shortages, illness and starvation among residents of the city, and growing fury and civil unrest. The war was ended under humiliating terms for the French, including the surrender of Alsace-Lorraine – and the people of Paris saw it as little more than a surrender by a weak government. Adolphe Thiers, the leader of the ever more unpopular government, saw the placement of the cannons in Montmartre, under the control of the left-leaning National Guard, as a threat to his government. He wanted them under his own control, and sent his men to take them.

The officers of the National Guard, stationed to protect the hard-won guns, refused to surrender them. Crowds formed around them. People would not let the cannons go. The headmistress of a local school was particularly furious. Her name was Mademoiselle Michel – and she screamed at the officers trying to seize the guns and whipped up the people to support and defend the cannons. Women covered the guns with their bodies, and the headmistress did so too. The soldiers, ordered to fire on the crowds and prostrate women, refused. Instead, they turned their weapons on their officers. A socialist revolution had begun. The Paris Commune was born.

\* \* \*

Clémence Louise Michel was born on 29 May 1830, in the small village of Vroncourt in the Haute-Marne region, due east of Paris. Her mother Marianne Michel was a servant in the home of local landowner Étienne-Charles Demahis. It was acknowledged locally that this man's son and heir – Laurent Demahis – was romantically involved with Marianne and was in fact Louise's father. Despite her illegitimacy, the Demahis family treated Louise as their own – for a time at least. Raised in the Demahis château, she enjoyed a privileged childhood not uncommon for the illegitimate children of wealthy families, much like the fortune of George Sand's older half-brother Hippolyte. Her grandfather educated her, and put volumes of Voltaire, Rousseau and the other leading Enlightenment thinkers into her hands. Her grandmother taught her music, to sing and play piano. Later in life, reflecting on this time in her memoirs, Michel looked back with nostalgia, and wondered if she had ever deserved it.

This peace would be shattered, however, with the deaths of her grandparents. Laurent had married since the birth of Louise, and his new wife, once her in-laws were gone, would not suffer her husband's illegitimate daughter to hang around her house. Until the age of twenty Louise had been known by her grandparents' name, Mademoiselle Demahis, but after their deaths she was forced to give up that name. However, she was not turned out penniless; clearly there was some money settled, as she went to a new town to pursue teacher training. She left the name Demahis behind and took her mother's name instead. From then on, she was known as Louise Michel.

Even during her seemingly want-free childhood, Michel showed signs of the rebel and the writer she would become. In her teens it was evident that she never intended to marry. Always bold, at twenty she sent ardent fan mail and poetry to Victor Hugo, who – surprisingly – replied. The fervour of the young Michel impressed him, and they began an epistolary friendship that lasted years. Originally signing her name Louise Demahis, she took to signing off letters and poetry as 'Enjolras' – the young, doomed revolutionary of *Les Misérables*. After some years working as a teacher and running various schools in the Haute-Marne and a brief stint in Paris, she finally moved to Paris permanently at twenty-six.

The following years were critical for her career as writer, teacher and activist. She opened the doors of her Montmartre school, aimed at educating the working-class children of the *quartier*, and continued with the innovative teaching methods she had begun developing: bringing animals into the classroom, taking children outside and writing plays for her students to perform. Creative approaches to teaching may be more accepted now, but these were radical, ground-breaking techniques in nineteenth-century Paris, especially in the deprived areas that were the focus of Michel's efforts. This was the beginning of Michel's deep involvement in the community of Montmartre. Then, as now, teachers wore all manner of hats in caring for their charges; they were responsible for not only their pupils' academic development, but also their broader well-being in an age with little in the way of social care, acting as the educated, accessible lynchpins of deprived communities. In her role as teacher, Louise Michel became deeply aware of the social issues affecting her students and their families, and saw the poverty of the district up close. Michel worked tirelessly to support her Montmartre community, especially the underprivileged women, teaching them to read and write, and advocating for their rights. She became involved with André Léo's *Société pour la Revendication des Droits Civils de la Femme* (Society for the Vindication of Women's Civil Rights), where she championed the national cause of girls' education.

Her radical political and philosophical ideas also soared during this time. She immersed herself in reading scientific and philosophical texts, declaring herself an atheist and materialist. Rejecting the Catholic Church as an oppressive force supporting social hierarchy, she believed that society should be understood and improved through reason, science and social action, rather than religious faith. She joined the Union of Poets and became actively engaged in political movements, attending socialist meetings where she met influential revolutionaries, not least Théophile Ferré, who would become her close friend (perhaps her lover) and revolutionary partner. Michel's political stance hardened during this period, particularly her anti-clerical views. She grew increasingly opposed to the Second Empire and the policies and position of Napoleon III and Empress Eugénie. She condemned Napoleon III's authoritarianism, the suppression of democratic freedoms, censorship of the press, and the regime's repression of political dissent. Michel was also critical of the regime's militaristic ambitions and the widening gap between rich and poor, which she saw as emblematic of an unjust system that needed radical change. She fiercely criticised the Catholic Church's alignment with the authoritarian regime.

By 1870, as political tensions in France rose in the lead-up to the outbreak of the Franco-Prussian War, Michel's activism intensified. In January, she attended the massive funeral of journalist Victor Noir, killed by Prince Pierre Bonaparte, a cousin of the emperor. The death sparked fury across Paris; this injustice was seen as emblematic of the imperial family's arrogance and disdain for the people. His funeral became a mass protest, attended by more than 100,000 protestors and mourners. A month later, Michel also participated in a demonstration in support of imprisoned republican generals. The war broke out in July, with Napoleon III captured at Sedan on 2 September, Empress Eugénie fleeing Paris on 4 September, and the harrowing Siege of Paris commencing on 19 September. During the siege, Michel worked hard for her community, struggling to keep her school open despite the shortages, and providing food for her students with the help of her friend Georges Clemenceau, mayor of Montmartre. Her revolutionary fervour became more visible as she helped organise the Comité de Vigilance des Citoyennes du XVIIIème Arrondissement, a women's vigilance committee that played a key role in mobilising women during the siege.

When the Paris Commune was proclaimed in March 1871, following the attempted seizure of the cannons, Michel took on a leadership role. She worked to mobilise women in support of the

Commune, organising day-care for children, recruiting women as ambulance workers, and even defying gender norms by giving sex workers jobs among the respectable working classes, arguing for their right to be part of the new social order. Michel herself joined the struggle as a soldier and nurse with the Montmartre battalion, participating in battles at Clamart, Neuilly and Issy-les-Moulineaux, at which the militias of the Commune fought the soldiers of the new Versailles government as they attempted to take back Paris. Michel became known as the 'Red Virgin of Montmartre' – a reference to Joan of Arc – for her fearlessness and commitment to the cause, and of course her unmarried status. The comparison stems from their shared roles as women who took up arms, defied traditional gender expectations, and became symbols of revolutionary struggle and national resistance.

The Paris Commune was a radical and brief revolutionary government that controlled Paris from 18 March to 28 May 1871. Michel's leadership and courage during the months of the Commune solidified her place among the key figures of Paris's history. The movement developed into a bold experiment in socialist self-government, which tied in with her burgeoning anarchist ideals. Elections were held in late March, and the Commune was established with a council largely made up of workers, intellectuals and artisans. The Commune implemented progressive policies, including the separation of Church and state, free education for all children, and improved working conditions. It also allowed workers to take over abandoned businesses, aiming to empower the working class and create a more egalitarian society.

The Paris Commune was not just an experiment in governance but also a flashpoint for intense controversy. Its radical socialist policies and anti-clerical actions, such as seizing Church property and taking priests hostage, alarmed conservatives and the bourgeoisie, both in France and abroad. The Commune's emphasis on workers' rights and the redistribution of wealth, and its defiance of the Catholic Church, provoked a sharp backlash from those who saw it as a threat to the established social order. The revolutionary government was further discredited by its cold-blooded execution of many clergy as the Versailles government moved against it. Archbishop Georges Darboy was widely regarded as a hero, even among those who supported the Communards, having organised assistance for the wounded during the Franco-Prussian War and remained at his post throughout the siege. He and other priests were captured, and the Communards attempted to exchange them for political prisoner Louis Auguste Blanqui. When these negotiations failed, he and the other priests were shot, an act ordered by Théophile Ferré. This move contributed to the Commune's reputation as a violent, lawless movement.

Tensions escalated; the French government regrouped and prepared a brutal military response. In May 1871, government forces launched an assault to retake Paris, leading to one of the bloodiest episodes in French history, known as *La Semaine Sanglante* (The Bloody Week). From 21 to 28 May, Versailles troops stormed the city, their blue and red uniforms stark against the smoke-filled streets, massacring tens of thousands of Communards, many executed even after they had surrendered. Michel was in the thick of the fighting, alongside the other women of the Commune. In Michel's words: 'The women, during those days of May, erected and defended the barricade at Place Blanche. They held on until death.' In last-ditch attempts to subvert the authority of the Versailles troops, Communards in turn set fire to private homes, state buildings and national monuments across the city: the Tuileries Palace, Palais-Royal, Hôtel de Ville and Palais de Justice all burned. Ordinary Parisians were horrified as their monuments blazed, and some never truly recovered from the trauma of seeing their city in flames. Notre-Dame, however, was spared.

The scale of the repression was unprecedented, with entire neighbourhoods reduced to rubble, the bodies of Communards lining the streets. Louise Michel, who had fought valiantly until the end, initially evaded capture. However, when she learned that the authorities had taken her mother hostage, Michel surrendered to ensure her mother's release, displaying once again her characteristic selflessness and dedication. She was, however, profoundly affected by the trauma of losing her comrades and the sheer scale of the brutality visited upon the people of the Commune.

Her heroism during the Bloody Week was matched by her courtroom performance later that year, where she proudly admitted to her role in the Commune and even took responsibility for actions she had not committed. She refused to seek leniency and defiantly requested the death penalty. Her fierce defence of the revolution made headlines across France, and she openly declared, 'If you let me live, I shall never cease to cry for vengeance.' Victor Hugo wrote his poem 'Viro Major' in her honour, a homage to her bravery, heroism and virtue.

While she awaited sentencing from her cell in the dreaded Clermont Detention Centre, she received the following letter of reassurance from a close friend. This letter serves as a poignant reminder of Louise's life beyond her role as a revolutionary and an anarchist:

Paris, July 18, 1883

Dear and kind Louise,
I have just come from your mother's house, where Mrs. Biras gave me your letter. Your mother is well, she was very happy to see me. She thinks that you are still in St Lazare, and we arranged that she will always think that. Don't worry, your mother's rent has been paid, and we gave her 100 francs yesterday; she was happy with it. We will always be there for you. Your mother won't have to leave your house, I promise you. And you, dear Louise, how are you? I wish I could kiss you, you must be bored, but I know that you will always be brave. My husband sends you his kind regards,

and the children asked me not to forget to kiss you for them, and I kiss and hug you so much, of course. Mrs. Biras told me to thank you for the lace you gave her. She thinks you made it, that's why it is very precious to her. I saw your three cats, and Moustache came to me. Paul gets along well with him.

Paul and I are going to visit your mother again tomorrow. She asked us to come and really loves me. So we do come.

Don't worry about your mother, dear Louise, and you must write us the most you can. In your next letter, could you tell us if we need to send you money and how much? We will do it.

See you soon, with much love from everyone,

L. Vaughan

However, perhaps on account of her gender and the public outpouring of support, Michel was spared the death penalty, and instead sentenced to deportation. After months in prison, in August 1873, she and other Communards were transported to New Caledonia in the south-west Pacific Ocean, aboard the ship *Virginie*. During the long journey, she formed lifelong friendships with fellow exiles, including other celebrated revolutionaries Henri Rochefort and Nathalie Lemel. Upon arrival in December 1873, she began her life in exile. Even in this penal colony, Michel's revolutionary spirit still found ways to express itself. She would spend seven years in exile in the remote community.

In her memoirs, Louise Michel openly identifies as an anarchist, a cause to which she converted during her time trapped on the ship which transported her to New Caledonia. As a young woman, she had initially felt a general compassion for the oppressed, which later developed into an idealistic but broadly vague commitment to revolutionary change. During her time in New Caledonia her ideas developed much more concretely in the form of a deep support for the anarchist movement. She affirmed later that the January 1883 *Manifesto of Lyon* fully encapsulated her political ideology, underlining this by reproducing the document in its entirety in her memoirs.

The *Manifesto of Lyon* strongly reflected the values of the Paris Commune, particularly its emphasis on direct action, anti-authoritarianism and self-governance. Like the Commune, the manifesto rejected centralised political power and instead championed a society organised through decentralised, worker-managed structures. Both movements shared a belief in grassroots revolution rather than parliamentary reform, and both saw the state as an oppressive force that needed to be dismantled rather than reformed.

New Caledonia had been established as a French penal colony in 1853, following French annexation of the island as part of its broader colonial ambitions. Political prisoners enjoyed a good deal of freedom, and Michel was allowed to come and go and interact with other prisoners and the local population more or less as she pleased. She came into contact with the indigenous Kanak people, who had attempted to resist French colonisation, and quickly immersed herself in their struggles and culture. Michel learned some of their languages and contributed to the first French–Kanak dictionary. Her sympathy for the Kanak people deepened, and she also formed connections with Arab deportees from Algeria, exiled by the French, further broadening her understanding of colonial oppression.

In 1878, five years after Michel's arrival on the island, the Kanaks launched a pro-independence revolt against French settlers who had taken their most fertile lands. Unsurprisingly, Michel sided with the Kanaks rather than her fellow French Communards, who mostly supported the colonial authorities. In a symbolic act, she gave her cherished red scarf, a relic from the Paris Commune, to two Kanak insurgents. Although she never saw them again, the gesture cemented her legacy in the region, influencing a protest group called the *Foulards Rouges* (Red Scarves) years later. Michel's admiration for Kanak culture shocked her French compatriots, but she embraced their music and dance, and even suggested starting a Kanak theatre.

In 1879, Michel left West Bay for the capital, Nouméa, where she became a teacher, but her time in exile was drawing to a close. In 1880 the French government issued a general amnesty for the Communards and, her sentence commuted, she returned to France, smuggling in her five beloved cats. Upon her arrival in Paris, she was greeted by a crowd of 10,000 people at Saint-Lazare station.

Michel's return to France marked a new phase in her activism. In January 1881, she attended the funeral of Louis Auguste Blanqui and continued to engage with the anarchist movement. In July of that year, she participated in an anarchist congress in London, alongside influential figures such as Peter Kropotkin and Errico Malatesta. Her ideas were growing more radical; in 1883 she led a demonstration of the unemployed at the Esplanade des Invalides in Paris, carrying a black banner to symbolise the devastation caused by the crushing of the Paris Commune. At this workers' demonstration, Michel fully embraced the black flag as a symbol of anarchism, distancing herself from the red favoured by others. Unlike red flags, which were often tied to socialist and communist movements, the black flag represented anarchism's rejection of all hierarchical structures, including the state and political parties. This protest was one of the most significant moments in her anarchist activism. The demonstrators demanded bread and work for the unemployed and some looted a bakery, which the authorities used to justify their harsh crackdown. The police dispersed the protest with violence, and Michel was arrested as the ringleader.

Louise Michel's anarchism was deeply rooted in both revolutionary action and personal conviction. She championed direct action and resistance, believing that true social change could only be achieved through uprising rather than gradual, governmental reforms. Michel rejected centralised authority, and instead supported a society based on voluntary cooperation, mutual aid and self-management. She emphasised solidarity with the oppressed, particularly workers, the poor and women.

For her role in the workers' protest, Michel went into hiding for three weeks before turning herself in for arrest. In her trial, she defended herself with characteristic defiance and, though the jury recommended leniency, she was sentenced to six years in solitary confinement, of which she served three. During her time in prison, Michel wrote her memoirs and continued to build her reputation as a revolutionary writer and thinker. In December 1884, she was temporarily released to be by her mother's bedside, thanks to the efforts of influential friends including Georges Clemenceau and Henri Rochefort. Michel's mother died in January 1885, a loss which had a profound impact on Michel; all through her years of activism and exile, the pair had remained close and corresponded regularly despite the distance and Michel's imprisonment.

By January 1886, Michel was released from prison for good, at the age of fifty-five. Although her health was declining, she remained active in Paris's political and cultural scene. In 1888, Michel survived an assassination attempt while giving a speech in Le Havre. Pierre Lucas, a former circus clown who opposed anarchism, shot her twice, injuring her ear. Her speech that day was part of her ongoing campaign to promote anarchist ideas, which centred on issues like workers' rights, social equality and the need for a revolutionary change to dismantle oppressive systems. Her message resonated with many workers and activists; but it also attracted opposition from those who feared the destabilising effects of anarchism or saw it as a threat to the existing social order. Pierre Lucas was one of these opponents. Despite her injuries, Michel refused to press charges against him, asserting that he attacked her due to societal failings.

In 1890, Michel moved to London, where she would spend much of the rest of her life. In London, she found relative freedom from police surveillance and devoted herself to working with the poor in the Whitechapel area, teaching refugee children and caring for abandoned animals. However, she remained politically active always, her London years filled with publications and conferences. She continued to advocate for revolution, education and social justice until the end of her life. Anarchism was now also at the forefront of her personal agenda, and she embarked on numerous speaking tours promoting the ideals of this movement.

Her activism remained undeterred by age or distance. In 1904, she travelled to Algeria, a colony then under harsh French rule. During her visit, she expressed her solidarity with the Arab and Berber populations, denouncing colonial authorities. Her speeches in cities like Algiers and Oran condemned the atrocities of colonialism, aligning the Algerian cause for independence with her broader anarchist vision of universal emancipation.

It was during another speaking tour, this time in southern France, that Louise Michel died in January 1905, aged seventy-four. Her funeral on 22 January was a momentous event. Between 50,000 and 120,000 people turned out to pay their respects to the Red Virgin of Montmartre, and bearer of the black flag of anarchy. At the time, it was one of the largest funerals ever seen in France. She was buried beside her mother at the Levallois-Perret cemetery, close also to the final resting place of Théophile Ferré.

Louise Michel's legacy is complex, shaped by her experience of straddling two social worlds – the bourgeoisie and the working class. As the child of a servant and likely the son of a landowner, she experienced both privilege and marginalisation, giving her a unique perspective on the injustices of society. This dual identity may have fuelled her sense of self-invention, as some historians argue that Michel carefully crafted her own legend through her actions and writings. As a woman who fought for both women's rights and broader social change, she became known as one of the greatest female revolutionaries in French history.

Her feminist and anarchist views on education, particularly her critique of the gendered differences in schooling, were radical for the time. Michel's life was a continuous struggle for a better world, one defined by equality, liberty and justice. From her days in the Paris Commune to her exile in New Caledonia, and finally to her tireless work in London and France, she lived as a revolutionary and died as one, leaving a legacy that continues to inspire anarchists, feminists and fighters for justice around the world.

Portrait of Berthe Morisot by her sister Edma, 1865.

# 12

# Berthe Morisot

## 14 January 1841–2 March 1895

The dark wooden palette is balanced in the crook of the artist's arm, filled with a thousand shades of white, stretching from the stark titanium to creamy smudges with hints of yellow, colder pools with notes of grey. The hand of the artist flies expertly, passing over her canvas, dabbing the different shades in quick, feathery brushstrokes.

Outside, the muted hum of Paris drifts upwards – creeping in around the frame of the Haussmannian window: the clatter of hooves, distant chatter, the rumble and crunch of wheels over cobbles, a muffled bark – but in this quiet room, the world is narrowed. The city seems quite distant from this intimate scene. Light filters through white curtains, illuminating the face and white muslin of a sleeping infant in its cradle. A translucent lace veil is draped mist-like over her, held in place by her mother's bright hands: another layer of protection. The artist's hands work busily, dabbing the pale rose and blues, all to capture the sheen of diffused, muted light on soft, fragile skin.

Beside the cradle, a young woman leans forward, her gaze fixed tenderly on the sleeping child. One hand supports her tired cheek, the other smooths the fine lace edge of the cradle's cover. Her dark hair is pinned up simply, wisps escaping around her face, and a black ribbon stylishly encircles her throat.

A HISTORY OF FRANCE IN 21 WOMEN

The artist adds a final touch, and signs her name. Setting the brush aside, she wipes her hands on her smock, adding still more streaks of pigment. Light catches on her dark hair, her profile sharp with concentration, softening only as she turns back towards her subject, telling her sister she can relax at last.

Berthe Morisot allows herself a rare, quiet smile. The painting is finished.

\* \* \*

On 15 April 1874, three years after the end of the Franco-Prussian War and the crushing of the Paris Commune, this painting – *The Cradle* – was shown at an unusual exhibition opened in Paris. It was held, unconventionally, in a photography studio on the Boulevard des Capucines, kindly lent by Félix Nadar – a photographer, caricaturist, writer, hot-air balloonist; he was a nineteenth-century Renaissance man – for the proceedings. The walls were a deep red, and the paintings were selected and hung by the artists themselves. They were quite different from the sort of painting Parisians were used to.

Thirty-one artists had their work included, and together contributed some 200 artworks. The work shown was infused with vibrant colour and light, rendered in dabbing, abstract brushstrokes. The scenes were lively, capturing movement, energy, nature – fleeting moments in daily life. The style was a far cry from the traditional, precise types of painting and composition favoured by the rigid Salon de Paris. The Salon guarded academic artistic practice and served as the gatekeeper of prestige. However, things were changing in France, and revolutionary spirit was in the air. The Belle Époque was about to begin, and this new artistic revolution lay at its heart.

The artists were not unified politically. Pissarro was an anarchist and an ardent supporter of Louise Michel, whom he knew personally. Ottin and Meyer had been Communards. Others were more conservative, still others more liberal. They were also not unified by a single style or technique: there were paintings, sketches on paper, sculptures and ceramics. What unified them was that they were doing something different. These artists, peddling their expressive new style, were going to change the face of French art for good.

In later years they would be known as the Impressionists, and this was their first exhibition.

Alongside the names of the men whose work featured at this exhibition – including Monet, Pissarro, Cézanne and Renoir – was listed a female name: Berthe Morisot.

Berthe Morisot, the first female Impressionist, exhibited an impressive ten paintings at this first exhibition, establishing herself at the centre of the movement. Her work differed from that of the men exhibiting around her, in so far as all but one of them presented women in candid poses.

The most striking of these works was *The Cradle*. Morisot painted it in Paris in 1872, and it portrays her sister Edma tenderly watching over her sleeping daughter, Blanche. Today, it is held in the permanent collection of the Musée d'Orsay and was shown again at an Impressionist retrospective in 2024, 'Inventing Impressionism', which sought to recreate the original Impressionist exhibition, right down to the red walls, and marked the 150th anniversary of the original exhibition.

*The Cradle* was Morisot's first exploration of the theme of motherhood, which would become a favourite subject in her later works. A gauzy veil hangs between the viewer and the infant, but Edma looks directly at her daughter, a quiet intensity in her gaze. The fact that the viewer is slightly excluded creates a still-greater sense of intimacy between the mother and child, and of maternal protection, as it is Edma who seems to have drawn the curtain, a shield between her daughter and the world. She became her sister's favourite model in the 1870s, and numerous paintings of her featured in the exhibition. Later her own daughter Julie joined Edma as one of Morisot's most painted subjects.

The Impressionists aimed to capture fleeting moments in an ever-changing world. The paintings they made were not static, immoveable, but transient. They rejected grand scenes of history painting and instead focused on recognisable moments from quotidian life. They painted parents and children, peasants, farmers at work, and embraced the 'plein air' mode of painting outdoors, their work infused with sunlight and informed by the elements. They used colour to invoke change, transition and the pace of daily life. Nothing was fixed, stayed or contrived. They captured natural life as they saw it.

This style had both advantages and disadvantages for women. Less technical in some ways, it might have been perceived as a more accessible style of painting for women who could not afford rigorous academic art tuition; at the same time, the style was not easy to master, and female painters did not enjoy the same liberties as male ones. While Manet could visit brothels and paint prostitutes, women painters certainly could do no such thing or even roam the cafés and bars of Belle Époque Paris looking for suitable subjects. Women who wanted to paint scenes from daily life were often limited to scenes of their own family lives. For some, however, this was no limitation at all, but an opportunity for profound, intimate reflection.

Berthe Morisot made a study of the intimate lives of aristocratic Parisian women, and showed her work in all but one of the eight Impressionist exhibitions between 1874 and 1886. Her deft, feathery brushstrokes drew adulation, as did her portraits of women in unstaged settings, guard down, without artifice. She claimed a space for herself right at the centre of this new, boundary-pushing and male-dominated artistic movement, and never compromised her artistic vision. She had immense artistic talent, but even so, her career would not have been possible without the support of her family, and specialised early training.

## BERTHE MORISOT

Berthe Morisot had come into a world on the cusp of transformation. She was born on 14 January 1841 in the quiet, provincial town of Bourges, which lies at the very centre of mainland France. Hers was an artistic family: her father, Edmé Tiburce Morisot, had studied architecture at the École des Beaux-Arts, while her mother, Marie-Joséphine-Cornélie Thomas, was the great-niece of Jean-Honoré Fragonard, one of the last great Rococo painters of the *Ancien Régime*. Both Berthe and her sisters were encouraged to practise art and drawing from their childhood. She and her elder sister Edma had a particular talent for it, nurtured by their parents and many tutors. Theirs was a privileged, bourgeois upbringing; such opportunities were not available to many women. It is especially striking then that Berthe would eventually transcend this sheltered world to take her place among the art world's great rebels.

The Morisots moved to Paris in 1855 during a time of profound transformation and cultural upheaval. The Second Empire was taking shape under the rule of Napoleon III, who, despite his authoritarian tendencies, fostered a golden age of art, public works and modernisation. Paris was in the midst of being remade into a modern capital, with the sweeping boulevards lined with trees and elegant buildings with matching, ornate, cut-stone façades that always spring to mind when one visualises the city. Under the direction of Baron Haussmann, the same prefect who had helped George Sand regain custody of her daughter, the medieval and maze-like streets of 'Old Paris' were being replaced with grand avenues, wide boulevards and formal parks. The quarry of Buttes Chaumont – which had enjoyed a less than illustrious history, first as a site to display the bodies of executed criminals, then as a dump, slaughterhouse and storage facility for sewage – was replaced with a picturesque park, with dramatic craggy cliffs and Grecian temples. The Bois de Boulogne and Bois de Vincennes were redesigned too, inspired by London's Hyde Park. These changes not only improved infrastructure but provided new spaces for leisure, social interaction and artistic inspiration – a gleaming Paris made for promenading and, perhaps, for painting.

Growing up amid the rapidly changing Parisian landscape, Berthe and Edma found inspiration, and a society sympathetic to artistic ambition, even occasionally among women. That said, the art world of nineteenth-century Paris, while flourishing, was not an easy one for a woman to navigate. The Académie des Beaux-Arts presided over the scene with an iron fist, dictating the standards of 'acceptable' art, and the Salon de Paris was its grand display. The Salon de Paris, the official annual art exhibition sponsored by the French government, was central to the art world during this time. To be an artist was to seek acceptance in the Salon, an annual exhibition that defined reputations. Here, academic painting – a style focused on historical, religious and mythological subjects rendered with perfect, often polished realism – reigned supreme. It was not a system sympathetic to artistic innovation. Napoleon III, recognising the growing dissatisfaction among avant-garde artists who felt excluded from the Salon, famously authorised the Salon des Refusés in 1863 to display works rejected by the traditional Salon jury. This decision not only allowed revolutionary artists like Édouard Manet to present their unconventional paintings but also paved the way for the Impressionist movement that would follow.

Women artists were largely ignored by the Salon or given space only in the lesser categories of landscape or still life. And the only art school that mattered, the École des Beaux-Arts, was closed to women entirely until 1897. That said, for all that women were excluded from formal training with the academy, somewhat bizarrely they were not excluded from showing their work at the Salon, and before long Berthe and her sister would both achieve this pinnacle of artistic achievement and showcase their work there.

## BERTHE MORISOT

Despite these barriers, Berthe and her sisters were encouraged to pursue the arts, albeit within socially acceptable bounds. In 1857, as Berthe turned sixteen, her mother enrolled the sisters in drawing lessons under Geoffroy-Alphonse Chocarne, whose academic style felt restrictive and uninspiring. Yves – Berthe's other and less artistically inclined sister – abandoned the lessons after only a few sessions, but Berthe and Edma begged for a new instructor. Their request led them to Joseph Benoît Guichard, an artist who took them out of the drawing room and into the Louvre itself, where they cut their teeth copying works of the Old Masters. He sensed their talent, and also their ambition. He warned the girls' mother: 'my teaching will make them painters, not minor amateur talents. Do you know what that means? In the world of the *grande bourgeoisie* in which you move, it would be a revolution, I would even say a catastrophe.' Berthe's mother, unperturbed by the threat of catastrophe, continued to encourage her daughters, finding them the best tutors.

When she was twenty, Berthe was introduced to the Barbizon painter Jean-Baptiste-Camille Corot, and this proved a turning point in her artistic career. Under Corot's influence, Berthe began to experiment with plein air painting. While liberating for Berthe, it also presented challenges: for a woman to paint outside in Paris was a rarity and often met with both curiosity and condescension. Writing in her journal, Berthe shared how setting up her easel in a park attracted stares, laughter and, often, judgement. To preserve her privacy, she found ingenious ways to work in relative isolation, painting from boats or enclosed gardens, a private revolution within the public world.

This flexibility of approach would stand Berthe in good stead in the years to come. By the 1860s, Paris stood on the brink of an artistic upheaval. Academic standards were under fire, and a young generation of artists were rejecting the constraints of Realism. They chose relatable rather than lofty subjects, scenes of life previously dismissed as unworthy of 'art'. They saw the beauty in the mundane. For the Salon, their work was too raw, too unfinished. Yet for these artists, this unfinished quality, or *non-fini*, was the very point, and Berthe had a remarkable eye for it.

In 1864, Berthe reached a milestone in her artistic career when the Salon de Paris finally accepted two of her landscapes, *A Souvenir of the Banks of the Oise* and *Old Path at Auvers*. Edma also exhibited work at the Salon that year, and the sisters must together have been ecstatic. While the Salon was certainly male dominated – with more than ninety per cent of the work presented by male artists – the Morisot sisters were not the first women to be granted the honour of showing their work. Early trailblazers had included other female artists Élisabeth Vigée Le Brun (1755–1842) and Rosa Bonheur (1822–99) – these women had paved the way for the acceptance of the Morisot sisters, whose success in turn continued to make the case for the inclusion of female painters in the elite art world. Berthe's work was also selected for six subsequent salons. In recognition of his daughters' success, Monsieur Morisot had a studio constructed for Edma and Berthe in the garden of their Passy home.

She was noticed by art critics, who usually ignored newcomers to the Salon, and received a mixture of praise and somewhat backhanded compliments by misogynistic critics not yet ready to really make room for women. Critic Paul Mantz wrote of one of her still lifes:

> Since it is not necessary to have had a long training in draughtsmanship in the academy in order to paint a copper pot, a candlestick, and a bunch of radishes, women succeed quite well in this type of domestic painting. Mlle Berthe Morisot brings to the task really a great deal of frankness with a delicate feeling for light and colours.

While Mantz and his colleagues made snide comments, Berthe and her sister persevered, quietly reshaping the role of women in art.

## BERTHE MORISOT

While Berthe was embraced – albeit somewhat backhandedly – by the establishment, her interests were more closely aligned with those who challenged it. Before long, she began to diverge from traditional landscapes and café scenes and began to explore intimate, female spaces – the interior of her own world. While her male colleagues painted cafés, bars, boulevards, brothels, Berthe began to focus on quiet moments in women's lives, on private spaces and gardens. Throughout the 1860s and 1870s, she honed her vision as a painter.

She and her sister Edma, until this time thick as thieves, collaborators, supporters and aligned in their artistic vision, finally split onto divergent paths. Edma chose to put aside her artistic career in favour of marriage and starting a family. Edma and Berthe had worked together, painted each other, exhibited together and kept each other company on their path as female artists in Paris. But in 1869, at the age of thirty, Edma married a naval officer and moved away from Paris. The separation was hard for Berthe and marked the beginning of a very different phase in her career, a phase she would have to navigate on her own. This perhaps played some role in bringing her to the nascent Impressionist movement.

Morisot's early career was also marked by a complicated and sometimes fraught friendship with Édouard Manet. Their relationship was one of mutual admiration but also tension, particularly around their artistic boundaries. Manet wrote to a friend: 'The misses Morisot are delightful; it's just a pity that they don't happen to be men. However, I suppose they could, as women, serve the cause of Painting by marrying Academicians and give the Old Buffers a shock.' This dismissiveness among Berthe's future Impressionist colleagues, even after she had been accepted by the Academy, was unfortunately pervasive. For all that, Manet was struck by her, both her looks and her talent. He asked her to pose for him many times, creating some of the most famous images of her, including *The Balcony* in homage to Goya – emphasising her beautiful 'Spanish' eyes. In fact, Manet is responsible for my favourite portrait of Berthe Morisot, in which, dressed stylishly in black, she reclines against a red background. Her large eyes under her dark fringe draw in the viewer, challenging them, inviting them.

In 1870, when Morisot showed Manet her painting *The Mother and Sister of the Artist*, intending to submit it to the Salon, Manet took liberties with her work, retouching the figure of her mother and transforming her into a darker, more sombre presence. Morisot was furious, recounting her annoyance and consternation in a letter to her sister:

> He cracked a thousand jokes, laughed like a madman, handed me the palette, took it back; finally, by five o'clock in the afternoon we had made the prettiest caricature that was ever seen … And now I am left confounded. My only hope is that I shall be rejected. Mother thinks this episode funny, but I find it agonising.

This frustration spoke to the frequent dismissal of her artistic agency by male peers. Despite this, Manet's influence lingered, though it was arguably Morisot's influence that deepened his own approach to colour and lightness of touch.

As already discussed, the outbreak of the Franco-Prussian War in 1870 threw Paris into turmoil, ushering in the end of the Second Empire and giving way to the brief, turbulent rule of the Paris Commune. These events reshaped the city and the very essence of French society, with citizens experiencing first-hand the fragility of peace. Morisot had been stuck in Paris during both the siege and the bloody, destructive and short-lived age of the Commune, and she was horrified by what she witnessed, writing, 'I have come out of this siege absolutely disgusted with my fellow men, even my best friends … selfishness, indifference, prejudice – that is what one finds in nearly everyone.' She was also horrified by both the destruction wrought by the Paris Commune – no artist could remain unmoved by the sight of Paris's beautiful buildings burning – and the brutality of its suppression. She followed the politics closely: Adolphe Thiers, the president who ordered the 'Bloody Week', was a close family friend. It is a sign of trauma, not indifference, that none of Berthe Morisot's artistic subjects reflected the suffering and horrors she lived through. She was profoundly affected by the hardship and brutality of 1871 and dogged by bouts of depression, introspection and potentially eating disorders at various points in her life. Often, she isolated herself. Like many of her fellow artists, Berthe found catharsis in painting the return to 'normal' life – after the terrible year of 1871. She did not paint scenes of anguish and destruction, but rather the beauty to be found in the quotidian. Her paintings highlight the fragility and value of human life, and the transience of beauty and of moments of peace. Her painting became more confident; she stopped deferring to Manet, and he in turn realised that he had much to learn from *her*. Out of the malaise of 1872 came one of Manet's most striking portraits of her: *Berthe Morisot with a Bouquet of Violets*. Meanwhile, she was pushing the boundaries of what painters could do with light, arguably further than any previous painter. She was becoming a great artist. At the same time, she was captivating.

The Impressionist movement, in which Morisot was a driving force, was born in this era of upheaval, defying the traditions upheld by the Academy and the Salon. The Impressionists worked swiftly, prioritising impression over precision. As has been seen, in their first exhibition of 1874, Morisot was the first woman to show her work with the group.

The year 1874 also marked a new chapter in Morisot's personal life: she married Eugène Manet, Édouard Manet's younger brother, their romance kindled over plein air painting together in the summer of 1874. He proposed to her as they both sketched boats and, perhaps to her own surprise, Berthe said yes. We can never know if she loved him, or if she really loved Édouard, who was out of reach. It is undeniable that a profound emotional connection existed between Berthe and Édouard Manet, but it is also undeniable that he was married.

Despite this, the marriage was loving, and it was successful. Berthe appreciated the warmth and stability, the permanence, that marriage offered, and she began to paint her husband. Eugène was less ambitious than his brother, and was content to devote more of his time to supporting Berthe's career than advancing his own. Also a painter, he never received the same recognition as his brother or his wife, but was a devoted father and husband and frequent subject of his wife's paintings. Their marriage was a rare partnership of mutual respect, and Eugène's gentle encouragement allowed Berthe's artistry to flourish in the face of social pressures that would have confined most women. Their only child, Julie, was born in 1878. Julie would spend her childhood as her mother's model, and the sketches and paintings Berthe made of her daughter seem almost like a childhood photo album, catching her at every phase of life. Children are notoriously tricky subjects, and Berthe demonstrated herself to be one of the rare artists who could really capture the energy and vitality of children, particularly her daughter. They shared a remarkable bond, which Julie would eventually write about in her autobiography *Growing Up with the Impressionists*.

However, back in her professional sphere, things were not quite so peachy. The exhibition of 1874 was met with a mix of ridicule and intrigue. *Le Figaro* critic Albert Wolff described the movement as a gathering of 'lunatics', although Berthe's work was singled out for some selective praise: 'one woman whose feminine grace is maintained amid the outpourings of a delirious mind'. Indeed, it would take years for Impressionism to become respected as a movement, and a generation for it to become revered and acknowledged as one of the pivotal art movements of the nineteenth century.

## BERTHE MORISOT

Morisot rejected the coquettish poses that catered to a male audience. In works like *The Wet Nurse*, she explored themes of domesticity and labour, depicting a woman artist's efforts side by side with those of the wet nurse, offering a quietly radical perspective on the shared, uncelebrated work that enabled both domestic and artistic spheres.

By the 1880s, Morisot's reputation as an artist was solidified, and she was recognised as one of the Impressionists' most consistent and committed members. She would exhibit with the Impressionists in all but one of the following eight exhibitions, her only absence due to the birth of her daughter.

The critical reception had shifted too, with some of her harshest early critics now judging her among the finest in the group. Her works, though usually modest in scale, carried an expansive sense of space, emotion and light, often incorporating delicate whites that seemed to dissolve into the atmosphere. Critics described her brushwork with the verb *effleurer* (to touch lightly or brush against), reflecting her unique style that captured a sense of transparency and immediacy.

Her success was not confined to Paris. In 1887, her works were shown internationally in George Petit's International Exhibition in Paris and Paul Durand-Ruel's Impressionist exhibition in New York. Yet, despite her growing acclaim, Morisot remained focused on her close circle of friends, hosting Thursday soirées that attracted intellectuals and artists, including Degas, Whistler and Monet.

Morisot's final years were shadowed by loss. Eugène died in 1892, leaving her bereaved but resilient. She continued to work and advocate for her daughter, Julie, who inherited her mother's artistic sensibility and creative spirit. By 1894, the French state purchased *Young Woman Dressed for the Ball*, the first of Morisot's works to enter a national collection – an acknowledgement long overdue.

In 1895, while caring for Julie, who had fallen ill, Morisot herself contracted pneumonia. She died on 2 March, leaving behind a body of work that would be preserved largely within her family, passing into private collections and quietly influencing future generations of women artists. Her legacy was cemented not by the institutions that had long excluded her but by those who loved her, through her daughter's journals, the writings of her grandson Denis Rouart, and the devoted recollections of friends like Stéphane Mallarmé and Paul Valéry. Morisot's work, long marginalised by early critics of Impressionism – if not her colleagues – would later be recognised as central to the Impressionist movement, embodying both the quiet force of resistance and the transformative power of art.

Her paintings, intimate and introspective, offered a vision of modern life that celebrated not only the fleeting beauty of a world in flux but the steadfast resilience of a woman artist who dared to leave her mark. As she once wrote in her diary, 'I don't think there has ever been a man who treated a woman as an equal, and that's all I would have asked for – I know I am worth as much as they are.'

Berthe Morisot played a pivotal role in a cultural revolution that redefined not only French art but also the global artistic landscape. The birth of Impressionism in Paris was not just a new style of painting; it was a radical departure from the rigid traditions of the Académie des Beaux-Arts, signalling the beginning of modern art. By embracing this new, innovative approach, France re-established itself as the centre of the artistic world, particularly after the devastation and political turmoil of the Franco-Prussian War.

The significance of Impressionism goes beyond aesthetics: it was a statement of creative independence that attracted artists from all over the world to Paris. The city became a magnet for painters in subsequent decades, like James Whistler, John Singer Sargent and Vincent van Gogh, who were drawn to its vibrant, avant-garde scene. Paris was reinvented as the cultural capital of Europe, a hub where artists could experiment, collaborate and challenge the status quo. By fostering a spirit of innovation, France asserted its cultural dominance, influencing artistic movements well into the twentieth century. For artists, Paris smelled like freedom, and opportunity. Courtesan and cabaret culture inspired them, giving them access to models and female spaces with more freedom than possible in more conservative societies. Then, as now, choosing art over financial stability seems more understood and accepted in France. Beyond that, Haussmann's remade city was beautiful, with sweeping parks and boating lakes, aesthetic buildings, jumbled rooftops, places for elegantly dressed men and women to picnic and lunch on the grass, ballrooms, cabarets, ballets and operas. The Impressionists painted life, and Paris offered them this in abundance. And just short train rides away were the coasts of Brittany and the wheatfields of *France profonde*. The great train stations, the theatres, the freedom enjoyed by individuals and the less constrained sexual morals all attracted those with artistic souls to Paris. Degas painted the ballerinas, Morisot women and children at different stages of life, Monet the great train stations and boulevards, Manet the entertainments of the Tuileries and so much more.

Berthe Morisot, with her focus on intimate scenes of domestic life, contributed a unique and essential perspective to Impressionism, subtly but powerfully reshaping the role of women in art. Her work stood as not only testament to her artistic vision but also a quiet act of defiance against a society that sought to confine women to certain roles. The Impressionist movement, with its emphasis on modernity and freedom of expression, was both a reflection and a catalyst of France's cultural renaissance, making Morisot's contributions as significant to the nation's artistic heritage as those of her male counterparts.

Berthe was a central figure in the Impressionist movement and highly respected by her peers. Today her paintings are centrepieces of collections around the world. *The Cradle* and many of her other famous works hang in the Musée d'Orsay in Paris, *Summer's Day* at the National Gallery in London, *The Harbour at Lorient* in the National Gallery of Art in Washington DC, *The Psyche Mirror* in the Thyssen-Bornemisza Museum in Madrid. Her work resonates with viewers across the world, and she is now widely recognised as one of the most important and innovative of the Impressionists.

Sarah Bernhardt in *Gismonda* by Theobold Chartran.

# 13

# Sarah Bernhardt

*c*.22 October 1844–26 March 1923

In 2023 a large leather-bound ledger was displayed at the Petit Palais in Paris. It was part of an exhibition about the life of the legendary French star of stage and screen Sarah Bernhardt. But it was a curious choice, some thought. The book was *Le Livre des Courtisanes*. On page 158 was written in neat black ink the name Sarah Bernhardt, listed as a young courtesan, with the remarks that the then teenage Sarah was a favourite of 'old men and especially members of parliament'. This book was an official record of the high-class sex workers of Paris, kept for the sake of monitoring and regulating the slightly nebulous and certainly scandalous world of the demi-monde.

In Paris, the Belle Époque – literally 'the beautiful era' – was characterised by a sense of elegance and luxury, and a fascination with beauty and innovation. It refers to the pivotal moment – also called the *fin de siècle*, at the end of the nineteenth century and the dawning of the twentieth – when peace was enjoyed between the end of the Franco-Prussian War and the beginning of the First World War. It was a period of arts and pleasures and entertainment, with Paris as its hub. Artists like Monet, writers like Proust and performers like Sarah Bernhardt thrived, while the Eiffel Tower and Paris Métro exemplified modernity. Architecture and decoration took on swirling, colourful, floral patterns – known as the new art or *art nouveau*. The period also saw the rise of the bohemian lifestyle, with intellectuals, artists and the bourgeoisie mingling in a city that celebrated both high art and the avant-garde. Absinthe flowed freely in cabarets and bars, the cancan was the most popular dance, and the famous Moulin Rouge threw open its doors in 1889.

However, beneath the glittering surface, the Belle Époque also witnessed social tensions and inequalities that would later contribute to the upheaval of the twentieth century. There is no greater icon of this moment in Parisian history than Sarah Bernhardt.

Sarah Bernhardt not only came to prominence at the height of the Belle Époque; she became its poster girl. Parisian apartments and student dorms the world over would find themselves decorated with reproduction art nouveau posters of Sarah Bernhardt's turns in *La Dame aux Camélias*, *Tosca* and *Medea*. She soared to unprecedented heights of celebrity, achieving success across multiple continents and mediums, conquering the Paris stage, then those of London, before forging a successful career as a silent-film actress, as well as recording her voice. Nevertheless, her origins, while not poor, were certainly precarious.

Sarah Bernhardt was born Henriette-Rosine Bernard around late October 1844. Her exact birthdate is unknown, and she seems to have intentionally obscured it in later life. Her mother was Julie Bernard, a Dutch Jewish woman who made her way as a courtesan in Paris. She never revealed the identity of Sarah's father, although her primary lover at the time was Charles de Morny, who certainly took an interest in Sarah's upbringing. This was a powerful friend to have, as he was the half-brother of Emperor Napoleon III, who would come to power in 1848.

Her mother was an admired and sought-after courtesan in Paris, famed for her beauty and golden hair. Her career provided well for her; she was able to pay for nurses for her children and educate them privately at reputable convent schools. Indeed courtesans were such an accepted part of society that nuns made no objection to caring for their illegitimate children; their money was as good as anyone else's.

Prostitution in France was highly organised and stratified, and no pains were taken to conceal it. There was also comparatively little shame attached, especially for high-level prostitutes or courtesans, who occupied a recognised and upper social class. Even now, it feels inaccurate and reductive to call a courtesan a prostitute, because, while at the base level, these women were exchanging sex, love, companionship for financial support, it was a far more nuanced professional series of relationships than is attached to the modern conception of prostitution. They were glamorous socialites, fashionistas, artists and actresses: figures of admiration. So glossy and wealthy did these women seem that the teenage Coco Chanel was in awe of the courtesans who crossed her path, and even looked up to them for their refinement and elegance.

Courtesans, however, were simply the glittering tip of the iceberg. The rank of courtesan was aspired to by all women engaged in sex work – formally or informally. There were many, many rungs below. Firstly, sex workers were divided into two categories, *filles soumises* and *filles insoumises*. *Filles soumises* were those who had officially registered themselves as prostitutes with city authorities, something which gave them a certain legitimacy, but which came with regulations such as regular health checks – grim events – and a prohibition from plying their wares in public outside certain hours or near schools (for fear they might corrupt the youth). Unregistered girls, *filles insoumises*, escaped the indignities of the health checks, but lived in fear of arrest or exposure, making them still more vulnerable.

At the bottom of the heap were women who walked the streets soliciting clients at night or worked in one of Paris's many brothels. They led meagre, miserable, hand-to-mouth existences, and their life expectancy was not high, their lives blighted by poverty, incurable venereal diseases and violence. Above this rank was the complex social hierarchy of the demi-monde. It is important to note that not all of its members engaged in sex work in the typical way, yet at the same time it did exist outside the rigorous conservative morality of contemporary 'respectable' French society. It was within the ranks of the demi-monde that many actresses, including Sarah Bernhardt, her mother and indeed George Sand's mother, belonged. There were ranks in this world too: *grisette*, *lorette* and *courtisane*. Grisettes were girls usually with day jobs, like shop girls or seamstresses, who engaged in sex work, both formally and informally – for extra income or meals. A cut above the grisettes were the lorettes. Named after the area around Notre-Dame-de-Lorette in Paris, where many of them lived, lorettes were unmarried women who had relationships with wealthy or upper-class men in exchange for financial support, gifts or housing. Unlike grisettes, who worked for a living, lorettes primarily relied on their lovers for economic sustenance, and their relationships were often more transactional than romantic. But they had more security than grisettes, wearing finer clothes and living lives of comparative luxury.

Then above the lorettes were the courtesans – a whole class of their own – and women who used their sex work to achieve real power. Courtesans were celebrities in their own right and powerful men vied for their favours. The opulent world of nineteenth-century France under the Second Empire was the perfect setting for courtesan culture to flourish, in direct contrast with the strict moral confines of Victorian England. In France courtesans were proud, celebrated and admitted to high society. They could choose their lovers, and in many cases became influential figures and patrons of the arts. Colette's most famous story, *Chéri*, opens with a description of the languorous morning of a courtesan bickering with her much younger, wealthy lover, before going to dine with his mother and discussing his forthcoming society marriage to an aristocratic young woman. She seems unperturbed by her lover's upcoming marriage, just as his mother seems unperturbed by his older lover, and includes her in family discussions. They lived in luxurious apartments and mansions, travelled in ornate carriages, were followed by a train of servants and were corseted in silks and the latest fashions, adorned with bright gemstones. The prestige of actresses in the famous theatres often gave them the ability to vault the first ranks of prostitution, avoiding street walking and grisettery, even lorettery, and ascending almost instantly to the rank of courtesan. It seems that this is what Sarah Bernhardt managed, with the help and influence of her mother and her lovers.

However, this was not always the path she wanted to follow. At a young age, Sarah was determined to become a nun.

Sarah's early life was marked by her mother Julie's connections to powerful, upper-class figures. Raised by a nurse in Brittany due to her mother's frequent travels, Sarah's adventurous spirit and penchant for storytelling were evident from a young age. She later recounted a vivid, albeit likely fabricated, tale about falling into a fire as a child and being doused with milk, earning her the nickname 'Milkblossom'.

At age seven, Sarah was sent to a boarding school for young ladies in Auteuil, reportedly funded by her unknown father's family. It was there that she made her first foray into acting, playing the Queen of the Fairies in a school production of *Clotilde*. Meanwhile, her mother's prominence in Parisian society grew, as she mingled with influential politicians and aristocrats, including the blue-blooded Charles de Morny, rumoured to be Sarah's father. Morny would later play a crucial role in shaping Sarah's early career.

At ten, Sarah entered the exclusive Augustine convent school at Grandchamp, near Versailles, where she embraced her Catholic faith. Her mother may have been of Jewish ethnicity, but was not practising, and so while Sarah was conscious of her Jewish heritage, she was raised a Catholic. The nuns were kind to her, and she loved the order and the security offered by the convent. She described her first school mistress as having large, beautiful eyes 'like George Sand's'. She became captivated by the idea of becoming a nun, a dream that was complicated by her strong will and dramatic flair. One infamous episode involved Sarah organising a full Christian burial for her pet lizard, for which she was accused of sacrilege. Her religiosity, though fervent, would remain as complex and contradictory as her identity throughout her life. She made no secret of her Jewish descent, not least in choosing the name Sarah as a stage name and publicly declaring herself to be a member of 'the great Jewish race', but also described herself most often as a Catholic, although in certain interviews claimed atheism instead. When all was said and done, however, and when she knew herself to be dying, she received the last rites from a Catholic priest.

Her family were dead set against her taking orders. Becoming a nun was expensive, and while it seemed she had been left some money by a mysterious father, it was to be given to her on the occasion of her marriage. The young Sarah remonstrated that she would marry the good Lord and become a bride of Christ to unlock the fortune to pay for her career as a nun, at which her mother and her lovers and friends, who had formed a sort of career-counselling panel, scoffed. Indeed, it was at this family meeting, which seemed like a guidance-counselling session from hell, that it was first suggested that Sarah become an actress, and, implicitly, a courtesan. There are even reports that Sarah's mother Julie planned to auction her daughter's virginity to the highest bidder, something Sarah desperately fought against. Morny – her mother's powerful lover – was so struck by the passion and vehemence of her resistance that he suggested that she take to the stage, and it was he who sponsored her first steps in the world of theatre. Following this, her guardians took her to the Comédie-Française for a performance of *Phèdre* by Racine, which moved the young girl to tears. Her sobs disrupted the show; she was consoled by Alexandre Dumas *fils* who declared her a star.

## SARAH BERNHARDT

All the signs seemed to point to the theatre as the right next step for Sarah. Her mother had no wealth of her own, only support from lovers, and thus she wanted her daughter to be independent. Acting seemed an appropriate halfway house between sex work, respectability and Sarah's own ambitions. She clearly had a flair for drama, and this would give her glamour, a practical skillset, and a position to attract wealthy suitors should she want them. Morny secured Sarah an audition for the prestigious Paris Conservatory. With coaching from Dumas, she delivered an impassioned recitation of La Fontaine's fable *The Two Pigeons*, which won over the sceptical jury, securing her a place at the Conservatory in 1860. Over the next two years, she studied under prominent actors Joseph-Isidore Samson and Jean-Baptiste Provost, who taught her the balance between grand gestures and simplicity. It was during this period that she began to use the name Sarah Bernhardt, emphasising her Jewish lineage, perhaps in an effort to link herself with the most famous actress of the day – Rachel Félix, also Jewish, who died young in 1858 when Sarah was just thirteen. Her legacy doubtless loomed large as Sarah started her theatrical training.

It seems, as demonstrated by her listing in *Le Livre des Courtisanes*, that Sarah did engage in high-level prostitution during her acting training. Until fairly recently, the word 'actress' did carry connotations of higher-class sex work in France. Work has always been unstable for actresses, and salaries often low, a bad review or social faux pas enough to destroy a career. Nowadays in France, actresses and artists who clock up a certain number of hours of work one year can receive an 'intermittence' or a salary the next – aiming to mitigate the instability of the work while acknowledging its cultural value. This was not the case in Paris in the nineteenth century. Unmarried women, even talented professional ones, were extremely vulnerable to a turn of the wheel of fortune. George Sand's numerous novels emphasised this.

As a result, many women, and particularly actresses, engaged in what today we would term prostitution across the different strata of the demi-monde. In some instances, this could be simply following the conventions of the day, which included actresses sleeping with reviewers to ensure good reviews – which was not expedience at all but exploitation. It was not the case that reviewers were impartial until sexual favours were offered, but rather that unless sexual favours were offered, the reviewer was likely to torpedo a career. Sarah had first-hand experience of this. Her stage debut for the Comédie-Française as Iphigenia in Racine's play of the same name earned scathing reviews from the critic Francisque Sarcey, whom she famously refused to sleep with. She was devastated, and this could have ruined her career. Nevertheless, her talent prevailed and she kept her job – just.

In the end it wasn't a bad review which ended Bernhardt's career at the Comédie-Française, but her fiery personality. During a ceremony to honour Molière, Bernhardt's sister Regina, who had recently also joined the company, accidentally stepped on the train of the very senior actress Zaïre-Nathalie Martel, which caused Martel to shove Regina so hard that she fell and struck her head on a marble column, causing her to bleed. Incensed, Sarah slapped Martel in retaliation, and, refusing to apologise, was promptly dismissed. Her family, dismayed by her behaviour, distanced themselves, and Sarah found herself out of work at a pivotal point in her career.

Bernhardt soon managed to join the Gymnase, a less prestigious, boulevard theatre specialising in light comedies, but scandal followed when she recited politically charged, anti-imperial poetry by Victor Hugo at a royal reception, offending Emperor Napoleon III. Indeed, on her recital of 'Oceano Nox', the emperor and empress abruptly walked out, followed by members of the court. Victor Hugo's work had been banned previously, given his anti-imperial views. Her final role at the Gymnase, as a Russian princess, was poorly received, and her own mother deemed her performance 'ridiculous'. Disillusioned, Bernhardt abruptly quit the theatre in 1864 and decided to travel, adopting a more liberated lifestyle akin to her mother's, though she soon discovered that she was not suited to the life of a courtesan. While – when successful – they enjoyed greater levels of freedom, their livings still depended on pandering to clients and patrons, and Sarah struggled to bend herself to the will of others. She was too free a spirit to be a kept woman and needed to be in command of her own destiny.

Her travels led her to Belgium, where she met Henri, Hereditary Prince de Ligne, with whom she had an affair. The romance was cut short when Bernhardt learned of her mother's heart attack and returned to Paris. It was after this affair that Bernhardt discovered she was pregnant with what would be her only child. Timing and other circumstances have led many to speculate that the child's father was indeed the prince, but this has never been conclusively proven. On 22 December 1864, she gave birth to Maurice at the age of twenty, raising him on her own while continuing to perform minor roles at the Théâtre de la Porte Saint-Martin. Significantly, she gave him her own surname, refusing to carry any shame for having an illegitimate child.

Her acting career was on the back foot at this point, but in early 1866 her fortunes changed when she secured a reading with Félix Duquesnel, the director of the Théâtre de l'Odéon, who was captivated by her talent, intelligence and resilience. Although co-director Charles de Chilly initially had reservations about her thin figure and reliability, Duquesnel recognised her potential and hired her, even paying her salary out of his own pocket. Bernhardt initially struggled with roles in eighteenth-century comedies that didn't suit her naturalistic acting style, but she soon found her footing and began to shine, especially in male roles, which became a hallmark of her career. In 1867, she took on her first male role in Racine's *Athalie* and gained further acclaim in 1868 with her portrayals of Anna Damby in Alexandre Dumas's *Kean* and Cordelia in *King Lear*, solidifying her reputation as a rising star.

The year 1868 was a breakthrough, especially with her performance as the minstrel Zanetto in François Coppée's *Le Passant*, which earned critical acclaim and led to a command performance for Emperor Napoleon III. Her success at the Odéon, her most beloved theatre, marked a period of personal and artistic growth. During these years she formed a close friendship with the then sixty-five-year-old George Sand, performing in several of her plays at the Théâtre de l'Odéon, including the adaptation of *François le Champi*, *Le Marquis de Villemer* and *L'Autre*. By 1869, Bernhardt had met with so much success that she moved to a far larger apartment in central Paris, joined by her mother and grandmother, and she began her famous collection of animals, starting with dogs and turtles but soon progressing to big cats like cheetahs. Who knows what her traditional Jewish grandmother – who had moved in to care for the infant – made of this decadent menagerie?

In 1869, a house fire shattered her new life. She lost many of her possessions and grieved particularly for portraits of her family, as well as her jewels:

> I had not much jewellery, and all that was found of the bracelet given to me by the Emperor was a huge shapeless mass, which I still have. I had a very pretty diadem, set with diamonds and pearls, given to me by Kalil Bey after a performance at his house. The ashes of this had to be sifted in order to find the stones. The diamonds were there, but the pearls had melted.

This fire was a catastrophe. She was on the rise, but not yet wealthy, and the loss of all material possessions and her home was enough to ruin her. Fortunately, however, she was popular. Friends rallied round, a charity concert was held, and before long Bernhardt moved into a still-bigger property, which she furnished even more decadently than the last, and populated with an even greater menagerie, including cheetahs.

The 1870s would perhaps mark the high point of her career, but were also the years in which she established herself as more than an actress and glittering figure of the Belle Époque: a staunch patriot.

In July 1870 war broke out between France and Prussia. Emperor Napoleon III clashed with Otto von Bismarck, the Prussian chancellor, over Prussia's effort to put a Prussian prince on the throne of Spain, which Napoleon III saw as a direct threat to his domains and influence in Europe. The war was to become a disaster for France. The Prussian army was more experienced and better prepared than the French forces, and had long been so. Voltaire had quipped a century earlier that 'where some states have an army, the Prussian Army has a state'. It was a formidable force in Europe, and Napoleon III would have done well to proceed with more caution.

After the declaration of war, things spiralled quickly for France. In the first week of August alone, the French were defeated at Wissembourg, Spicheren and Wörth. The Prussian army routed the French forces again and again. As the war intensified, Bernhardt took the initiative to transform her beloved Théâtre de l'Odéon into an infirmary for wounded soldiers. She personally applied to the Préfet de Police for essential supplies, using her influence to secure a vast quantity of provisions, including food, alcohol and other necessities to care for the injured. She dressed as a nurse, and played this role with aplomb, personally tending to the wounded and the dying across the stage of the theatre and collecting them in ambulances herself. She slept at the Odéon for weeks, dedicating herself fully to her patients. In September 1870, Emperor Napoleon III was captured at the Battle of Sedan, ending the Second French Empire with his abdication.

In January 1871, as the Germans began a full-scale bombardment of Paris, Bernhardt was forced to close her theatre-hospital, but still offered shelter to twenty wounded men in her own apartment. The bombardment was relentless, and eventually Paris had no choice but to capitulate.

After the armistice in January 1871, Bernhardt, now exhausted and emaciated from months of intense work, managed to negotiate her way through the German lines to reunite with her family, including her mother, sister and son Maurice. They returned to Paris, only to find the city under the control of the Paris Commune. As has been seen, that movement was swiftly snuffed out, and Bernhardt returned to the stage, and in late 1871 was tempted back to the ranks of the Comédie-Française. In gratitude for her return, and in tacit acknowledgement of her rising celebrity status, she was given the highest rank the company could offer. She was still not yet thirty.

From here, her career went from strength to strength. She built a mansion in Parc Monceau and began to tour to support her increasingly lavish lifestyle. Of one of her performances in London, an audience member, George Arthur, wrote, 'she set every nerve and fibre in their bodies throbbing and held them spellbound'. Even though she was performing in French, the power of her voice and movement transcended language barriers and captivated English audiences too. It was during these years that her reputation for excess and idiosyncrasies really took hold. She wore a stuffed bat on her head, was rumoured to sleep in a coffin, and filled her apartment with still more wild animals.

Sarah Bernhardt was muse to many artists, and countless contemporary portraits exist of her – some painted like icons with saintly gold-leaf backgrounds, others depicting her in costume, perhaps as a heroine of the stage, or an odalisque. Some present her as herself, regal, alluring, opulent and idiosyncratic. One of Sarah's most significant relationships, which likely had romantic undertones if not overtones, was with female artist Louise Abbéma who frequently made artworks inspired by Sarah. Indeed, it was a particularly striking portrait of Sarah in 1875 that launched her to fame; another famous work depicts them both together, boating in the Bois de Boulogne.

For all this, Sarah was a talented artist herself, creating beautiful and emotive sculptures. One, entitled *Après la Tempête* and depicting a Breton mother cradling the lifeless body of her child in the aftermath of a fatal storm, was exhibited at the Paris Salon in 1876 and took the silver medal. Another of her famous pieces was a bas-relief of Ophelia at the moment of her death, drowning and wreathed in flowers. In 1879, she presented a bust of Louise Abbéma at the salon, where it was well received. Perhaps her most moving portrait of Louise is, however, not of her face or even her body at all, but actually a lifecast sculpture, of Louise's hand grasping hers – a portrait of their relationship. It is impossible to say if they were lovers or if their bond was deep but platonic, but all the evidence points to a relationship that was much more than a typical friendship.

The 1880s brought Sarah one of her most famous roles – Marguerite in *La Dame aux Camélias* – and her first US tour. Written by Alexandre Dumas *fils* in 1848 and first published in 1849, *La Dame aux Camélias* was a romantic tragedy based on Dumas's real-life love affair with the famous courtesan Marie Duplessis. The heroine – Marguerite – may well have resonated with Sarah Bernhardt given both her and her mother's experiences working as courtesans in Paris.

On 15 October 1880, at thirty-five years old, Sarah Bernhardt and her team boarded a ship from Le Havre bound for the United States. It would be her first of nine US tours, and would last seven weeks. Many were sceptical about what success she might achieve, as Americans were not known for their love of French theatre, and when asked if she would perform in English Sarah replied: 'I prefer to play in good French rather than in bad English.' To assist audiences, the script was translated and printed. From

October 1880 to May 1881, Bernhardt gave 156 performances to millions of Americans, with tickets priced at twenty-five dollars each. On her debut in New York, she received twenty-seven curtain calls. Later in the same trip, Thomas Edison recorded her reciting a speech from *Phèdre*. She became famous the world over. Oscar Wilde wrote *Salome* for her, but she was never able to perform it while the playwright languished in Reading Gaol.

Her career continued unabated; she continued her relationship with Louise Abbéma who created numerous portraits of her and raised her son Maurice. She also became more politically vocal as time passed and her influence grew. In 1894, a Jewish army officer named Alfred Dreyfus was accused of leaking classified military secrets to Germany. He was put on trial for treason and convicted – but the case stank of antisemitism. The evidence was weak, and Dreyfus's Jewish background made him a prime target for scapegoating. He was shipped off to the remote penal colony on Devil's Island, near French Guiana – and ostensibly left to rot. But his supporters in France were rallying. Antisemitism was surging in France at this time, and Sarah Bernhardt, now in her mid-fifties, found herself the victim of many vitriolic diatribes and illustrations that attacked her Jewish background. Needless to say, the case resonated with her.

In 1898 Émile Zola penned his famous open letter titled '*J'Accuse …!*', calling out the army's antisemitism and challenging the conviction. Sarah Bernhardt was moved by the letter and wrote to him to offer support. She rallied the theatre community too to support Dreyfus. She even wrote to Dreyfus personally in prison, and received backlash for this, but remained undeterred, even when it caused a rift between her and her beloved son, who rejected Zola's arguments. It was a polarising case in France, and one that exposed deep-seated antisemitism across French society. '*J'Accuse …!*' helped turn public opinion and highlighted the injustice and prejudice behind the conviction, and the loud protests of influential voices across multiple spheres forced the army to revisit the case. Dreyfus was eventually released in 1899 and exonerated fully in 1906.

In 1894, the same year that the Dreyfus Affair began, Sarah Bernhardt made one of the most important strategic partnerships of her career. She was introduced to Alphonse Mucha, commissioning a poster from him to advertise her new turn as *Gismonda*. The result was a two-metre-high art nouveau portrait of Bernhardt dressed in gilded Byzantine robes. Bernhardt was so pleased by the elegant, striking, mosaic-patterned poster that she ordered 4,000 copies and gave Mucha a six-year contract to make new posters for her. This partnership cemented the reputations of both painter and model; Alphonse Mucha's depictions of Bernhardt, the greatest actress of her generation, are still famous the world over, and copies are sold by the banks of the Seine to eager tourists. I discovered Sarah Bernhardt at the age of twenty-five, and only subsequently realised that she was the red-haired woman in the picture that had hung over my bed since my early teens.

In 1906 she sustained a serious leg injury while playing Tosca in Rio de Janeiro – in the final act the eponymous heroine throws herself from the ramparts of the Castel Sant'Angelo to commit suicide, and Sarah, who was always very physical in her roles, flung herself from the wall as usual, only the mattress meant to break her fall was misplaced. Her leg never fully healed.

When Sarah was sixty-nine and winding down her career, the First World War erupted across Europe, triggered by the assassination of Archduke Franz Ferdinand, before escalating into a brutal conflict over territory, national pride, and power between the Allied and Central Powers. France, positioned on the Western Front, bore the brunt of battles that devastated its north-eastern regions, as trench warfare and new military technologies led to unprecedented destruction and death. More than a million French troops would be slaughtered on the battlefields of the

Western Front. Bernhardt played a key role in supporting the war effort. Though she was made a Chevalier of the Légion d'Honneur that year, she was also facing financial difficulties due to debts incurred by Maurice's gambling addiction. On the outbreak of war, she rushed back to Paris, only to be asked by the French government to relocate for safety to a villa on the Bay of Arcachon.

A year after war broke out – 1915 – she had her leg amputated. In spite of the fact that this catastrophic injury caused her great discomfort, it never stopped her touring or performing, and she continued to work at nearly full tilt. Refusing a wheelchair, she designed a litter to be carried around in. She was also determined to contribute to her country in its time of crisis. She joined a troupe of famous French actors and travelled to the front lines, including the Battle of Verdun and the Battle of the Argonne, inventing the concept of performing for the soldiers and the wounded. Propped up on pillows in an armchair, she delivered a rousing recitation of '*Les Cathédrales*', a patriotic poem by Eugène Morand. Her ability to inspire courage in war-weary soldiers despite her age and physical limitations was mesmerising to those who beheld her.

The First World War was a defining catastrophe for France, shaping its modern history and marking its people. Nearly 1.4 million French soldiers were killed, and millions more wounded, creating a 'lost generation' that altered the fabric of French society. The conflict shattered the optimism of the Belle Époque, replacing it with a more sombre and reflective national psyche. Economically, France was left with billions in damages, facing the monumental task of rebuilding shattered towns and infrastructure and restoring farmland. Politically, the war sowed seeds of instability, as disillusionment and the desire for peace at almost any cost influenced France's cautious stance in the lead-up to the Second World War. France's national memory, steeped in the trauma of trench warfare and collective sacrifice, would be reshaped by memorials and literature reflecting the war's horrors; the French landscape still bears scars from the conflict.

Following her tour of the battlefields, Bernhardt returned to Paris and starred in two short patriotic films, including one based on the life of Joan of Arc and another titled *Mères Françaises*. These films were designed to encourage French patriotism and urge the United States to join the war effort. That same year, she embarked on an American farewell tour, on an explicit mission to encourage US participation in the war – performing patriotic and nationalistic pieces designed to instil in them the spirit of resistance to German tyranny. She set sail for France once again in late 1918, her ship docking on the eleventh day of the eleventh month – Armistice Day. Even as the war drew to a close, she remained a symbol of French resilience and patriotism, and her efforts during the conflict were highly praised.

In the early 1920s, Bernhardt continued to tour, perform and lecture. Her health, however, was in decline, and in 1922, while rehearsing a new play, *Un Sujet de Roman*, she collapsed, and fell unconscious for an hour. Despite this, she attempted to take on the role of Cleopatra in *Rodogune* and began filming *La Voyante* from a makeshift studio in her home. In March 1923, Bernhardt collapsed again and died on 26 March 1923, from uraemia. Her funeral was attended by 30,000 people, marking the end of a legendary career.

\* \* \*

Today, an artefact that testifies to Bernhardt's stage career, illustrious social circle and eclectic taste is tucked away in the collections of the Victoria & Albert Museum in London.

It is a real, human skull.

Not only that; it has been decorated.

A gift from none other than Victor Hugo to Sarah following her triumphant turn in *Hernani* in 1877, it is inscribed on the cranium with the following verse:

*Squelette, qu'as-tu fait de l'âme?*
*Lampe qu'as-tu fait de la flamme?*
*Cage déserte qu'as-tu fait*
*De ton bel oiseau qui chantait?*
*Volcan, qu'as-tu fait de la lave?*
*Qu'as-tu fait de ton maître, esclave?*

Or:

Skeleton, what have you done with your soul?
Lamp, what have you done with your flame?
Empty cage, what have you done with
The beautiful bird that used to sing?
Volcano, what have you done with your lava?
Slave, what have you done with your master?

By inscribing it on a real skull and gifting it to Bernhardt, known for her vivacity and fascination with death, Hugo created a memento mori – a fitting gift for Bernhardt who thrived on the intensity of life and art. Bernhardt's reputation has outlived her. She is celebrated as the first true celebrity actress, paving the way for Hollywood and influencer culture today. Her image survives as an icon of her times, immortalised in the Alphonse Mucha posters that adorn the walls of college students across the world. She is an emblem of decadence, art, passion and – above all – Belle Époque Paris.

Colette and Missy, early twentieth century.

# 14

## Colette

### 28 January 1873 – 3 August 1954

It is early evening on 3 January 1907, and on the dusky stage of the Moulin Rouge, usually the haunt of cancan dancers, a curious spectacle is being played out. An aristocratic woman, dressed in drag as an archaeologist in a velvet suit and necktie, stands centre stage. She paces the stage slowly, consulting a heavy tome of ancient lore, while a sarcophagus looms in the background. Suddenly, a mummy jumps up from the sarcophagus, wrapped head to toe in bandages, which are then comically unwound by the archaeologist. The scene teeters between comedy and eroticism, as underneath the bandages is revealed not a desiccated corpse, but a sprightly and curvy young woman, adorned with a sheer skirt and a bejewelled, orientalist golden brassiere. Her midriff and legs are left exposed, her feet bare, as though she has stepped out of some dream of the Nile – part ancient ritual, part Belle Époque fantasy.

Fully divested of her bandages, with her body on show and a pseudo-Egyptian headdress perched atop her bob cut, the resurrected mummy proceeds to perform an exaggeratedly sensual dance for the archaeologist, who gawps in awe at the spectacle, along with the riveted audience. The scene suddenly climaxes as the archaeologist, unable to restrain him/herself a moment longer, embraces the vision and the pair of women share a passionate, lingering kiss.

The house goes wild. The police are called. The woman playing the archaeologist, who is also the author of the piece, is replaced by a male actor for two nights, but it's still too scandalous, and the police shut it down.

The preening young woman who emerged from her bandage cocoon is none other than the writer Colette, an icon of French literature who, after a messy divorce which has left her broke, has decided to pursue a career on the stage, in the company of her aristocratic female lover. Colette is just beginning to reclaim her own agency and independence, and will soon build her reputation as a great writer, a daredevil and scandal maker of Belle Époque Paris. Her journey to the stage of the Moulin Rouge, from the sheltered Burgundian countryside, began seven years earlier, at the very turn of the century.

* * *

It is 1900. A new century dawns, and the Belle Époque in full swing. Literary France is thriving, and artists and writers are gravitating towards Paris, the heart of creative expression and innovation. The French capital basks in a brief period of peace and creative fervour. The grand Exposition Universelle has thrown open its gates, transforming the city into a gallery of modern marvels. Crowds revel in the cutting-edge exhibits: a giant Ferris wheel – the *Grande Roue de Paris* – hoists gleeful passengers high above the skyline, and a futuristic moving sidewalk carries visitors from Les Invalides to the Champ de Mars. By night, new electric lights in the sweeping art nouveau style twinkle on the Pont Alexandre III – illuminating the newly revealed ornate, golden Fames statues, allegories of Art, Science, Industry and Commerce, each accompanied by a rearing Pegasus. The lights from this bridge spread across sprawling fair pavilions, while glamorous soirées spill from salons and cabarets – artists, writers and socialites toasting art and innovation in the warm Parisian night. In this festive summer, the city also inaugurates its first Métro line beneath the boulevards and hosts athletes from around the world for the 1900 Summer Olympics – an event so fanciful that it even features hot-air balloon races drifting across the sky.

Amid this excited hubbub, an unlikely literary sensation is taking shape. A new novel is flying off the shelves, into the hands of the clamouring public.

Set far from Paris's hectic boulevards, *Claudine à l'École* recounts the tales of a young girl navigating life in rural Burgundy; it is a coming-of-age story, and perhaps the first to speak with real insight and honesty about an unselfconscious female sexual awakening. Set in an all-girls school, it is amazing, the public reflect, how well the middle-aged male author has captured the intimate experiences of a teenage girl.

The first instalment in the Claudine series, with its taboo-busting portrayal of same-sex attraction and various scandals, all told in the first person, entertained and resonated with readers. The central character, speaking with eyebrow-raising candour, represented a rebellion against societal norms. The heroine became, in the words of the modern American critic Judith Thurman, 'the first teenager of the century'. Almost overnight, the Claudine books became a cultural phenomenon in France.

*Claudine à l'École* was published under the decidedly masculine name 'Willy', nom de plume of one Henry Gauthier-Villars. 'Willy' was known widely as a prolific author, except he wasn't. He employed a slew of ghost writers to churn out a stream of products, including reviews, letters, articles, poems, plays and, eventually, novels. He was a literary entrepreneur; not a bad idea, *if* employees are treated fairly. However, Villars's model certainly muddied the waters of authorship and moral rights, and soon turned outright illegal and exploitative once he had the good fortune to marry.

Back in 1893, Villars, then thirty-four, had wed the twenty-year-old Sidonie-Gabrielle Colette. Soon he realised he had struck gold. Not only was his young bride beautiful and inventively stylish, but she was gifted with prodigious creative talent and a turn of phrase of which Villars could only dream. Colette was promptly forced to write for her husband. This was how the Claudine novels came to be, and bear 'Willy' on the title page. Yes, the ground-breaking little book, so accurately capturing the adolescent female experience, was in fact written (under coercion) by a young woman and *not* a middle-aged man. *Quelle surprise.*

* * *

Sidonie-Gabrielle Colette, known to history simply as Colette, was born on 28 January 1873 in Saint-Sauveur, a small town in the heart of Burgundy. Her rural surroundings filled her with a lifelong love for the natural world, an appreciation nurtured by her beloved mother, Sido, whose presence permeates Colette's work.

Colette's father, Jules-Joseph Colette, was a retired military officer who had served as a captain. He had lost a leg fighting the Austrian Empire in the Second Italian War of Independence, which ended his military career. After this, Jules-Joseph became the local tax collector in Saint-Sauveur. They were not wealthy, and there was no dowry to be settled on Colette, which made it unlikely that she would ever 'make a good marriage'. That said, she was bright, lively and vivacious, capturing the attention of a certain visitor to Burgundy, there to settle his illegitimate child with a wet nurse in Saint-Sauveur. The man in question was Willy, that fixture of Paris literary circles so well known for his wit and charm, but with something of a reputation for loose living.

Willy was persuasive, more businessman than artist. To Colette, young and eager to explore a world far beyond the provinces, marriage to Willy presented an entrance into the much-mythologised bohemian Paris of the Belle Époque. She imagined herself on the arm of a famous literary figure, discussing new ideas flourishing in the arts and philosophy. The allure of Willy's world was undeniable and, at first, she revelled in it. It marked a departure from her rural upbringing, and a heady and intoxicating one at that.

Once married, the illusion began to crack. While Willy encouraged her to start writing, likely sensing her potential, he did not encourage her to build her own reputation as a writer, harnessing her talents to enhance his business instead. Colette was to be his next source of material, providing fresh, quirky, sensual characters and narratives. At first the work felt cathartic for Colette, allowing her to explore her past and express her voice, but soon her talent would become a source of conflict between her and her husband.

Enter *Claudine* in 1900. Despite the book becoming a significant cultural phenomenon, Colette's name was nowhere to be seen on it. Willy, claiming authorship, received all the royalties and public acclaim, while Colette remained in the shadows. Despite the fame and financial success the books brought, or perhaps because of this, Willy continued to regard Colette's labour and talent as his own property to exploit. Stories circulated of Willy locking Colette in a room, demanding she write until she produced pages to his satisfaction. Willy pushed her to create narratives that blended youthful exploration with hints of scandal – an approach that was controversial yet proved commercially lucrative. Colette's talent was at his disposal, and he wilfully exploited it. The bonds of marriage were different then. Wives still swore to obey their husbands and, given that their resources were meant to be pooled, and especially since Colette may have agreed at first to Willy using her work, there was little legal objection to Willy's appropriation of her work.

Nevertheless, this was a period of artistic awakening for Colette. Willy was not a two-dimensional villain. He inspired Colette, taught her her trade, and no doubt contributed something to the success of the Claudine series. Colette did acknowledge that she would never have become a writer if not for him, and so, for better or worse, it seems she did not regret the marriage, even if she did regret staying with him so long, and his manipulation of her.

Claustrophobia and freedom would emerge as key themes in her work, and the hallmark of Colette's writing would be her ability to capture nuanced and complex characters. Her characters were honest, and remarkably uncontrived. In many ways she can be seen as George Sand's successor, although their style is drastically different. Sand's writing, with its simple sentence structure and pared-back prose, proves easy for a non-native speaker; Colette's is a minefield, complex and occasionally jarring. But her characters are lazy, sensuous, passionate, modern, cutting, human. She was a brilliant writer who brought subversive, alluring and surprising characters to life. Chéri and Léa – the protagonists of her most famous short stories – are two of the greatest and strangest lovers of all time.

The voice she employed when writing Claudine, and the tightrope the character walked between social expectations and personal desire, reflected Colette's own experiences closely.

The second and third Claudine novels similarly seemed to mirror Colette's own life, and certain elements of her life with Willy. It seems that after an initial period of adjustment and difficulty in married life, during which Colette discovered her husband's affairs, and found herself mistreated by him, she became freer and began to carve out her own independent social life, and to explore more fully and more openly her own same-sex attraction. Willy, at least not a hypocrite, turned a blind eye to his wife's extramarital affairs with women, and potentially also encouraged them as good fodder for more books. In one of the stranger episodes of their married life, Colette began an affair with a Southern belle from Louisiana named Jeannie Urquhart. Married to a far older man, Urquhart was forging a career as a writer in Paris under her married name, Georgie Raoul-Duval.

Intrigued, and presumably not wanting to miss out on the action, Willy – without Colette's knowledge – also began an affair with the same woman.

The relationship with Georgie was Colette's first widely known homosexual relationship, and it was far from trouble-free. Colette was twenty-eight when they met, and still married to Willy, but the pair were instantly attracted to one another and their romance began immediately. When Colette discovered that Willy was sleeping with her too, she was initially outraged, before being persuaded to join in and form an unlikely *ménage à trois*. They travelled together as a throuple, before more 'infidelity' was uncovered, with both Colette and Willy dismayed to discover that Georgie had been sleeping with both of them individually, rather than as part of the agreed *ménage à trois*. After this, in 1901, the relationship fell apart for good, and the irate Colette poured her side of the story into the third of the Claudine books – *Claudine en Ménage*.

This affair was the most significant, but Willy and Colette were both known for their extramarital liaisons and sexual fluidity by this point. Colette had several other lovers during her marriage after the breakdown of the relationship with Willy, the most significant of which – and perhaps the defining relationship of her life – was with Missy, or Mathilde de Morny. Granddaughter of none other than Hortense de Beauharnais on one side, making her the great-granddaughter of Empress Josephine, and perhaps of Nicholas I, Tsar of Russia, on the other, Missy was a fixture of aristocratic French society, and in the style of George Sand always dressed in men's clothing and unabashedly smoked cigars in public. Indeed, Missy took her cross-dressing and arguably transgender lifestyle far beyond what George Sand had done, presenting herself in almost all ways as male. It is also worth noting that Missy's father, Charles de Morny, was the principal lover of Sarah Bernhardt's mother, and Charles certainly took an interest in Sarah's upbringing and career. It is too great a leap to seriously suggest that Missy and Sarah Bernhardt were sisters, but it was certainly not beyond the realms of possibility, and the two certainly knew of each other.

In 1800 the government of the French Republic had passed a law requiring women to apply for specific permission – usually on medical grounds – to wear trousers publicly, a *'permission de travestissement'*. Somewhat shockingly, the law stayed in place for 213 years, only being officially repealed in 2013. That said, the rigour with which it was enforced waxed and waned, and it seemed the elite and those who moved in influential bohemian circles could more or less get away with it. Missy was a captivating and notorious figure. A talented artist, she made a name for herself as a sculptor.

Missy met Colette in 1905, as Colette's marriage to Willy was on its last legs, and they formed a deep romantic connection. When Colette formally separated from Willy, they bought a house together and openly lived as a couple – while homosexuality had been legal in France since the Revolution, this remained a radical act in the early twentieth century.

Colette separated from Willy in 1906 and their divorce was finalised in 1910. With this part of her life definitively closed, Colette was ready for a new chapter. She pivoted from writing and towards performing. Left fairly broke by her divorce, with Willy retaining control of the earnings from *Claudine*, acting also gave her a quick income stream. More than this, Colette enjoyed the physicality of the stage and the thrill of playing for a live audience. She undertook specific training as a silent 'mime' actress – perhaps self-conscious about her lingering Burgundian accent. She performed in the Moulin Rouge and La Cigale, among other venues, singing, acting and posing scantily clad in *tableaux vivants*. She liked to scandalise.

And perhaps her greatest scandal yet came in 1907 when, as we saw at the start of this chapter, she kissed Missy in front of a huge audience at the Moulin Rouge during *Rêve d'Egypte*. Established in the heart of Montmartre in 1889, the Moulin Rouge had swiftly become an icon of Belle Époque Paris's heady sexual and artistic underbelly; there was the scandalous cancan dancing, led by cabaret icons like Jane Avril and La Goulue, alongside performances from boundary-pushing performers.

Following their scandalous kiss, the police were called and the show cancelled.

The police prefect who attempted to prosecute them was the thoroughly objectionable Louis Lépine; generally on the wrong side of history, he also served as an oppressive governor general of Algeria. For all the obstacles they faced, Colette and Missy stayed together until 1912, and bought a manor house together in Brittany, where they could be together away from prying eyes.

Following the end of her relationship with Missy in 1912, Colette turned her attention back to writing. That is not to say she did not write during her years of performing; her 1910 novel *La Vagabonde* draws on her experiences during this time, depicting a young female writer – recently divorced – who decides to pursue a music hall career. The parallels could not be more pronounced. However, it was her literary output in the years after 1912 that would cement her as a literary icon in her own right. At last, she was fully free of Willy's influence, confident, no longer naive about the industry, and ready to wield her voice. Today, Willy's reputation is primarily as the controlling husband of the woman who *actually* wrote some of the bestselling French books of all time. Colette's reputation is as a giant of literature, who redefined the French *roman*.

In 1912, Colette married Henry de Jouvenel, a journalist and editor at the newspaper *Le Matin*. This marriage brought Colette financial stability and a new set of social connections. Through Henry, she gained entry into the world of French journalism, where she wrote articles, reviews and essays that would broaden her understanding of the human condition and further hone her literary skills. Her experience in journalism sharpened her eye for detail and enriched her ability to capture the subtleties of human relationships, skills that would continue to define her novels. In 1913, Colette gave birth to her only child, a daughter whom she named Colette de Jouvenel. However, her marriage to Henry de Jouvenel was as tumultuous as her first. Colette was fiercely independent, and her need for creative freedom often clashed with the traditional values held by her husband. Their relationship gradually deteriorated, leading to a separation.

During the First World War, she leaned into her journalism even more; somehow juggling the demands of motherhood, wifely duties, writing novels and taking turns in plays, Colette managed to compose reams of articles. These were mostly published in *Le Matin* – one of the most widely circulating papers in France – and she even had a weekly column in the paper. When it came to her writing about the war itself, she shied away from traditional war reporting on strategy, which did not suit her style or expertise, and instead zoomed in on the human cost of the war, and the experiences of individuals.

Throughout the 1920s, Colette's reputation as a writer continued to grow. Her novels became more nuanced, exploring the complexities of love, ageing and personal identity. *Chéri*, published in 1920, was one of her most celebrated works, telling the story of a young man in a long-term relationship with an older woman, an affair fraught with both passion and melancholy. The novel reflected Colette's own experiences and observations on love's transient nature, as well as the painful tension between desire and societal expectations. *Chéri* struck a chord with readers, and its success further solidified Colette's reputation as a major literary figure. At a time when writers like Proust and Gide – who admired her – were also dissecting the intricacies of human desire and identity, Colette's work stood out for its female gaze and intimate realism.

Her writing was already having a ripple effect, encouraging other writers to be bolder, to dare to explore themes generally considered taboo, and beginning to change the face of French literature, in keeping with the social transformations of the 1920s. Her ability to capture the subtleties of desire and the challenges of ageing resonated deeply in a society that was grappling with changing attitudes towards love and relationships.

In *Chéri*, Colette masterfully crafts the story of Fred Peloux, known as Chéri, and his older lover, Léa de Lonval. The character of Chéri was initially introduced through a series of stories Colette published in *Le Matin* in 1911–12. He was raised in an opulent but shallow world of retired courtesans, and his mother, a member of this circle of ageing beauties, spoiled him with superficial luxuries. His relationship with Léa is a blend of power and play, one-upmanship and genuine affection, marked by Léa's experience and Chéri's youthful arrogance. Their affair is a continuous battle for dominance, where the thrill lies as much in verbal sparring as in physical intimacy. The descriptions of Léa grooming the young, teenaged Chéri, who for all his youth has much more wealth and social power than her, feel reminiscent of the relationship between Diane de Poitiers and Henri II.

As the novel begins, Chéri is about to marry a suitable young woman named Edmée, signalling the end of his affair with Léa. Although Léa has faced such partings many times, this separation unexpectedly leaves her heartbroken, revealing her deep, hidden love for Chéri. Meanwhile, Chéri, trapped in a conventional marriage, finds himself bored and yearning for Léa. Their eventual reunion is fraught with unspoken emotions and unresolved tensions. Despite recognising their genuine love, neither can let go of their rivalry, which has shaped their relationship, and now acts as a barrier to genuine love. In their final moments together, Léa understands that she has kept Chéri dependent on her for too long. In an act of self-preservation and strength, she forces him to return to his wife, acknowledging that she can no longer serve as both lover and mother. The novel ends with Chéri fleeing Léa's home in turmoil, unable to reconcile his desires with the expectations of adulthood.

*Chéri* draws heavily from Colette's own life experiences and observations of the French social elite. The dynamic between Chéri and Léa mirrors Colette's relationships with younger lovers after her first marriage. The theme of an older woman entangled with a younger man reflects Colette's exploration of the tension between love, power and independence – an issue she grappled with in her own life. Like Léa, Colette had been involved with men significantly younger than herself, most notably her stepson Bertrand de Jouvenel. This still-shocking 'affair' with her teenage stepson, carried on under his father's nose, lasted around five years, starting when Bertrand was approximately sixteen, and had a huge effect on both lovers, including – unsurprisingly – ending Colette's marriage to his father. The novel's exploration of the ageing courtesan's struggle to balance her desires with the reality of growing older likely reflects Colette's own fears and experiences of ageing in a society that prized youth and beauty.

*Chéri* was followed by *Le Blé en Herbe* (usually known in English as *The Ripening Seed*) in 1923, another novel that explored the nuances of youth and the inevitability of change, themes that had come to define her work.

In her later years, Colette's personal life remained as complex as her fiction. She married Maurice Goudeket, sixteen years her junior, in 1935. This relationship, unlike her previous marriages, was characterised by companionship and mutual respect. Maurice, a devoted partner, supported Colette's work and gave her a sense of stability she had rarely known before. Their relationship endured through the political turmoil of the Second World War, a period that brought both personal and professional challenges for Colette. Living in Nazi-occupied Paris, Colette faced difficult decisions, especially concerning her husband's Jewish heritage. Though her public life was tainted by her occasional contributions to pro-Nazi publications, her personal actions demonstrated her loyalty and protective instinct towards Maurice, as she risked much to shield him from the dangers of occupation. Indeed, her wartime allegiances and decisions were pressured when Maurice was interred in a POW camp, and she had to pull strings to get him out. While her record is not spotless, she was far from open collaboration.

Despite the controversy surrounding her wartime choices, Colette's literary output continued to flourish, and her works remained in high demand. In 1944, she published *Gigi*, a story that once again explored themes of transformation and societal expectations. This was an escape from the perils of the Nazi occupation and tells the story of a young girl groomed to become a courtesan, only for her wealthy suitor to offer her marriage unexpectedly. *Gigi* was adapted into a successful stage play starring Audrey Hepburn and later a film featuring Leslie Caron, cementing Colette's legacy as one of France's most celebrated writers.

By the time of her death on 3 August 1954, Colette had become a symbol of resilience, defiance and creative freedom. She was the first woman in France to receive a state funeral, a testament to her influence on French culture and her lasting contributions to literature. Her life's journey from provincial Burgundy to the literary salons of Paris, from an oppressed young wife to an independent author and cultural icon, remains one of remarkable transformation and self-discovery.

Colette's success, her enduring popularity and her extraordinary state funeral reflected significant shifts in French attitudes towards women, sexuality and societal norms. Her life and legacy served as a barometer of the cultural changes that were taking place in France, particularly in the first half of the twentieth century.

Her works continue to captivate readers with their exploration of human desire, identity and the pursuit of freedom, themes as relevant today as they were in her time. Through her novels, Colette offered an unflinching look at the lives of women, forever changing the landscape of French literature and inspiring generations of writers.

From her rural childhood in Burgundy to her luxurious final days in her Palais-Royal apartment, Colette lived unapologetically on her own terms. She displayed the same defiant spirit and literary flair as George Sand before, and her writing was her path to independence and freedom. Though she resisted aligning with feminism, which she viewed as limiting, Colette continually flouted social conventions, carving a path as one of France's most liberated women. She pursued sexual freedom without apology, much like her contemporary Sarah Bernhardt, maintaining open relationships with both men and women. A trailblazer, Colette was one of the first women to report from the front lines during the First World War and among the earliest novelists to adapt her works for cinema. Her grave at Père Lachaise remains adorned with flowers from devoted readers. Renowned for her sensual prose and deep insights into human relationships, Colette captivated literary giants like Marcel Proust, André Gide and Jean Cocteau. With over eighty volumes to her name, she solidified her place as one of France's great literary icons, celebrated on screen by new adaptations that capture the wild, free spirit of her extraordinary life. Walking in the gardens of the Palais-Royal where Colette spent her final years, you can almost feel the ghost of the frizzy-haired trailblazer contemplating, flirting and critiquing from the shadows.

Coco Chanel in the early 1950s.

# 15

# Coco Chanel

## 19 August 1883–10 January 1971

'My life didn't please me, so I created my life.'
Coco Chanel

Chanel worked with her ten fingers, her fingernail, the edge of her hand, her palm, her pin and scissors, right on the garment, which was a white vapour of long folds, splattered with crumbled crystal.

Sometimes she falls to her knees before her work and embraces it, not to revere it, but to chastise it ... to soften some expansion of tulle ... The fiery humility of a body before its favourite task! Chanel is like the prostrate washerwoman who beats the washing, like the hard housewives who are trained day after day, twenty times a day, to genuflect like nuns. This professional training of the body leaves her thin, a little hollowed out by fatigue. At the moment, she's offering me a neck full of black hair that's growing with vegetal vigour. She speaks as she works, in a low, deliberately restrained voice. She talks, teaches and repeats, with a kind of exasperated patience. I can make out repeated words, sung like essential musical motifs: 'I hate little things ... How many times do I have to say that breadth makes you thinner? I won't tire of saying it again ... Press there, give ease here ... No, no little things on a fabric that defends itself ... No, don't constrict ... I won't tire of saying it again ...'

It is only a moment, but one of total muteness, of fierce retreat, an ephemeral petrification from which the mouth suddenly escapes – bending lips, with sad corners, impatient, tamed, punished by sharp teeth ...

The closed eyelids suddenly reveal two glittering granite-coloured eyes, the colour of mountain water in the hollow of a sun-drenched rock.

Colette wrote this description of Coco Chanel, in her 1932 work *Prisons and Paradise*.

Coco Chanel was two things before she was anything else. She was an artist and she was an opportunist. She was industrious with exacting standards, and made her collections herself. In the 1920s, at the height of her fame, Winston Churchill was astounded that during a society getaway in Scotland, Chanel broke away from the party to tweak and alter garments with her own hands, busily tucking and pinning, while the other guests quaffed champagne.

Her eye for fashion, her talent for design and her skill with shears and a needle and thread were unrivalled. She was shrewd. She took no prisoners and sought to survive. She did not care for the life she was born to, and so she made herself a better one. One that glittered with pearls and diamonds and reposed in fine silks.

\* \* \*

Beneath all the luxury now associated with the Chanel brand – the fine tweeds, the twisted pearls, the aroma of Coco Mademoiselle, Chance and No. 5, and the butter-soft leather of the coveted 2.55 bags – is a slightly incongruous truth: Coco Chanel came from poverty. Her father, Albert, was a peddler; her mother, Eugénie, a laundress. When Chanel was born in 1883, the couple was not only unmarried, but totally broke. Eventually they bowed to societal pressure and tied the knot, but it brought them little good fortune, only many more children to feed. When Eugénie Chanel died at just thirty-two, her daughter Gabrielle Bonheur Chanel was eleven and the second eldest of six; the youngest, Augustin, would die at six months old. None of the family was destined for a happy life. Even Gabrielle – not yet Coco – whose life was marked by glamour and flashes of joy, found true happiness evasive. Until her dying day she lied constantly about her age, her origins, her family; she never married, watching while her lovers married others.

When Eugénie died, Albert Chanel made a difficult choice. He gave away his children. His two surviving sons, both aged under ten, were sent into serfdom as unpaid farm labourers, fed and sheltered in exchange for work, but little more. The three girls, Julia, Gabrielle and Antoinette, were taken to a convent – a stark place of cool stone at Aubazine.

Here, the young Gabrielle Chanel cannot have been much loved. But she was taught the skills and given the inspiration and discipline that would carry her through her career and make her name last centuries. Late in life, Coco Chanel would quip, 'some people think luxury is the opposite of poverty. It is not. It is the opposite of vulgarity.' There was no wealth in the habits of the nuns, stark black and white, impeccably neat and pristine, adorned with rosary beads, and the odd chain. These colours, styles and motifs would form the basis of Chanel's signature style. It is not too great a leap of faith to think that Chanel's little black dress was inspired by the ankle-grazing habit of a novice nun. It is not hard either to see how rosary beads informed her strings of pearls. The young Gabrielle's eyes must have scanned over those habits, and thought what she might have made of them, with a nip here, a tuck there, some fluting, some darts, pleats, and getting rid of those awful sleeves. These were the images, the shapes, the colours, that permeated Gabrielle Chanel's adolescence. The monochromatic nuns taught her simplicity of style. Just as importantly, they taught her to sew.

Her childhood before the convent was chaotic and somewhat squalid. When her mother died, she and the other children were crowded into a one-room apartment, with a strong smell of unwashed bodies and disease. For the rest of her life, Chanel valued cleanliness and purity above all else in her designs. The nunnery may have marked the breaking up of her family, but it also gave her a security and orderliness she had never known before. When she encountered courtesans later in life, she was unfazed by their lack of respectability; she just noted that they were glamorous and clean. Chanel wanted always to be glamorous and clean.

At eighteen, she left. She and her sister began to perform for petty cash in side-street cabarets. They weren't exotic dancers: they sang and danced jolly songs, fully clothed. But they did sleep with the rich men who watched them, and Gabrielle Chanel earned the nickname she would use for all of her life, Coco, after the chorus in her signature song, about a crowing cockerel, who crowed in French (not English) – so instead of *cock-a-doodle-doo* he went *cocoricooooo*!

Her renditions clearly were charming, because Chanel found her first wealthy lover who would become her first wealthy sponsor, Étienne Balsan, at one of these shows. A former cavalry officer, Balsan liked horses and owed his wealth to textiles, two passions he would impart to Chanel during their long affair. He invited her to be a mistress, one of many, at his Château of Royallieu. The building had once been a monastery, but Balsan reconsecrated its once hallowed halls for pleasure. He kept many mistresses there together, including renowned courtesan Émilienne d'Alençon, and their lives consisted of sensual and pastoral pleasure: riding out, picnicking, drinking and lovemaking. Balsan and his friends shared the girls in the château, but it seemed the girls shared the men as well, as before too long Chanel's affections had transferred – irrevocably – from Balsan to Arthur 'Boy' Capel, a polo player from a middle-class family on the rise.

Boy would be the great love of Coco's life. But, like her, he was an opportunist, and while he backed Chanel in her first shop and stuck with her until his death, when the opportunity for him to bolster his status through marriage to a wealthy aristocratic society darling came along, he took it. Boy Capel married Diana Wyndham in 1918, after he had already been Chanel's lover for ten years. History doesn't relate where Chanel was on the day her great love married the twenty-five-year-old Diana, but she wasn't raising a glass at the reception.

Capel and Balsan, who apparently managed their jealousy in the arms of other lovers, both agreed to give Chanel the capital and connections needed to open a luxury milliner's shop in Paris. The premises found for the young Chanel was 21 Rue Cambon, in Paris's prestigious 1st arrondissement. The boutique was given the name Chanel Modes, and it was the beginning of everything. Capel and Balsan threaded the needle, and Chanel went to work.

She worked with alacrity. The hat shop on Rue Cambon was a long way from the cloisters at Aubazine, and she knew she had a chance. She took it.

Chanel Modes grew into other boutiques in the fashionable resort towns of Biarritz and Deauville, adding elegant dresses and sailing jackets to its wares. While France was in the midst of the First World War, Chanel's business thrived, her pared-back and practical aesthetic catching the mood of the time. The businesses were so successful she was able to pay back much of the initial investments. Her love life expanded too, and soon included a refugee Russian prince, Grand Duke Dmitri Pavlovich of Russia, one of Rasputin's murderers. Having escaped the Russian Revolution, he was one of many Russian aristocrats who flooded France in the aftermath of the Bolshevik triumph.

By 1918, Chanel had purchased the permanent premises of the Chanel couture empire, at 31 Rue Cambon – just a few doors down from her first hat shop. Chanel – the brand – is still found at this address in Paris.

In addition to her success as a couturier (she was officially registered as such in 1919), Chanel established herself as a fixture of high society and a patron of the arts. Her best friend was Misia Sert, and together they patronised the avant-garde performances of Sergei Diaghilev – the notorious impresario of the Ballets Russes – and composer Igor Stravinsky as they made their first strides in Paris. Chanel designed costumes for the Ballets Russes, notably for *Le Train Bleu*, written by none other than Jean Cocteau and choreographed by Bronislava Nijinska, sister to the legendary dancer. She also boasted Pablo Picasso and Salvador Dalí among her roster of eccentric and fashionable lovers. Her achievements and liaisons during this period of her life – the time of her great flourishing – are too many to detail. Perhaps her most significant romantic conquest was Hugh Grosvenor, Duke of Westminster, an English aristocrat whose 'incalculable' wealth made the fortunes of Capel and Balsan pale by comparison. He was nicknamed Bendor, after a cherished racehorse and familial heraldic dispute that dated back to the Middle Ages.

But tragedy shadowed every success. Boy had died in a car accident in 1919, an event from which Chanel never truly recovered. But onwards and upwards; outwardly at least she continued on the path chosen and took many more lovers, but her heart may truly have been buried with Boy.

Her success as a designer and society sensation soon reached the ears of New York film magnates, and Samuel Goldwyn of MGM fame – introduced to her by Dmitri Pavlovich – offered her upwards of the equivalent of $75 million in today's money to go to New York and design costumes for films. Subtle and minimalist, her designs didn't translate well to the screen, and while it wasn't a total failure, she didn't make the splash she'd hoped for, and soon headed back to Paris. The deal had doubtlessly appealed to Chanel, despite her success and roster of wealthy clients; even she had had to slash her prices in the wake of the Great Depression, whose reverberations had hit Europe as well as New York.

Back on the arm of Bendor, Chanel made valuable connections among the English political elite. She holidayed with Winston Churchill, who admired her salmon-catching skills in Scottish rivers. During their 1927 sojourn, he wrote to his wife:

> Coco is here in place of Violet [the duke's former wife]. She fishes from morn till night, & in 2 months has killed 50 salmon. She is very agreeable – really a gt & strong being, fit to rule a man or an empire. Bennie very well & I think extremely happy to be mated with an equal – her ability balancing his power. We are only 3 on the river & have all the plums.

Chanel said of Churchill, 'Winston is a dandy and a visionary.' Evidently, the pair were on first-name terms, Churchill never visiting Paris without calling on Coco, even after the end of her relationship with Bendor. He confided in her his great disappointment at the marriage of Edward VIII to Wallis Simpson, and the catastrophe of the abdication. It was perhaps through her connections to Churchill that Chanel received an invitation to the coronation of George VI.

The tweeds of the English countryside and Scottish Highlands would inform the styles Chanel sketched in Paris. And her well-known connections to Britain's wartime prime minister would make her a valuable acquaintance of the German officers who would soon be storming Paris.

Chanel's fashion business – with its simple, good-quality and understated styles – had boomed during the years of the First World War. It had also helped that her Biarritz boutique was about as far from the fighting as one could get, and those who flocked to the coast for escapism indulged in the little luxuries it offered. Her modern, boyish twists on femininity also found an eager audience in the roaring twenties. During these interwar years, Chanel – both woman and brand – flourished. Her name and her social life and her designs were omnipresent in the magazines of the day. And she was on the arm of the Duke of Westminster, and decorated his new Highland estate, including installing 'the first bidet in the Highlands'. There were even rumours of marriage, but such a thing never materialised. When queried on this, Coco is said to have quipped, 'There have been several duchesses of Westminster. There is only one Chanel.'

But war was coming to France. In Germany, Hitler and the far right were gathering support. In France, Coco was also dabbling in far-right nationalism. The duke was a confirmed antisemite and homophobe, sympathetic to German fascist politics. This was not unusual for the time, but still hateful, and it seems he was particularly outspoken – he was a member of both the Link and the Right clubs; this may well have influenced Chanel's views.

With the outbreak of war, Chanel closed up shop. She declared 'this is not a time for fashion', which retrospectively seems quite admirable but at the time seemed like a dereliction of duty. Four thousand workers were laid off just when they needed income, routine and security the most. Chanel retained only a skeleton staff to sell perfumes and accessories in the boutique. As her seamstresses scrabbled for work, Chanel stayed at the Ritz and was often glimpsed retreating to the hotel's air-raid shelter, with a servant trotting behind, carrying her gas mask on a cushion.

Other designers continued to work throughout the war, notably Christian Dior and Pierre Balmain, and received criticism as collaborators, for creating decadent ballgowns to grace German bodies as they danced with Nazi lovers in the stolen ballrooms of Paris. But they were not true collaborators. Dior used the money he earned from selling gowns to Nazi wives to fund his sister's

Resistance activities, and to try to purchase her safety after she was deported to Ravensbrück.

Chanel may not have made dresses for German women, but she was couture's greatest collaborator. She lived in the Nazi-occupied Ritz on Place Vendôme. She even went so far as to engage in a sexual affair with a high-ranking Nazi officer, thirteen years her junior, and to try to squeeze her Jewish business partners out of the business. So, Chanel did not design for the Nazis, but she did sleep with them – as will be seen – and she had no problem with ratting out the Jews.

For some years, Chanel's perfumes had been mixed and distributed by a man named Pierre Wertheimer, along with a series of partners, with whom she had made an agreement in the mid-1920s to manufacture, market and distribute Chanel perfumes. Chanel was to receive ten per cent for her intellectual copyright, the rest of the profits going to Wertheimer and his investors, who were doing the heavy lifting. However, when she saw his success, she began to regret the agreement she had made and tried to take back the business. Under French laws, her lawsuit failed; she had after all entered into the arrangement freely and there had been no double-crossing.

When the Nazis occupied France and ushered in a slew of antisemitic laws, Chanel tried again. She tried to take full control of the business, dispossessing Wertheimer using an antisemitic law that facilitated 'Aryans' taking over Jewish businesses. Beginning in 1941 she began petitioning the Nazi government to be given sole control of Chanel Perfume, and she also claimed the Wertheimers had 'abandoned' the business, because they fled France fearing persecution, deportation and murder by the Nazi regime. Wertheimer had seen this coming and handed over the business to a trusted colleague of a French Catholic background, which foiled Chanel's attempt to increase her revenues using new antisemitic legislation.

After this, she began an affair with Baron Hans Günther von Dincklage – a man with a direct line to Himmler and Goebbels, two of the most senior overseers and instigators of the Nazi regime. Some have tried to romanticise, or skim over, Chanel's liaison with von Dincklage. They make the case that love is love, and it was an extreme and dangerous time. But he was a Nazi, and an illegal occupier of France. Some of Chanel's biographers have waxed lyrical over his charm, education and classical good looks, as if these explain her behaviour – appealing to their largely female readership with a line almost of 'well, who could resist?' and 'she was bored'. I have no doubt that he was charming and handsome, but the truth is many resisted. Many, many Germans were tall and handsome and had ready charm and sensitive sides. This should not have been enough to gloss over the fact that they were agents of a genocidal regime, illegal attackers of France's sovereignty. If women like Catherine Dior could risk their lives delivering messages for the Resistance, and survive torture and interrogations at Ravensbrück, Coco Chanel could have moved to a slightly less high-profile hotel and picked more suitable candidates for her affection. She was not a village girl missing all the young men, or someone alone and vulnerable. Perhaps she did see her affair as insurance or protection, but she had other routes available to her, and dining nightly with Nazis, sleeping with a jack-booted officer, and trying to use antisemitic legislation to her advantage are not the actions of someone vulnerable and desperate. They are the actions of someone expedient, and in this context without scruples.

Sympathisers have also pointed to the fact that von Dincklage and Chanel spoke English together, as a way of distancing him from the evil he represented. But Chanel wasn't making a bold statement in insisting on English; she simply didn't speak German. And there were swastikas emblazoned on her lover's caps and jackets that were draped over the chairs in her suite at the Ritz. No amount of charm and perfect English can wash away the blood of the Jews, the Romani, the political resisters, the French innocents from the hands that clasped Coco Chanel, in the sanctuary of a Ritz apartment, flowing with champagne, during the years of the war. While resisters were shot, Jews gassed and Catherine Dior tortured, Chanel laughed and danced and made love with a Nazi officer.

More than this, she undertook a mission for them: Operation Modellhut took place in 1943. Chanel was supposed to use her contacts to convey a message to Winston Churchill from the SS regarding a faction of leading Nazis desiring to break away from Adolf Hitler and negotiate a separate peace with England. She travelled to Spain at the height of the war to attempt to get an audience with her old friend Churchill, but she was denied, and the mission was a flop. Decades later it was revealed that she had her own code name as a Nazi agent – Westminster.

Coco Chanel never showed remorse for her wartime actions, only defensiveness. Maybe they were born of her hard-honed survival instinct – which had always led her to cling to men who could protect and help her – rather than latent antisemitism and Nazi sympathies. But other women did better, and in far tougher circumstances.

However, while the evidence of Chanel's wartime liaisons and collaborations is incontrovertible, documents have also been uncovered that purportedly link Chanel with the work of the French Resistance, and these were displayed alongside those proving her involvement as a Nazi agent at a 2023/4 exhibition in London. Nevertheless, specialist historians have cast doubts on the validity and even authenticity of Chanel's Resistance file, which is bizarrely thin, and links her with parts of the network active in the Balkans – hardly her milieu. The other awkward fact is that in the aftermath of the war, Chanel left Paris, stayed out of the limelight and kept her head down, perhaps out of shame for her collaboration. If she had been a Resistance operator, that would have been to her credit and might have cleared her and rehabilitated her image.

The Nazi occupation of Paris was marked by fear, treachery, oppression and scarcity. It was a time of great hardship for the people of the city. The Nazis imposed strict curfews and regulations, there were food shortages and extensive rationing, Jews were deported, and ordinary people lived in fear of being denounced for resistance by their neighbours. Nazi occupation brought out the very worst in some, the best in others.

In August 1944, Hitler ordered his henchman Dietrich von Choltitz, the final commander of Nazi-occupied Paris, to raze the city. Even a confirmed Nazi like von Choltitz could hear the mania in the Führer's voice. He refused this final order, and surrendered the city to the Free French Forces on 25 August 1944. The liberation of the city was a glorious day in the history of France, and joy reigned in the boulevards and avenues of the French capital. The relief, the disbelief, the euphoria were so great that they bordered on hysteria. But for collaborators, who fixed fake smiles to their faces, and clapped quietly with furrowed brows, it was a time of great anxiety. What would happen to them?

A committee was convened to try to prosecute collaborators, but there were many summary executions too. Women known to have had German lovers had their heads violently shaved and were paraded through the streets, publicly shamed. Chanel probably never seriously feared this, but it must have been distressing and unnerving to behold such violence happening to others less guilty than she. The French actress Arletty, of almost unrivalled popularity since her turn in the classic film *Hôtel du Nord*, was arrested and imprisoned for eighteen months as penalty for her affair with a Nazi officer. It was house arrest in a luxury mansion, but still. She famously quipped of her wartime affair: '*Si mon cœur est français, mon cul, lui, est international*' ('If my heart is French, my ass is international').

This period of rough justice, known as *épuration sauvage*, lasted until Charles de Gaulle returned to Paris from exile in September 1944 and established official courts to prosecute those accused of collaboration. However, in late summer 1944, shortly after the liberation of Paris by the Allies, Chanel was arrested at the Ritz by two members of the French Forces and interrogated. There was – as yet – little evidence of crimes available to her accusers, although her affair with von Dincklage was widely known. The depth of her espionage work and support for the occupiers was not yet known. She was released quickly, and rumours circulated that Churchill had intervened on her behalf.

Nevertheless, Chanel's reputation in Paris was in tatters. Chanel – wisely – thought it best to withdraw from the society of the newly liberated Paris. She entered into a sort of self-imposed exile in Switzerland, accompanied by none other than her Nazi lover von Dincklage. Their relationship continued for more than a decade and was not one of necessity brought about by the war. She also continued to support the convicted Nazi intelligence officer Walter Schellenberg financially into the 1950s, even paying for his funeral and offering ongoing support to his widow. This is a clear act of generosity from Chanel, but one that shows where her loyalty lay.

She lay low for several years, increasingly frustrated by what she considered to be backsliding in fashion. Her practical, empowered clothes were replaced by Dior's New Look – more feminine and restrictive. In 1954, she decided enough was enough, and moved to re-establish her fashion house in Paris. Surprisingly, it was to Wertheimer that she turned for financial backing. Being a businessman first and foremost, Wertheimer said yes.

Chanel was in her seventies by now, but nevertheless her renaissance was a success. Chanel had one more signature invention to 'drop' – this would be the iconic 2.55 bag, released in February 1955. Her new collections went from strength to strength, and some of the most glamorous women of the day wore Chanel suits, not least Jackie Kennedy, who pushed the classic Chanel suit to new heights of fame when she appeared on international news in a blood-spattered pink Chanel set following the assassination of her husband.

Coco Chanel never retired and worked tirelessly as the chief designer of her fashion empire until she died on the morning of 10 January 1971 after a short illness. She died as she lived, in a suite at the Ritz. Her funeral mass, held in the 8th arrondissement at the grand neoclassical Church of St Madeleine, was as great a leap from the circumstances of her birth as it is possible to imagine. Her coffin was lavishly decked with flowers: camellias, orchids, roses. Among the offerings was a pair of scissors formed of white camellias with a card reading, 'To Mademoiselle from her mannequins.' Her body was quietly interred in Lausanne where, in the words of her successor Karl Lagerfeld, 'she continues to promote the brand even in death'. Her grave is adorned with flowers, carefully grown into the shape of the double entwined Cs that once blazed down at her from the mullioned windows in the abbey of Aubazine. Her headstone is simple, but fierce. Five stone lions snarl at visitors, above a simple cross, and the inscription 'Gabrielle Chanel – 1883–1971'. In death, her assumed identity of Coco is appropriately stripped away. As her contemporary, the designer Pierre Balmain, said, she 'always dared, always strips, never adds, there is no other beauty than the freedom of the body.'

Chanel liberated women. She made comfortable stylish, and sexy. She was irreverent and lived as she liked. She didn't write, she wasn't a heroine of her country – quite the opposite. She was flawed, arrogant, often mean-spirited and self-serving. She was no saint. But her style, her talent, her vision and her force of will were undeniable. She has become an unlikely heroine of French women ever since. Her style and her determination to build the life she wanted for herself have endured as her legacy. Her war record blights her reputation. Maybe she is an anti-heroine – but when we think of the evolution of modern France, and of the modern Parisienne, it is impossible to ignore her.

Paulette Nardal (*back*) and her sisters, Lucie (*left*) and Jeanne (*right*) in Clamart, 1935.

# 16

# Paulette Nardal

## 12 October 1896–16 February 1985

'The Martinican woman has entered the city of men.'
Paulette Nardal

In September 1939, Paulette Nardal was coming to the end of a two-month sojourn in her native Martinique. She was forty-two and had a significant career as a writer and teacher under her belt already. Undeterred by news of war, she was preparing to return to Europe, to Paris, where she convened a Black literary salon with her sisters – the first of its kind.

She had booked her passage on a banana carrier, but, arriving at the marina in Fort-de-France, found that it had left ahead of schedule. Odd. War had just been declared in Europe, although no one yet had any comprehension of how terrible the conflict would be or how long it would last. The ship had wanted to leave as quickly as possible. Nonplussed, Paulette managed to secure a berth on the next departing ship – the SS *Bretagne*. She might have been safer staying in Martinique, and knew this on some level, but when life-altering disasters erupt, there is often a level of denial surrounding them. Paulette had planned only a short trip to Martinique and needed to return to Paris to organise her affairs.

After a month at sea, Paulette's ship was off the English coast, and almost in sight of her destination. Disaster struck. The war had spread fast in Europe. German aggression was as yet unchecked and the SS *Bretagne* was torpedoed by an undetected German U-boat. Panic reigned, and Paulette recalled hearing German guns apparently targeting the lifeboats. In vain she tried to swing herself into one of the undamaged boats, bobbing at the water line, but failed. She waited on board as long as she could, considering simply going down with the ship. Eventually, as the ship burned, she jumped into a life raft. Landing badly on the lurching surface, she shattered both of her kneecaps on impact.

Given the urgency of the situation and the boat's proximity to England, passengers were evacuated to Plymouth, and Paulette spent eleven agonising months recuperating in Plymouth hospital, even while German bombs rained down on the city. Following her discharge, she returned to Martinique, not wanting to experience any more of the horrors of wartime Europe. This had been a disastrous, transformative chapter in the life of a remarkable woman. Despite this setback, she would never stop writing, and never stop fighting for change and the rights of women of colour.

\* \* \*

It's a sunny afternoon in September and I'm on the train to Clamart.

This is a suburb to the south-west of Paris. Not too fashionable, not too convenient; I might never have come here if not for this particular mission. As I make my way to 8 Rue Hébert, I look up at the pretty art deco building of white cut stone that seems to dominate the street. Curious, I approach the windows of the ground-floor, street-facing apartment, and try to peer in, but the curtains are drawn, presumably to keep out nosy passers-by like me.

I have come here to discover an often ignored chapter in Parisian literary history.

Salon culture is pivotal to the history of Paris, and the history of French literature and culture. Hosted in someone's home – usually a fashionable woman with at least a large drawing room – salons were comprised of creatives and intellectuals who met to discuss the arts and ideas. Literary salons were all the rage in eighteenth-, nineteenth- and twentieth-century Paris. But they were largely whitewashed. Paulette Nardal challenged this – leading by example, and establishing an important Black literary salon in Clamart. It was here, in this unassuming apartment, that she and her sisters nurtured the ideas that would form the foundation of the Négritude literary movement.

Paris – while always a hub of literary innovation – remained very narrow in other respects. While salon culture might have been progressive in terms of gender, given that women were usually hosts, it had also been exclusive – racially at least. Transgender, homosexual and non-binary people all managed to break in – but people of colour rarely found the doors of fashionable salons open to them. Alexandre Dumas was, perhaps, the exception that proved the rule.

Paulette Nardal was the first Black person to study at the Sorbonne, and the first person to host a Black salon in Paris. Her journey to the Clamart apartment, where she lived with her equally literary sister Jeanne, was long, and started many miles across the sea in the French Caribbean.

The island of Martinique is 435 square miles. It has volcanic origins and is covered in lush jungle. It is crisscrossed by rivers and waterfalls, and around it glitters the Caribbean Sea. In the centre rises the ominous peak of the active volcano Mont Pelée. While living in France, Paulette would long for her homeland, writing wistfully of her memories of the landscapes of Martinique:

> In my homeland, it's perpetual summer. The coconut trees with their heavy fruit lean toward the sea with its odours of seaweed, and the long tails of their leaflets rub against each other, like silk rustling. Standing before the delicate and uniform green of the chestnut trees in France, my thoughts

evoke the sombre mass of mango trees, breadfruit trees, sandbox, and fern.

Today, the island is home to roughly 385,000 residents. It is one of France's poorest *départements*, and fifty-two per cent of the land belongs to the island's richest one per cent. It is a deeply unequal place, caught between two identities. Partly, it is a French *département*. But it is also a post-slavery island; the legacy of slavery endures, and the social structure is still defined along racial lines. However racially stratified the island is now, it was worse in 1896, the year of Paulette's birth. The same was true of Paris.

The life and work of Paulette Nardal epitomise the power of intellectual resistance against the forces of racism and colonialism. As a Martinican writer, translator and intellectual, Nardal was not only a forerunner of the Négritude movement but also a pioneering figure in Black feminist thought. Her contributions to the cultural and intellectual life of early-twentieth-century France are monumental, yet they have often been overshadowed by those of her male counterparts. This chapter aims to re-examine her contribution and highlight her role as a bridge between the Caribbean and African diasporas and as a crucial architect of the Négritude movement.

\* \* \*

Paulette Nardal was born on 12 October 1896 to a middle-class Black family in the town of Le François on the east coast of Martinique. The town is approximately twenty kilometres from Les Trois-Îlets where, 133 years earlier, Empress Josephine was born. For all their geographical proximity, the circumstances of these births were worlds apart. Where Josephine was born to a white family, with enslaved people fetching and carrying for her, Paulette's grandparents had themselves been enslaved. Paulette's great-grandmother Sidonie Nardal and her grandfather had been born into slavery in the sugar-producing region of La Trinité in Martinique – but they were recognised as free people in 1850 and 1854 respectively. Thus, the circumstances of Josephine's birth and Paulette's represented two radically different sides of the island, and the great dichotomy in its identity. But the two women had one thing in common – they would both move to Paris and become pivotal figures in the cultural life of the French capital, and it was Paulette, not Josephine, who was honoured with a golden statue in the opening ceremony of the 2024 Paris Olympics.

Martinique had been colonised by France in 1635, beginning a long and brutal era of exploitation. French settlers quickly overwhelmed the indigenous Carib population and established the sugar cane plantations that became the island's economic backbone. To fuel this plantation economy, the French imported enslaved Africans, forcing them to live and labour under the rules of the oppressive Code Noir of 1685. The conditions for enslaved people were dire: they toiled long hours under harsh supervision, suffered brutal punishments and lived in deplorable conditions. The abolition of slavery in 1794, inspired by the ideals of the French Revolution, was short-lived; Napoleon reinstated slavery in 1802, prolonging the suffering of the African population. It was only after widespread uprisings in 1848 that slavery was finally abolished in Martinique, with the writing into law of the decrees of abolitionist Victor Schoelcher, leading to a new era where former slaves were granted citizenship.

That said, for many, the end of slavery did not bring true freedom. Martinique eventually became an overseas *département* of France in 1946, yet it continues to navigate the lingering effects of colonialism, racial inequality and economic disparity. The experience of Martinicans was not unique in the region; other French colonies like Guadeloupe, Saint-Domingue (Haiti) and French Guiana, where the plantation system and slavery were equally central to colonial economies, experienced similar hardships.

Paulette, despite belonging to a bourgeois family who had risen from slavery to a comfortable, educated and dignified life, still experienced adversity in Martinique. She was six years old when the island's capital, Saint-Pierre, was destroyed in a freak eruption of the long-dormant Mont Pelée, reducing the city to ruins. Beyond this, the shadow of slavery loomed large in Paulette's life. The decrees of Victor Schoelcher that had freed her grandparents hung framed on the wall of the family home – and to this day the Achille family, Paulette's maternal line, have kept a copy of the act of emancipation that freed their ancestors. While other families sought to minimise their Black identity and history of enslavement, the Nardals wore it proudly, almost mocking the other Creole families who endeavoured to suppress this part of their identity.

In one generation the family managed to leapfrog from enslavement to a new class of bourgeoisie, developed a great love for high French culture, and started to prize education above all else. Paul Nardal, Paulette's father, studied engineering at the École des Arts et Métiers in Paris and was the first Black engineer in Martinique. He cherished the memory of the years he spent as a student in Paris, and the opportunities they brought him, and he doubtless recommended that path to his daughters, who before long would follow in his footsteps. Paulette's mother Louise Achille taught piano. No Creole was spoken in the house, only French, and the notes of classical music were heard in the halls. The family were highly cultured, valuing progress, social mobility and intellectual thought. Paulette was the eldest of seven sisters in a family with no sons: Paulette, Émilie, Alice, Jeanne, Lucie, Cécile, Andrée. In an era where it was uncommon for men, let alone women, to attend university, all were encouraged to pursue higher education.

Paulette finished secondary school in Martinique, after which she spent time in the British West Indies with the aim of honing her English language skills – which were eventually perfect. This gave her a broader experience of Caribbean and colonial culture, beyond that of her own island, and perhaps gave her a taste for travel. She took up teaching herself on her return to Martinique, but did not settle long in this profession, although it would always remain part of her life. In the short term she craved travel and broader experiences, and wanted to make an impact with her own writing. Her curiosity and ambition would soon draw her to the cultural and intellectual capital of the world – Paris.

Paulette arrived in Paris in 1920, in a city on the brink of reinventing itself, and picking itself up from the hardships of the First World War. Paulette admitted to feeling something like culture shock when she first arrived, observing in her writing the contrast between the life she left in Martinique and the new world she inhabited in Paris. The racial dynamics were different between the colony and the capital. In Paris, she encountered both opportunities and challenges as a Black woman navigating a predominantly white society and trying to break into intellectual circles.

She had arrived with comparatively little money, but a huge intellectual drive and cultural appetite. She enrolled at the Sorbonne, the first Black person to do so, and wrote her thesis on *Uncle Tom's Cabin*, the abolitionist (yet still problematic) novel by white American author Harriet Beecher Stowe. She embraced the frenetic life on offer in the capital. Josephine Baker was in town, and *joie de vivre* was back in fashion after the dark years of the war. For all this, she was nevertheless taken aback by the attitude that she encountered to her race. While France was not segregated, racism – both intentional and not – was pervasive, as was disdain for the 'colonies'. Paulette would later reflect, 'It was in France that I became aware of my difference.' For all that 'Black Culture' was decidedly fashionable in Paris at this time, it was not appreciated or discussed the way Paulette wanted it to be. Yes, Josephine Baker was the most talked-about performer of the decade, but she had shot to fame in a banana skirt. There was a craze for somewhat fetishised variations of Black culture and arts – not the kind of cultural experience Paulette was interested in. She did not want to be viewed as exotic or 'other' and was determined to present her ideas and creativity intellectually and on her own terms.

Following completion of her studies, after a brief stint back in Martinique, Paulette threw herself with renewed vigour into a new cultural life in Paris. She was determined to make waves and began working as a journalist and expanding her literary network.

In 1929 she published a short story titled 'En Exil' in *La Dépêche Africaine*, a prominent newspaper. The story follows Elisa, an elderly Martinican woman living in Paris, employed as a domestic worker. She is peripheral, almost completely unseen there, marginalised and unrecognised by the white French around her. There is a happy ending: Elisa is rescued by her son – now a successful businessman – who arrives to take her back to the homeland she has been dreaming of amid the drudgery and isolation. But the story goes deeper. As observed by Annette Joseph-Gabriel, as Elisa commutes on foot to her work, she passes the hallmarks of white privilege and French colonialism. She is heckled by entitled students on Rue des Écoles, the street on which Paulette herself had studied and must have felt alienation, and her job is situated on Rue Cuvier, named after a French 'scientist' who dissected the dead body of an African woman, Sarah Baartman, who in life had been exhibited at freak shows in France due to her curvy, African physique – completely atypical in Europe. Cuvier wrote an anatomical text on her body; far from being scientific, it was deeply racist and reinforced colonial thought through pseudo-scientific connections. He asserted that his experiments on Sarah Baartman proved that some races were closer to animals than others. He then mutilated her body and preserved parts of it. This all took place in 1815, but in 1929 when Paulette was writing, parts of Sarah's body were still on display for gawping tourists in Paris's Musée de l'Homme. It was not until 1976 that her remains were removed from display, and 2002 that they were finally returned to the country of her birth, South Africa. The world Paulette inhabited, and the world of her writing, was infused with the abhorrent legacy of slavery, exploitation, racism and French colonialist attitudes.

Throughout 'En Exil' Elisa does not utter a single word. She is presented as voiceless and othered in the French capital, suffocated by the history of oppression around her. Elisa is also affected by issues of class as well as race. For a working-class, elderly Black woman, domestic work was one of very few professional opportunities open to her. Through this narrative, Nardal delves into the complexities of identity and belonging, themes that resonated deeply with many Black women in the diaspora.

'En Exil' is in many ways typical of Nardal's literary output. In all of her work, Nardal wrote through a Black, woman-centred lens, and explored the relationship between home and exile. Above all, she wanted marginalised people in French territories to reimagine and embrace new roles in society, and to view political structures on different terms.

Other Black intellectuals were making waves in Paris at this time, and Paulette thrust herself among them. She met René Maran, author of *Batouala*, and a fellow Martinican. Maran attracted both praise and criticism for his scathing indictment of colonisation in this book, subtitled *Véritable Roman Nègre (A True Black Novel)*, which won the prestigious Prix Goncourt (France's equivalent of the Booker Prize) in 1921. He hosted a literary salon on Fridays and invited Paulette to attend; there she would encounter members of the Harlem Renaissance movement, a push by African-American artists to use culture as a tool for emancipation.

She was captivated and inspired by the work produced by this group. After drifting in Paris for some time she eventually settled on Rue Hébert in Clamart, and there she began to host her own salon, joined there by four of her sisters, Cécile, Alice,

Jeanne and Andrée, and their cousin Louis-Thomas Achille, who was like the brother they never had. Louis was enrolled in the English *Khâgne*[5] and brought other students to his cousins' salon, among them Léopold Sédar Senghor, who in turn introduced Aimé Césaire to the group – the father of Négritude. If Césaire was the father, then Paulette was the mother. She never claimed this herself, instead referring to herself and her sister Jeanne as 'pioneers' of the movement, who paved the way for the men. Joseph Zobel would hail her as the 'godmother' of the movement.

The network of intellectuals that formed around the Nardal sisters set about creating new, independent intellectual spaces. These included support groups for discussions, publications, and even platforms for the performing arts. Historians recognise this loosely connected group for its role in bringing together Black luminaries during the pre-Négritude era. However, their regular meetings and concerts, along with their extensive work as literary critics, musicians, journalists, translators, editors and activists, went well beyond the activities of a typical salon. Louis-Thomas Achille, reflecting on that period, highlighted the uniqueness of the Sunday gatherings at the Nardal residence:

> A dominant feminine mood ruled the tone and the rituals of these convivial afternoons, not at all like a business circle or a masculine club. The furniture of the two connecting rooms, the living and the dining room, did not reproduce in any way the decor of a salon of the traditional bourgeoisie of France or of the Antilles. Some English armchairs, airy, comfortable and light, furnished the accommodations for the conversation, which took place rather naturally also in English. There was neither wine, nor beer, nor French cider, nor whisky, nor exotic coffee, nor even creole ti-punch

---

5 A two-year academic programme focusing on the humanities.

to refresh the throat. Only English tea cut into these meetings, which never went beyond the dinner hour.

Paulette excelled in her role as hostess, facilitating deep conversation and the exchange of ideas: 'Her charm acted as a catalyst,' asserted John Paynter, an African-American poet who frequented Rue Hébert, and went with Paulette and her sisters to watch Josephine Baker perform.

But what exactly was the Négritude movement that emerged from those Sunday afternoons in Clamart? It was a cultural, literary and political movement that emerged in the 1930s among Black intellectuals in the French-speaking world, particularly in Paris. It sought to reclaim Black identity and pride by celebrating African culture and heritage, rejecting colonialism, and opposing the dehumanising effects of Western racism, in literature and beyond. In addition to Césaire and Senghor, key figures included Léon Damas from French Guiana, who used poetry and essays to critique colonialism and advocate for a unified Black consciousness. Paulette Nardal and her sister Jeanne's writings and gatherings laid the intellectual groundwork for Négritude by fostering dialogue on racial identity and cultural affirmation, significantly influencing its male leaders. For all that, it is only in recent years that Paulette and her sisters' contributions have begun to be widely recognised.

Paulette co-founded *La Revue du Monde Noir* (*The Review of the Black World*) with her sister Jeanne in October 1931. This was a ground-breaking journal that provided a platform for Black artists and intellectuals to publish their works and engage in critical discussions about race, culture and identity. *La Revue du Monde Noir* was a bilingual publication, with articles in both French and English, reflecting the Nardal sisters' commitment to fostering dialogue across the African diaspora. While *La Revue du Monde Noir* was presented as apolitical, the very act of founding a journal dedicated to Black culture in 1930s Paris was inherently political.

Despite its importance, *La Revue du Monde Noir* struggled to secure consistent financial support and ceased publication after just six issues in April 1932.

In the final issue of the journal, Nardal published an essay titled '*Éveil de la Conscience de Race*' ('The Awakening of Race Consciousness'). In this essay, she examined the growing racial awareness among Caribbean intellectuals and argued for the necessity of racial pride and solidarity. Nardal wrote, 'It is essential for the awakening of race consciousness that we recognise and reclaim our history, our culture, and our identity as Black people.' This essay is a powerful testament to Paulette's belief in the importance of collective consciousness for the empowerment of Black communities. Paulette's influence on the Négritude movement can be seen in the writings of its most prominent figures. Senghor later acknowledged the impact that Paulette's ideas had on his own thinking. In a 1987 interview, Senghor stated, 'It was the Nardal sisters who were really the ones who taught us what we were trying to do later on with Négritude.'

Throughout the 1930s, Paulette continued to be active in both feminist and anti-colonial movements. She was involved with several feminist organisations, including Ad Lucem per Caritatem and the Union Féminine Civique et Sociale (UFCS). Her activism was not limited to France. In 1935, she became deeply involved in the demonstrations against the Italian invasion of Abyssinia (now Ethiopia), an event that galvanised anti-colonial sentiment across the African diaspora. Nardal helped to found the Comité de Défense de l'Éthiopie (Committee for the Defence of Ethiopia) in Paris, and much of her writing and activism during this period focused on bringing attention to the plight of the Ethiopians. The invasion of Ethiopia was a turning point in Nardal's political engagement, deepening her commitment to Pan-Africanism and the defence of African sovereignty against colonial aggression.

As we saw earlier, Nardal sustained significant injuries on the SS *Bretagne* in 1939, and after recovering in Plymouth returned to

Martinique. Initially, she worked as an English teacher for dissidents who wanted to support General Charles de Gaulle's Free French Forces. In 1940, she became a teacher at the Convent of St Joseph of Cluny, a school for young girls, where she continued to promote education as a means of empowerment for women.

In the years following the Second World War, Paulette Nardal's activism took on a new dimension as she focused increasingly on the political and social empowerment of women. In 1944, she founded Le Rassemblement Féminin (The Women's Gathering) to encourage women to participate in the 1945 elections, the first in which women were allowed to vote in France. The organisation did not support any particular political party but aimed to educate women about their rights and responsibilities as citizens.

In 1945, Nardal also founded a journal, *La Femme dans la Cité* (*Women in the City*), which ran until 1951. The periodical emphasised the importance of women's involvement in politics and social work, urging women to take an active role in shaping their communities and their nation. Paulette's commitment to women's rights extended beyond journalism and activism. She played a key role in launching the idea of a maternity hospital in Martinique, which eventually led to the establishment of La Maternité de Redoute, later replaced by L'Hôpital de la Mère et de l'Enfant. This project was part of her broader vision of improving the health and welfare of women and children in Martinique.

In 1946, Paulette Nardal was nominated to serve as a delegate to the United Nations, where she worked as the West Indian representative on the Committee on Non-Self-Governing Territories in New York. She was the first Black woman to hold such a position, and her work focused on advocating for the rights of people in colonial territories and promoting the decolonisation process.

Paulette Nardal's legacy continues to inspire new generations of scholars, activists and artists. Her life's work stands as a testament to the power of intellect, resilience and cultural pride in the face of oppression. In considering the development of French literary culture, the relationships between France and its former colonies, and the experiences of the Caribbean French, it is essential to include the work and insight of Paulette Nardal, and to give her and her sisters the recognition they deserve in the history of French literature. France is very much more than just 'the hexagon', and its cultural heritage is more complicated than one might at first expect. Integrating writers like the Nardal sisters into the canon of French literature is a crucial step towards rectifying the way French literature is understood and taught, and ultimately offers a richer vision of what it means to be French.

Josephine Baker dancing the Charleston. Photographed by Stanisław Julian Ignacy Ostroróg – or Walery – in 1926.

# 17

# Josephine Baker

## 3 June 1906–12 April 1975

'The most sensational woman anybody ever saw, or ever will.'

Ernest Hemingway

In 1914 – the year war broke out in Europe and France was brought to its knees – something sinister took place a long way away, in the kitchen of a wealthy white woman in St Louis, Missouri. It had been a normal day, but now she was angry, very angry. Her Black maid had been careless with the housework, overboiling the water, causing some of the plates she was washing to crack. On discovering the damage, enraged, the woman plunged the maid's hands into the boiling water. The girl screamed in agony, as her skin blistered before her eyes. The maid's name was Freda Josephine McDonald, and she was just eight years old.

When asked to visualise Josephine Baker, most will rummage around in their memories and call up a black and white photograph of a mischievous-looking woman, nude except for a brief skirt made of silk bananas and a collection of beaded necklaces, staring down the camera with a provocative pose. The *danse sauvage* – performed in this ironic costume – was Josephine Baker's break-out moment. It took place at Les Folies Bergère, a famous cabaret in Paris. It was the height of the Jazz Age – *Les Années Folles*, 'the crazy years' – and the City of Light had just found its new darling. The hedonism of this era rode the wave of the economic boom and *joie de vivre* that swept Europe and the USA in the aftermath of the First World War. People came out from the shadows of the trauma of what had passed, determined to seize the day, and live like they'd never lived before. In Paris, it was a time of liberation, pushing boundaries and reclaiming a stolen youth. The arts flourished as writers and artists flocked to Paris. France roared back to life.

The little girl from St Louis who loved to dance, who had married and divorced twice before she turned seventeen and went on to take Paris by storm while still a teenager, is perhaps the greatest emblem of French values. In 2021, Josephine Baker was given a final honour by the country she credited with making her who she was. She was inducted into the French Pantheon, in a ceremony presided over by President Macron. She was the first Black woman and the third Black person in history, to receive this highest honour.

Freda Josephine McDonald was born in 1906 into a life of poverty. Her father, likely white, never acknowledged her – and she was raised by her African-American mother along with three siblings. The family struggled, and Josephine was sent out to work as domestic help from the age of seven. But she loved to dance. Later in life she would quip, 'It's all a question of luck. I was born with good legs.' Those legs would carry her to stardom.

At age eleven, she witnessed the St Louis race riots which saw at least thirty-nine Black Americans lynched – although the real death toll was likely far higher than the official figures. The memory of this night haunted Josephine for the rest of her life:

> I can still see myself standing on the west bank of the Mississippi looking over into East St. Louis and watching the glow of the burning of Negro homes lighting the sky …

## JOSEPHINE BAKER

> We children stood huddled together in bewilderment ... frightened to death with the screams of the Negro families running across this bridge with nothing but what they had on their backs as their worldly belongings ... So with this vision I ran and ran and ran.

And she did run. Her life in St Louis was miserable, scraping by and scavenging – and there have even been reports that her mother prostituted her as a child. When the opportunity to escape St Louis presented itself, thirteen-year-old Josephine seized it. In secret, she joined a vaudeville troupe; she was already a fantastic dancer. Marriage perhaps seemed another way out and she was married *twice* before her sixteenth birthday. The first marriage, to one Willie Wells, lasted less than a year. At fifteen she married William Howard Baker, and although that marriage was equally short-lived, she kept his name for all of her life.

After various turns as a chorus dancer and dresser with the Dixie Steppers, Josephine bade goodbye to St Louis and headed to New York City. She started out as a chorus girl in the all-Black musical *Shuffle Along*, and next took a starring turn in *Chocolate Dandies*. Later, she performed on the Harlem club scene during the Harlem Renaissance. It was here that she caught the eye of Charlotte Dudley, an American expatriate based in Paris, who was in town to recruit Black performers for a new show called *La Revue Nègre* at the Théâtre des Champs-Élysées. Josephine signed up at once.

*La Revue Nègre* brought a spectacle of blackness to white French audiences. The musical opened on 2 October 1925 and was nothing short of a triumph. Josephine stood out as a star on the rise: she differentiated herself from the other performers with her larger-than-life remarkable energy, sexiness and comedy. She appeared mostly nude and trailing feathers, and let herself be carried away by the music and the lights and the thrill of the huge audience. The *danse sauvage* was improvised but was such a hit that it became her signature turn during those early years in Paris. Simply put, she stole the show. From *La Revue Nègre*, Josephine was recruited to star in a new show at the still more prestigious Folies Bergère. Suddenly, Josephine Baker was the toast of Paris. She moved in creative and high-society circles. Ernest Hemingway was so impressed with her that he declared her 'the most sensational woman anybody ever saw'.

At Les Folies Bergère, Josephine gyrated in her banana skirt, dancing in elaborate, exotic and often minimal costumes to a radical Charleston tempo. The videos that survive of that routine might just be the first filmed instance of twerking, and in 2006 Beyoncé would salute Baker's daring and reclamation of offensive racial stereotypes by wearing a banana skirt herself to perform 'Déjà vu'.

At the same time as she was performing, Josephine was going into business and capitalising on her fame. She opened her own nightclub, Chez Josephine, on Rue Fontaine, and with the help of her manager launched a range of beauty products, Bakerfix and Bakerskin, so Parisians – both Black and white – could emulate her signature look. In 1927 she starred in the silent film *Siren of the Tropics*, making her the first Black woman to play a leading role in a feature film. She also began to record music, and the 1930 song 'J'ai deux amours' established Baker as a major player in the recorded-music scene as well; she danced, acted, sang and was a comedienne too.

Josephine was delighted by the levels of freedom and success found in unsegregated Parisian society. Nevertheless, white Parisians of the interwar years were still racist, and they were still ignorant. They didn't want to see Josephine singing classical music or doing what the white singers did. They wanted something different. She was billed as '*sauvage*' – wild, exotic. Instead of letting this stop her, Josephine played up to the racial clichés her audiences expected. She played it to her advantage – and she was brilliant. Nevertheless, she did take care to address more explicitly the pain of racial discrimination and hypocrisy in her music – perhaps most notably in the song '*Si j'étais blanche*' ('If I were white') – asking white men if they really needed her to be white to please them. The last lyric runs, somewhat hauntingly, '*Faut-il que je sois blanche pour vous plaire mieux?*' ('Do I have to be white to please you better?') Life for a Black woman was not easy in France, but it was so much better than in America.

Josephine's success in France was not mirrored in America or indeed Europe's more racist and conservative countries such as Austria and Italy. In Vienna, when her second film, *La Revue des Revues*, was advertised across the city with giant posters, depicting Baker nearly nude and dancing sensuously, papers branded her a 'Black Devil' and churches rang the bells when her train arrived in Vienna, to warn good people to stay out of the streets and avoid glimpsing her. In Germany, a six-month engagement in Berlin was cut short due to fears for her safety amid racist protests; in Italy, Mussolini simply banned her. This was of course not entirely because of her race – they also objected to her risqué routines – but she drew considerably more ire than similar white performers. They hated her because she challenged convention, threatening patriarchal and racist social structures. She was a free Black woman, living her best life, and earning far more money than most of the men seeking to curb her success.

When Josephine travelled back to America to perform, she was met with vitriolic and negative reviews, many infused with racism. Josephine was reminded of the inequality she had left behind from the moment she arrived. As her boat docked, she saw scores of African Americans awaiting its arrival. At first, for a moment, she thought they were fans coming to welcome her, before realising they were domestic staff coming to collect their white employers. That realisation set the tone for her entire US sojourn. Things went from bad to worse; when she reached her chosen hotel, staff refused to install her in the suite she had booked, and she struggled to find alternative accommodation.

She returned to Europe and married French Jewish industrialist Jean Lion. This marriage not only solidified her connection to France but also allowed her to officially renounce her US citizenship, a gesture that symbolised her disillusionment with her home country's systemic racism. Embracing French citizenship instead, Baker found a new sense of belonging and purpose in the nation that had celebrated her as a ground-breaking entertainer and welcomed her as an icon of modernity and liberation. This marked the beginning of a deeper involvement in French cultural and political life, shaping her legacy as a performer and activist.

After her disappointing tour of the States in 1936, Josephine returned to France on the luxury liner *Normandie*; on board she met the owner of the Château des Milandes, a spectacular Renaissance château in the Dordogne. Josephine, undoubtedly bruised by the tour and looking for a haven, decided to visit. She fell in love, and Château des Milandes would become the most enduring passion of Josephine's life, except perhaps her love for music. The château exudes fairytale charm: circular towers, fluttering flags, gorgeous stained-glass windows, sweeping lawns and formal gardens, all commanding panoramic views of the Dordogne Valley. For Josephine, still the young girl from Missouri at heart, the region was infused with magic: a landscape of rolling hills dotted with Renaissance and medieval castles.

Dating from the fifteenth century, the spiral staircases and vaulted ceilings of the château murmur with echoes of French history. Josephine saw her refuge in the stone walls and immediately decided to rent it. She bought it a decade later – all in all keeping it as her primary residence for over thirty years. She remodelled it to her taste, tiling the kitchen with playful, illustrated tiles depicting animals for the children she hoped to have, and designing a grand art deco bathroom in the style of her favourite perfume bottle, by Jeanne Lanvin.

However, the paradise Josephine would build at Milandes, and the children she longed to have, would have to wait. The France

## JOSEPHINE BAKER

Josephine returned to – and became a part of – faced storm clouds overhead. Fascism was on the rise in Europe, and the Second World War was looming. The war would upend daily life for nearly every French citizen, but Josephine – a Black woman who had married into a Jewish family – was particularly vulnerable.

In 1940 the German forces commenced their *Blitzkrieg* campaign against France and its allies, which swiftly overwhelmed French defences, leading to the fall of France. By 14 June 1940, German forces entered Paris with minimal resistance, and an armistice was signed on 22 June, dividing France into occupied and unoccupied zones. Paris came under direct German control, subject to strict occupation measures. Resistance movements emerged across the country. An international star, famous across Europe, and having previously toured Germany and Austria, Josephine Baker had influence and star power, and she emerged as an ideal candidate for espionage work. Her fame and connections gave her a cover story for crossing international borders; even under occupation and the shadow of war, the show had to go on. People had to be entertained, money made.

The French Resistance's network of partisan groups stretched across France and fought the Nazis and the collaborative Vichy regime at every turn. The Vichy government held authority in the unoccupied zones of France, but in practice it was little more than a puppet regime. The officials collaborated with the Nazi regime, including deporting Jews to concentration camps. The Resistance was made up of cells of armed men and women across the country who formed guerrilla and partisan groups to attack and sabotage the occupying forces, and relayed intelligence to the Allied forces trying to defeat Germany.

The German occupiers were well aware of the Resistance activities, and punished members of the Resistance brutally. Torture and executions were frequent, as were deportations to concentration camps and reprisal massacres of innocents. In several instances, scores of civilians were executed in punishment for the death of one Nazi officer at the hands of Resistance fighters. Social status, gender, illness were no defence if someone was caught. Christian Dior's twenty-six-year-old sister Catherine was captured, tortured and sent to Ravensbrück concentration camp.

However, not everyone saw Josephine as their number-one choice for Resistance work. Some officers warned that employing a celebrity like this – who lacked training and was not French by birth – could lead to another Mata Hari incident. The Dutch-born burlesque performer was infamous in France in the years following the First World War; she had pretended to work for the French while secretly serving as a double agent of the Germans. When the French finally caught on, she was executed by firing squad. Hari's story was a cautionary tale against trusting flashy foreigners.

But Josephine convinced them.

Captain Jacques Abtey was sent to vet her. The officer was struck by her – her beauty, her passion for France and her un-diva-ish attitude offstage. When he first saw her, she was looking for snails to feed to her ducks. She told him simply, 'France made me what I am, and I am eternally grateful to the country. I am willing to give my life for France, you may make use of me as you see fit.'

He signed her up, and soon Josephine was running rings around Nazi officers as a full-fledged intelligence officer. She used her social status to report on overheard conversations at embassy parties, and soon she was using her international concert schedule (which still continued during the war) to carry coded messages across borders, encoded in her sheet music, with Captain Abtey posing as her voice coach. Perhaps unsurprisingly, the two began an affair.

These missions took Josephine across Europe, North Africa and the Middle East. She performed in Marseilles, Spain, Portugal, Algeria and Morocco, maintaining the pretence of being an entertainer while secretly working as a courier and spy, and always at great personal risk. There was not only risk of discovery, but also the hardship of life on the road in the midst of a world war. For several months, she lived in tents and out of the back of a jeep as she, along with Abtey and Si Mohamed Menebhi, the brother-in-law of the Sultan of Marrakech, drove 3,500 kilometres across North Africa – deserts and all, traversing Morocco, Algeria, Tunisia and Libya, before taking a plane from Egypt to Beirut. There she gave performances on behalf of the Resistance across Lebanon, Syria and Palestine, under the banner of Free France. For these efforts, Baker was made a second lieutenant of the Female Auxiliary Troops of the French air force in recognition of her propaganda work and courage. General Charles de Gaulle, who had established his headquarters in Algiers, recognised Baker's contributions and appointed her as an ambassador of the Free French Forces. In gratitude, he awarded her the Gold Cross of Lorraine, which she sold to support the Resistance in Egypt. Unsurprisingly, the relentless schedules and rough sleeping took a toll on her health, and she was hospitalised for months.

It remains unclear when the romance between Josephine and Captain Abtey ended, but it seems that, after the war, he returned to his wife. Despite this, he wrote a book, *La Guerre Secrète de Joséphine Baker* (*Josephine Baker's Secret War*), in which he praised her bravery, intelligence and determination, reflecting the deep admiration and affection he felt for her. For all this, when she fell on hard times later in life, there was no evidence that he rallied to help her.

In October 1944, Josephine finally returned to France, triumphant after her years of service to the Resistance. She disembarked in Marseilles wearing her military uniform, met by rapturous applause from a crowd of fans who had shown up to welcome the iconic woman back to her adopted home. She began a tour of Europe with Jo Bouillon, a French orchestra director who before long became her fourth husband. In 1946, recovering from surgery in a private hospital outside Paris, she was awarded the Medal of the Resistance for her contributions. Josephine's reputation as a

Resistance agent was now as firmly established as her reputation as a performer. She would eventually receive France's highest military honour, the Légion d'Honneur, and the Croix de Guerre, cementing her status as a war hero.

The next chapter of her life – one set in peacetime – was remarkably different. She had conquered the stages of Europe, and established herself as a war hero and true *citoyenne* of France, and now finally felt free to turn her hand to the two matters closest to her heart: motherhood and racial equality. She married Jo Bouillon in 1947 in the chapel of the Château des Milandes. Having suffered numerous miscarriages, and realising that she was unable to have biological children, Josephine decided to adopt a diverse family of children whom she called the 'Rainbow Tribe'. When discussing her motivations for so intentionally bringing together this diverse family, Josephine said in a speech:

> people will mingle more quickly and easily until racial purity gradually disappears, but I'd like to see this happen through love and not hate. Jo and I plan to adopt four little children, four little children raised in the country in my beautiful Dordogne. They will serve as an example of true democracy and be living proof that if people are left in peace, nature takes care of the rest ... I decided to adopt a family of unwanted children from all over the world, to prove that the colour of skin is no barrier to love.

Over time, she adopted twelve children – ten boys and two girls – each from a different part of the world, including North Africa, East Asia, South America and northern Europe. The children, all within a six-year age range, were raised at the Château des Milandes. Baker was determined to honour each child's heritage, educating them about their cultural backgrounds while integrating them into the local community. They attended local schools, played with village children and were involved in local events. Later in life, one of them, Akio, reflected that they had grown up as 'rural people', deeply connected to the land and community around. Over the years, several have spoken publicly about their mother and their childhood. They are now scattered around the world, and most carry their mother's memory fondly, despite the ups and downs of their childhood and adolescence. Jari, reportedly sent away by Josephine when she discovered he was gay, can still be found working in the restaurant Chez Josephine in New York; he is friendly and jovial, and has a loving memory of his mother, even though they were at odds. Another brother has written a book about his mother's legacy.

Off stage, Josephine's carefree attitude left her vulnerable. She was bad with money, sometimes badly advised, and often exploited by tradespeople and suppliers. Despite her noble intentions, Baker's financial situation began to unravel. The cost of maintaining Château des Milandes, which she had turned into a popular but badly managed tourist attraction, and supporting her large family was enormous. Although her husband initially supported her vision and acted as a loving father to the Rainbow Tribe, he soon grew concerned about the scale and cost of Josephine's vision for their family. He remonstrated with her about her determination to adopt more and more children while their finances were becoming so precarious, especially as their income had plummeted since she quit the stage to spend more time at home. By the 1950s, they were close to ruin, and the couple separated in 1957, divorcing finally in 1961.

By 1964, Baker's personal financial situation had reached a crisis point. She was deeply in debt and Château des Milandes was auctioned. Josephine resisted eviction for some months through the winter and barricaded herself in the kitchen to avoid being thrown out. Eventually, however, she was forcefully evicted by eight young men paid well for the task, who locked her out when she stepped out in search of more food. She spent a rainy night wrapped in blankets on the doorstep of the château, with only a loyal black cat for company. Gone were her hordes of admirers and her pet cheetah; the medals won for bravery were tucked away to gather dust. She was impoverished, alone and desperate. But her name still carried some weight, and she still had her friends, even if they would not lend her the thousands that she needed.

These friends, including Grace Kelly, intervened to help. Kelly had once walked out of a racist hotel in solidarity with Baker and as a testament to her friendship offered her and the Rainbow Tribe a villa in Monaco, a country where she had recently become a princess. Brigitte Bardot, who had never met Josephine, made a televised appeal to the French public, imploring them to help Baker keep her home. The French public responded, but the donations were not enough to cover Baker's extraordinary debts.

Determined to reclaim Château des Milandes, Josephine returned to the stage, hoping to earn enough to buy back her beloved home. In April 1975, she launched a comeback show at the Théâtre Bobino in Paris, celebrating the fiftieth anniversary of her Paris debut. The show was a success, receiving critical acclaim, and Baker's friends and admirers, including Princess Grace, Sophia Loren and Mick Jagger, attended the opening night.

However, the strain of the performance and the emotional toll of her recent struggles became too much for her weakened body. Four days after the opening, Josephine Baker was found in a coma in her bed, surrounded by newspapers filled with glowing reviews of her comeback show. She was rushed to hospital, but never regained consciousness. Josephine Baker died on 12 April 1975, at the age of sixty-eight, from a cerebral haemorrhage.

People are likely to remember Josephine Baker as a star, draped in feathers, couture, diamonds, topless and dancing the Charleston to rapturous applause. But Josephine Baker was much more than her performances, and her rags-to-riches story and remarkable strength of character were more gasp-inducing than any of her outfits. It was a time of reinvention, and while Chanel, the orphaned convent girl, cut understated dresses and grafted herself into the political elite, the scolded and scalded maid from Missouri leaned into all the overstated glitz and glamour that Paris had to offer, and – although not French born – stayed true to her principles of *liberté*, *égalité* and *fraternité* all of her life.

Edith Piaf, singing, *c.* 1940s–1950s.

# 18

# Édith Piaf

## 19 December 1915–10 October 1963

> 'Singing is a way of escaping. It's another world. I'm no longer on earth.'
>
> Édith Piaf

On an October afternoon in 1935, two girls worked their way through the bustling streets of Pigalle, the red-light district of northern Paris. The sky hung low and heavy, threatening rain, but that wasn't about to stop them. They were making their way down towards the Arc de Triomphe, where they thought they might find a wealthier crowd. They picked their spot, the corner of Avenue MacMahon and Rue Troyon, within sight of the arch. In front of the imposing Haussmannian façades and curling wrought-iron balconies, the smaller of the two stepped forward, and placed her hands on her hips. She took a great breath and began to sing. Her voice, a thousand times more powerful than her diminutive frame would suggest, cut through the air, halting the passers-by. Her companion wove through the thickening afternoon crowd, shaking a hat for coins, as her friend's voice transcended the urban din – trams, cars, chattering café-goers – and stopped people in their tracks.

The song was not exactly cheerful, but it had a pull. She was singing 'Comme un moineau', a song about living and dying like a sparrow. It suited her: tiny, scrappy and worn out by too many long nights and recent traumas.

As she sang, a well-dressed man paused to listen. Silver-haired, sharp-suited and with an air of sophistication, he considered the tiny singer whose voice rang out like an orchestra. He was intrigued and knew talent when he heard it. He let her voice engulf him – raw, powerful – it moved him.

As she finished the final note, he approached, commenting, 'You'll ruin your voice singing like that on the streets.' The girl shrugged and said she didn't have much of a choice – it was sing or starve. He reached into his pocket, handed her a five-franc note, and told her to show up at his club, Le Gerny's, the following week. 'For an audition,' he said.

The girls could hardly believe their luck and celebrated by drinking late into the night. They sought out Le Gerny's and peeked through the velvet-curtained windows: it was more upmarket than anywhere they had worked before. Despite their friends' warning that the offer might be too good to be true, that he might be luring them into a web of sexual exploitation or something of the sort, they believed this was the chance they had been waiting for, their shot at something better, and the good luck deserved after a spate of tragedy.

On the day of the audition the tiny singer was a bundle of nerves. But when she stepped onto the small stage at Le Gerny's, all of that melted away. She opened her mouth, and the room went still. Her voice rose and filled the space, not just with volume but with raw emotion and a thick Parisian accent. Louis Leplée, the dapper man who had invited her, watched with quiet satisfaction.

Leplée didn't hesitate. He offered the girl a contract to perform for the princely sum of forty francs a night, a small fortune for someone used to collecting loose change on street corners. There was just one condition: she needed to get herself some proper clothes, and a new name. Édith Giovanna Gassion wasn't catchy.

The singer, all of nineteen years old and barely 4'8", accepted on the spot. Thinking about the name, Leplée took in her petite frame, her fragility and the song she had been singing when he first saw her, and christened her 'La Môme Piaf' ('The Sparrow Kid'). In time, this would become simply 'Édith Piaf'.

\* \* \*

Édith Giovanna Gassion was born on 19 December 1915, in the midst of the First World War, in the working-class district of Belleville in Paris. Now a fashionable, up-and-coming neighbourhood, back then it was a slum. She was named, by her Algerian-Italian mother, after the British nurse Edith Cavell, whose execution by firing squad for helping Allied soldiers escape German-occupied Belgium had shocked the Western world a couple of months earlier.

Édith's parents were both performers – her mother was a singer, her father a contortionist – but neither was commercially successful or renowned. They performed in cafés, in the streets, in circuses. Her mother Annetta, performing under the name 'Line Marsa', struggled with substance abuse and poverty. She was married to Édith's father Louis Alphonse Gassion, but he travelled constantly for work and also during this time was serving in the French army during the war. It was a miserable existence for the young mother and child, scraping a living in Belleville, anxious for news from the front. Annetta gave birth to a second child, Herbert, in 1918, but it swiftly became clear she was struggling. Édith had already been surrendered to the care of her maternal grandmother, and Herbert was handed over to the state. Louis, seeing that Annetta's mother was little better suited to childcare than her daughter, took Édith to live with his own mother in Normandy.

However, it was not a pastoral country life that Édith was entering into, but a '*maison close*' or brothel in Bernay, a small town situated between Rouen and Caen. Édith's grandmother, Louise, was the madame of the establishment and she was not thrilled at the arrival of her sickly granddaughter. Nevertheless, she accepted the job. While she was not conventionally a 'respectable woman', she was a responsible and able one, and the sex workers she supervised were delighted with the arrival of the little girl. She was pampered by the women of the house, and for the first time in her life benefited from wholesome, healthy food. She was given milk, fresh air, constant attention and something very much like love. One woman in particular, 'Madame Gaby', took on the role of caregiver for the unwanted child. These women on the fringes of society became Édith's first family. A look at her early life gives a striking portrait of the poor underbelly of Parisian society in the interwar years. While Josephine Baker was performing in Les Folies Bergère and Hemingway was drinking in Parisian cafés and penning novels about the 'Lost Generation', Édith's mother was scraping a living on the streets and in the cabarets of Paris, battling addictions, while her daughter was raised in a brothel.

At three years old, Édith went blind from keratitis. The prostitutes who looked after her scraped together what little money they had to take her on a pilgrimage to St Thérèse of Lisieux. Édith later said of her childhood 'I lived in a world of sounds' and described identifying the women she lived with by touch, walking around with her hands stretched out to navigate. Seemingly miraculously, by age seven, her sight returned, something she would always credit to the intervention of St Thérèse, and she would carry the saint in her heart for all of her life.

Around this same time, Louis, back from the war, returned to claim his daughter. He bought a caravan and signed with a circus as a performer, taking Édith on the road with him. Various mistresses stepped in to fill the maternal role, with assorted levels of motivation and success. Their existence was precarious, but it

# ÉDITH PIAF

introduced Édith to the world of performing. Recalling her life at that time, Édith reflected: 'I lived in the trailer and did the chores ... My days started early, the work was hard, but I liked the constantly changing horizons of our vagabond life. It was a thrill to discover the enchanted world of the travellers, the fanfares, the clowns' spangled costumes, the lion tamers' gold-braided tunics.' Eventually Louis quit the circus and went solo, busking for his bread with Édith holding the hat to collect his 'earnings' – perhaps he clocked that a sweet seven-year-old was an asset in this context. The pair then realised that when Édith sang, they took in nearly twice as much as they did when Louis performed alone. She recalled that the first song she performed – the only one she knew – was 'La Marseillaise', met with rapture by postwar audiences. By her teens, street life had become second nature, and she had started to realise her voice could take her places. Yes, Édith's life with her father was hard, but she treasured his rare displays of paternal love, kisses, gifts, protection, pride.

Her upbringing did not involve a conventional education, but it made her adaptable and resilient, honing her survival instinct. That said, she was always fragile, always vulnerable. She related later to a journalist, 'I had gone through a particular apprenticeship in life and love', stating that her father had had a new mistress every three months, and that although they were 'more or less' kind to her, she had not had her mother by her side to teach her that love could be supportive and sweet. She remembers her father bringing her to a café in Faubourg Saint Martin in her teens and introducing her to a woman he said was her mother; she didn't recognise her at all. She also met her brother Herbert there for the first time. They played for a moment, then the pair were separated again.

At fourteen, she struck out on her own in Pigalle, singing earnest *chansons réalistes*, a genre of music of growing popularity, characterised by deeply emotional and often gritty portrayals of the hardships of everyday life. This choice resonated with audiences in the poorer neighbourhoods of Paris, the songs laden with themes like poverty, heartbreak and social injustice. Singing on the streets was how she made ends meet, accompanied by her friend Simone 'Mômone' Berteaut. The two were inseparable in these early years, hustling through the streets to scrape together enough money for a shared room. Édith was popular for the power of her voice, and the rough working-class accent she sang in. While Édith sang, Mômone drew the crowds and collected the sous and occasional francs tossed their way. They found something very close to freedom in those early years, living on their wits and singing when and what they wanted. There was no money to spare, but there was enough for their wants and they were quite close to being happy.

Yet street life was still harsh, still precarious, and this phase in Édith's life was soon to take a turn for the tragic. At seventeen, she began an affair with a delivery man named Louis Dupont, and they moved in together in 1932 in Belleville. To furnish their rooms, they grifted, hustled and stole, and thought nothing of it. Édith quickly became pregnant and continued to sing throughout the pregnancy: waltzes, tangos and her signature *chansons réalistes*. In February 1933 she gave birth to her only daughter, Marcelle, known as 'Cécelle'. By all accounts she was besotted with the child and had the support of her father and stepmother. But the poverty of their existence took its toll. Édith had to continue earning and brought her baby all over Paris with her while she sang. She grew tired of her lover, began affairs with other men, and then left him, despite his remonstrations and those of her family. Bringing Cécelle with her, she moved to Pigalle with Mômone, until Louis came to reclaim his child from what he saw as unfit living conditions. Perhaps he was right; Édith's new life, like that of her mother before, was fast and unstable. She became involved with a gang leader, Henri Valette, who was a criminal and probably also a pimp. Édith's friend Nadia was forced into prostitution by one of Henri's friends, who threatened her with a beating if she did not oblige; she drowned herself in the Seine. It was a hard world, and the glamour of the hedonism and bright lights must soon have worn off.

In the summer of 1935, she received worse news still. Louis arrived at her cabaret to tell her Cécelle had incurable meningitis. On 6 July, her daughter died at just two years old. The grief was crushing and they could scarcely afford the baby's funeral. There were conflicting reports that she turned to prostitution to raise the last ten francs for her daughter's burial.

Everything shifted in October of that year – just months later – when she was discovered by Louis Leplée on that corner by the Arc de Triomphe. Her debut at Le Gerny's was a sensation. The audience was captivated by her voice, which seemed to carry a lifetime of stories, and of loss, and Leplée gave her a regular gig. Soon after, Édith recorded her first songs with composer Marguerite Monnot, kicking off a career that would make her a legend. Leplée helped Édith refine her image and took her under his wing in the seedy world of Parisian cabaret. Leplée, who was gay, assumed a fatherlike role in Édith's life. He wanted to present her as she was, vulnerable and childlike, and let her voice speak for itself. He suggested she wear a simple black dress, emphasising her diminutive physique, and stood her alone under a spotlight in the centre of the stage, making her stark presence unforgettable. Under Leplée's guidance, she began to make a name for herself, not only in Paris but across France, touring, recording and singing on the radio.

Then suddenly, just as her star was rising, Leplée was murdered – shot in the eye in his apartment. The scandal nearly ruined Édith's career, with newspapers implicating her in his death. Though she was cleared of any involvement, her reputation took a hit. His death remains unsolved, but it was brutal, and his close association with Édith made life difficult, bringing press attention to her previous associations with unsavoury underworld figures.

Yet Édith was nothing if not resilient. She persevered, performing in lower-end cabarets like Chez Odette and L'Ange Rouge while gradually working to rebuild her public image. Her resilience attracted the attention of Raymond Asso, a songwriter who saw in Édith a kindred spirit. With Asso by her side, she redefined herself. Together they crafted songs that drew from her hard life on the streets and created a sound both raw and deeply personal, capturing the essence of her life and the soul of Paris.

And so, Édith kept singing, turning her struggles into songs that resonated far beyond the back alleys of Paris that inspired them.

Through these early years, Édith forged her identity on pavements, nightclubs and under the lights of small stages, building the dramatic, indomitable character that would soon capture the world's attention. She sang not only with technical skill but with raw, unfiltered power. This, after all, was Piaf's secret: not only was her voice technically impressive, it was imbued with her life, her experiences, her resilience, and it was this rough, piercing beauty that made her one of France's most enduring icons. She stood for all the downtrodden who refused to be crushed.

Before long, Édith was headlining at the Bobino, like Josephine Baker before her. As her fame grew, Piaf also performed at the Théâtre de l'ABC, where she shared the stage with Charles Trenet, a star of French *chanson* best known for 'La Mer'. The audience's enthusiastic response marked her as a new force on the Parisian music scene, and by the year's end, she had established herself firmly as a headline performer. She mixed with the musical elite of Paris, including Josephine Baker, who was also captivating interwar Paris at this time.

Beyond building her own profile, Édith lent her voice to causes beyond entertainment, performing at an anti-Franco rally in support of the Spanish Republicans, a rare political stance for entertainers of her time. This activism provides a glimpse into her commitment to the struggles of ordinary people. As her influence grew, Édith received an unprecedented honour in January 1938: a forty-five-minute programme dedicated to her on Radio-Cité. She was still only in her early twenties, but already becoming a cultural icon.

The Second World War upended Édith's life and career. Asso, her mentor and partner, was drafted to fight, a separation that left her anchorless. Then came 1940 and the German occupation of Paris. Despite the upheaval, Édith kept performing. That February, she met writer Jean Cocteau, who was so impressed with her that he cast her in his play *Le Bel Indifférent*. The play was a hit, demonstrating her versatility as a performer as well. She started touring, mostly in the unoccupied 'free zone' of Vichy France. Cocteau and Édith developed a close and lasting friendship. Indeed Cocteau was so profoundly affected by Piaf's death that it seemed to spur his own. Upon learning of her passing, he reportedly said, '*Ah, la Piaf est morte. Je peux mourir aussi*' ('Ah, Piaf is dead. I can die too'). Almost unbelievably, he died within twenty-four hours.

Édith returned to Paris in September 1940 and gave her first solo concert at the Salle Pleyel with a full orchestra. This marked her transition from music hall singer to full-on solo star. By 1941, she was performing all over France, commanding high fees and starring in the film *Montmartre-sur-Seine*, where she played Lily, a flower seller who rises to fame. The film firmly established her as the 'Little Sparrow' who captured the hearts of everyday French citizens.

For all her success, performing during the occupation made her a lightning rod for criticism, as it had done for couturiers who continued to sew for German clients. At one of her shows at the Théâtre de l'ABC, she concluded each performance with the rousing patriotic song, 'Où sont-ils, tous mes copains?', standing proudly under the French tricolour until German censors shut it down. In 1943, her fame was such that she went on a controversial tour of German POW camps. She later claimed she used her time there to help prisoners escape by taking photos with them, which were supposedly used to forge identity papers. True or not, the story added to her legend as a defiant, resilient figure.

By the liberation of France in 1944, Édith had become deeply tied to the spirit of the French people, channelling their suffering and hope through her songs. Often melancholic, these were filled with themes of love, loss and longing, which proved cathartic for the French people and resonated with a population that had lived under the strain of Nazi occupation. Postwar, she climbed only higher. She mentored Yves Montand, and expanded her career internationally, while still rooted in the Parisian culture that shaped her. Her resilience and connection to the city turned her into a timeless icon of French endurance. It was also this year that her father died, and she buried him with due reverence in Père Lachaise. The following year, she had her baby daughter Cécelle's remains exhumed and buried her there alongside him. When Édith's time came, she would rest there too.

In the aftermath of the war Édith Piaf wasted no time getting back to what she did best. In 1945, she co-wrote and performed what would become her most iconic song: 'La vie en rose'. Her team were sceptical about what success the song might have, and it was not immediately recorded. However, when Édith performed it live, audiences decided for them. It was an instant hit, capturing the hopes of a world looking for light after so many years of darkness. It would later become a timeless classic, eventually earning a place in the Grammy Hall of Fame. It is loved across the world, one of the most passionate romantic *chansons* of all time.

The following year, in 1946, Édith made some big career moves, leaving Polydor to sign with Pathé-Marconi (Columbia). She also met boxer Marcel Cerdan, though at that point it was just a fleeting introduction. A year later, the two would embark on a passionate and well-publicised affair that would have a profound impact on Édith's life and perspective on love. At the time of their meeting, her career was in full swing, and she started collaborating with the vocal group Les Compagnons de la Chanson. That spring, she starred in her second film, *Étoile sans Lumière*. By May, she was performing with a fifty-piece orchestra at the Théâtre de Chaillot, solidifying her reputation as one of France's top entertainers.

In 1947, she became involved again in the world of politics, performing at a French Communist Party rally where she met party leader Maurice Thorez. That September, she returned to the Théâtre de l'Étoile, where she performed alongside Les Compagnons de la Chanson once more. This time, their leader, Jean-Louis Jaubert, became her lover. In October, she took a leap across the Atlantic, boarding the *Queen Elizabeth* to try her luck in the United States. The early days of her American tour were tough; American audiences were initially unimpressed with her simple, stripped-down style, and although she sometimes sang for them in English, she was not an immediate hit. But a rave review by the influential critic Virgil Thomson in the *New York Herald Tribune* turned things around. She soon became a regular on *The Ed Sullivan Show*, performing there eight times, and her popularity in the US took off.

Around this time, her affair with Cerdan, who was married with children, was beginning to heat up and raise eyebrows. By 1948, their relationship was the stuff of tabloids. A week after losing his European-champion title to the Belgian Cyril Delannoit, Marcel made the front page of *France Dimanche* with the singer: 'Piaf brings bad luck to Cerdan.' Rumour swirled, but Édith continued to tour and perform relentlessly, on stage and on screen. Cerdan made history that September by becoming the middleweight champion of the world. Édith, ever the loyal partner, was often by his side, even flying back and forth between France and New York to see him. She spoke of him frankly as the love of her life. They were well matched, he a boxing legend born to a labourer's family in Algeria, and she a street performer who had become an international icon.

By late 1949, Édith had enjoyed a year of sell-out shows and great success with her song 'Hymne à l'amour' – written for her new lover. Cerdan was set for a rematch with Jake LaMotta (of *Raging Bull* fame). Édith, eager to see him, convinced him to fly to New York instead of taking a ship which would take much longer. She implored him to take the flight, to have more time together, and he agreed. The decision proved fatal. On 27 October, his plane crashed, killing everyone on board. Devastated, Édith refused to cancel her show at the Versailles cabaret in New York that night. Instead, she announced that she was dedicating her performance to Cerdan and broke down in tears as she sang 'Hymne à l'amour'. This was perhaps the most emotional and powerful performance of Édith's career, recreated by Céline Dion atop the Eiffel Tower in the opening ceremony of the 2024 Olympics. Grief-stricken, she took to the stage, and against all the odds made it through most of her set without breaking. Everything changed when it came to the 'Hymne à l'amour'. For the first time, her voice failed her, her eyes streaming, faltering on the final line '*Dieu réunit ceux qui s'aiment*' ('God reunites those who love each other') – she collapsed, grasping a velvet curtain for support. She confided in friends in the following days that she felt she had nothing left to live for.

In the early 1950s, Édith Piaf's life was spinning out of control, a chaotic mix of grief, health problems and drug addiction. Injured in a car accident, she became addicted to the morphine prescribed to manage the pain – perhaps it also dulled the grief of losing Cerdan. During this period, she took up with Eddie Constantine, but her erratic behaviour strained friendships. In 1952, she married singer Jacques Pills, with Marlene Dietrich maid of honour, but the marriage couldn't curb her addiction. Despite rehab, she was in and out of clinics between performances at prestigious venues like the Olympia in Paris. Singing was her purpose, her life, and even as her health deteriorated, she refused to step back from the stage.

By 1956, Édith was playing sold-out shows at Carnegie Hall, pushing herself despite doctors' warnings. She released one of her most vigorous songs, 'L'homme à la moto' – a cautionary tale of a Hell's Angel-type motorcyclist and his poor girlfriend Marie-Lou, which she sang with real fire. Her marriage to Pills ended that year, and she soon began a relationship with songwriter Georges Moustaki.

By 1959, her health was in serious decline, but nevertheless she embarked on another US tour, only to collapse on stage multiple times, horrifying audiences. Returning to France, she was hospitalised again but still kept on performing, against all medical advice. In 1960, just as many were muttering that her career was over, she made a magnificent comeback with the release of another song, 'Non, je ne regrette rien', a defiant swan song which echoed around the world.

In 1961, despite ongoing health problems, she kept touring and won awards, but exhaustion caught up with her. She began serialising her life story while battling illness and addiction. In 1962, she met and married the much younger Théo Sarapo, who became a supportive partner. By 1963, Piaf was barely holding on but continued to perform, including a final show at the Bobino. After several hospitalisations, she retired to the south of France, but her health took a severe turn. In October, Édith Piaf died at her villa, aged just forty-seven.

Her death was a national event. However, due to Piaf's wild lifestyle – her lovers, drinking and drug use – the Archbishop of Paris denied her a funeral mass. Yet, despite this, her burial at Père Lachaise drew a crowd of more than 40,000 devoted fans. Fifty years later, the Church relented and gave Édith a requiem mass at the St Jean Baptiste church in Belleville.

Her influence only grew posthumously, with her songs 'La vie en rose' and 'Non, je ne regrette rien' becoming symbols of resilience. Despite a life marked by turmoil, Piaf's voice came to define French culture, and the suffering endured by her generation, marked by loss. Her voice transcended language, culture and class and moved people around the world. Her legacy is as an icon of passion and endurance. She sang with her blood; she was the soul of Paris, and the voice of the streets.

Simone Veil at the Élysée Palace, 26 May 1977.

# 19

# Simone Veil

## 13 July 1927–30 June 2017

'Day after day, then, the four of us, Mama, my sister Milou, my brother and I, waited to leave for Germany, ignorant of both the date and destination, our one hope being that we would not be separated. No one had heard of Auschwitz and I never heard the name mentioned. How could we have the first idea of the future the Nazis had planned for us?'

Simone Veil, A Life, 2007

The sixteen-year-old Simone Veil – then Simone Jacob – arrived at the internment camp for Jews in Drancy in 1944, accompanied by her mother, her twenty-one-year-old sister Milou and her brother Jean, eighteen. Her second sister, Denise, had so far escaped arrest and was fighting with the French Resistance, although before long she too would be deported to Ravensbrück. Operational from 1941 to 1944 and infamous for its harsh conditions, Drancy became a central part of the Nazi system in France, and about 67,000 Jews were deported from there, mostly to Auschwitz where they were murdered upon arrival.

Antisemitism had deep roots in all parts of French society, both before and after the Second World War, as exemplified by the events of the Dreyfus Affair. Of course, many, including

Sarah Bernhardt, resisted, but the widespread prevalence of antisemitic views on an establishment and military level cannot be denied. The intolerance and discrimination only intensified under the Vichy regime, which aligned itself with the values and aims of the Nazi occupiers. The Vichy government implemented its own antisemitic laws even before being pressured by the Nazis, stripping Jews of their rights and excluding them from public life.

In October 1940 the Vichy regime, led by Marshal Philippe Pétain, passed the Law on the Status of Jews, which restricted the rights of Jews in France. In the summer of 1942, the French police conducted the infamous Vel' d'Hiv Roundup, arresting over 13,000 Jews in Paris, including thousands of children. Officials actively cooperated with these efforts, often going beyond what the Nazis demanded, and willingly deported Jews who were French citizens alongside foreign Jews.

This included the sixteen-year-old Simone Jacob and her family. Over 76,000 Jews were deported from France during the war, most of whom were murdered in concentration camps. Every member of Simone's immediate family would end up in the concentration camps. The three sisters, Simone, Milou and Denise, would be the only survivors. Her mother would die of typhus in Bergen-Belsen – rampant at that camp, the disease also claimed the lives of Anne Frank and her sister Margot. After being separated from the family, and sent to the Baltic states to work, her brother and father were never seen again. Most Jews who left on trains bound for this region were summarily executed. The three sisters would forever carry the memory of their parents and brother, and honour the memory of the six million Jews slaughtered by the Nazis. Instead of leaving France after the war, disgusted at the capitulation and collaboration that allowed French Jews to be deported even from the Vichy Zone, Simone made it her mission to improve the country that betrayed her. She was a Jew, but also a French woman, and she would not willingly be driven out of her country. She dedicated her life to battling prejudice and inequality in France, and the teenage girl who survived Auschwitz and had the number 78651 tattooed onto her arm would go on to be one of the most influential French women in twentieth-century Europe.

\* \* \*

Simone Jacob was born on 13 July 1927 in Nice on France's Côte d'Azur. Her family, while mostly secular, maintained a strong Jewish identity and were proud members of the local community. As Simone would later write, 'Being a member of the Jewish community was never a problem. It was proudly claimed by my father, but for cultural reasons, not religious ones.'

Her childhood was happy, straightforward and relatively sheltered. She threw herself into her studies and was close to her parents and three siblings. All this would change with the advent of the Second World War. With the 1940 German invasion of France, the Vichy regime in the south assumed control and began collaborating with Nazi Germany. Initially, the Jacob family escaped the worst dangers of occupation because Nice fell into the Italian-controlled zone. For a time, this offered them a fragile form of protection, and the young Simone saw her life continue largely unhindered. She saw her friends, studied and prepared for her baccalaureate. Meanwhile, her sister Denise, older, more headstrong and aware of the threats circling, began to take an active interest in Resistance activities. While the family felt no need to flee, they began to live more cautiously.

By 1943, to the Jacobs, the mounting threat felt too real to ignore as Jewish families across France faced intimidation, detention and deportation. The family decided to split up and acquired false papers. Denise escaped to Lyon, and joined the Resistance, keeping her Jewish identity to herself. Simone's father advised his daughters to stay away from Nice.

In March 1944, Simone, despite having stopped attending school for fear of arrest, sat her baccalaureate, and breathed a sigh of relief. Just as she celebrated finishing the exam, Gestapo agents accosted her, having somehow come to learn that she carried false papers. In a tragic confluence of circumstances, the messenger Simone had sent to warn her family that their papers were no longer secret was being followed. He accidentally led the Gestapo to the rest of the family, and in this way all three siblings and their mother were arrested. Only Denise and André, Simone's father, escaped – for the moment at least.

By April, Simone, Milou, Jean and their mother had arrived at Drancy. It was a grim place, situated just north of Paris, a cloister of modernist housing blocks surrounded by high fences that served as a temporary prison for French Jews and Roma. Then on 13 April 1944 they were packed onto cattle trucks as part of Transport 71 to Auschwitz. Before leaving, they heard a rumour that men over sixteen would be given the option to stay and work in France rather than being deported, and they insisted to Jean that it was better he take this option. This, despite their best intentions, was the worst advice they could have given him, and Simone carried the guilt for this the rest of her life. Jean did ask to stay, but those who escaped the deportations to Poland were not kept in France. Within weeks, they were sent with the infamous Convoy 73 to the Baltic states, where nearly all of them would work on digging up and disguising mass graves of executed Lithuanian soldiers to cover up war crimes, before being executed themselves.

Simone would describe their journey to Auschwitz in cattle trucks in her memoirs, stoically reflecting that although the conditions were cramped and miserable they were far 'luckier' than others, as the weather was mild and no one died on the journey, so they were spared the horror of travelling surrounded by corpses. Others were not so lucky. When Simone came to write about her experiences of deportation and internment, she did not shy away from describing the horrors and indignities she endured, although never strayed into graphic or overly emotive description. She was factual, and nevertheless infused her work with balance and optimism. She acknowledged the rare kindnesses she experienced from prison guards, whose small and clandestine acts of 'mercy' she credits with saving her life and the lives of her mother and sister again and again during her imprisonments. Acts of mercy from the guards were the closest they dared come to rebelling against the machine of the Nazi regime in which they were enmeshed, complicit.

The first of these acts of jarring, fleeting 'kindness' from the guards who were executing them was a moment that saved her from being sent directly to the gas chamber. When she replied honestly to the first person who asked her age on arrival at Auschwitz, telling her she was sixteen, it was muttered to her quickly, 'Whatever you do, tell them you are eighteen.' Simone recalled that a girl from Nice who had been arrested at the same time as her still had a bottle of Lanvin perfume in her pocket. When they saw that they were being stripped and their possessions confiscated this girl, Simone and two other teenagers sprinkled themselves with the remainder to prevent the guards enjoying it, a final act of autonomy and teenage rebellion. When women imprisoned with them asked in confusion what had happened to their friends and relatives sent to other parts of the camp, the guard replied by pointing to the furnaces and the black smoke billowing from the chimneys. At first, none of them comprehended what they meant.

At Auschwitz, Simone, her mother and her sister were set to work. It was hard labour, contributing to the enlargement and running of the death camp. One of the first jobs they were given was to work on extending the loading docks so cattle trucks of people could be unloaded more or less straight to the gas chambers. Simone recalls seeing truckloads of Hungarian prisoners arrive in this manner, and the sudden chill she felt as she understood what was happening.

Like many, Simone's survival was contingent on the whims of the guards and pure chance. She managed to keep her health, and for a long time so did her mother and sister. She was never separated from her mother or sister, or forced to wear the striped prison uniforms. She was not tortured, or experimented upon, but she was nevertheless horrified by the brutalities she witnessed.

Through another act of 'kindness' from an otherwise severe camp supervisor, Simone and her sisters were sent to Bobrek, where conditions were less harsh. The officer purportedly told Simone that it was because she was too pretty to be allowed to die in the camp, and then she personally arranged for Simone and Milou and their mother to be transferred. They stayed in the new camp from July 1944 to January 1945, and Simone observed with joy that conditions there were so much better that not a single prisoner died during their six-month internment.

In January 1945 they were forced to leave the camp to return to Auschwitz on foot when the guards received word that Soviet and Allied troops were advancing, commencing a death march in the freezing cold with 40,000 others; 'those who fell down were instantly shot'. They were jumbled in with the men who treated them badly. Veil recalled an encounter with a thirteen-year-old boy who had been abused by some of the male prisoners, in the absence of women, but was suddenly abandoned and no longer fed once women arrived. The women – now victims of the male abuse themselves – pitied him and tried to help.

After being sent from place to place they arrived at Bergen-Belsen, where conditions were beyond horrific. There was no food, and the bodies of the dead were abandoned in quarters of the living. Cannibalism occurred. It was here that Simone's mother died of typhus on 15 March 1945, after already suffering and surviving so much. Simone all her life attributed all of her achievements to her mother: the woman who gave her 'the motivation and the will to act'. The camp was liberated just a month later on 15 April. It was only upon her arrival at a sorting centre for survivors that Simone learned that her sister was in Ravensbrück. She wept uncontrollably on hearing the news, devastated that her sister, whom she had imagined living free in France fighting the Nazis, might have suffered the same fate, if not worse. There had been rumours that all the inmates of Ravensbrück were shot prior to liberation. They hurried to Hôtel Lutetia in Paris – the point of return for lost souls who had been abducted and deported during the war – and searched anxiously among the crowds of emaciated faces. But they did not find her. On making inquiries, they found that Denise had arrived back in Paris a few weeks before them. They were overjoyed, and soon reunited.

While initially devoting herself to quiet recovery, comforting grieving friends and relatives, and nursing Milou who had contracted typhus as well in the camps, Simone retained a strong sense of purpose, a desire to study. She received news that she had in fact passed the baccalaureate exams she had sat just before her arrest. Armed with this and support from surviving relatives, Simone decided to study law at Sciences Po. It was here, aged eighteen, that Simone Jacob met Antoine Veil, a fellow student at Sciences Po who had spent the war years in Switzerland. Within weeks of meeting, the couple became engaged, and on 26 October 1946 Simone and Antoine married. Simone was nineteen, Antoine twenty.

In the first years of their marriage, Simone supported Antoine's budding career, taking a step back from her own studies to focus on family. In a surprising decision, she accompanied Antoine to Germany for his work, living in the American-occupied zone while continuing to study law informally. Despite how little time had passed since the end of the war and liberation of the camps, Simone was determined not to let what the Nazis had done define her or hold her back – she was a survivor in the truest sense. She related in her memoir that many found it difficult to understand her choice to live there, but revealed that she never felt uncomfortable, as in the area they lived in they simply 'lived like

Americans' and were self-sufficient. It was there in Germany in 1947 that Simone gave birth to her first son, Jean, and just over a year later, her second, Nicolas.

In 1950, Antoine's work took them to Wiesbaden, where they stayed for two years before moving to Stuttgart in 1952. During this time, Simone's days were filled with family responsibilities, yet her ambition remained undimmed. She assisted Antoine with his work whenever possible, reading him newspaper articles and discussing politics as they drove. That summer would bring still more grief for Simone, however. Her sister Milou, who had been her constant companion in Auschwitz and whom she had nursed back to health in the aftermath of the war, was killed in a car accident. Milou's one-year-old son was also injured, and would die of his injuries in Simone's arms, despite initially seeming unhurt. The loss of Milou had a profound impact on Simone.

In 1953, the Veil family returned to France after Antoine passed the entrance exam for the École Nationale d'Administration (ENA), an elite institution known for training future French leaders. Back in France, Simone gave birth to her third son, Pierre-François, in 1954, bringing new joy to the family. But this period also marked a turning point in her personal aspirations. After the birth of Pierre-François, Simone expressed her desire to pursue a career in law more concretely by applying for the bar. To her consternation, Antoine, whom she had so diligently supported, told her it was 'out of the question' and that it was not 'a career for a woman'. Simone was shocked, and they rowed.

However, Simone – an astute diplomat and politician already – was able to guide Antoine to compromise, while preserving the integrity of their marriage and, instead of pursuing a career as a lawyer, she took examinations to become a magistrate. This was just the beginning of Simone's career in public service. She served as a magistrate for eighteen years.

During her time as a magistrate, Simone was instrumental in prison reform and improving the treatment of women in prison.

She also made strides in civil affairs, including advancements for women, particularly in the areas of parental rights and adoption. She helped secure dual parental control over family legal matters, a change that reflected her dedication to gender equality and her belief in the shared responsibilities of both parents. She was not, however, much in the public eye. When Valéry Giscard d'Estaing was campaigning for the presidency, he had made statements about bringing women into the government, and rumours began to swirl about who they might be. Simone Veil's name was circulating – much to her consternation. Rumours became reality, and Giscard invited her to join his government as health minister, apparently at the recommendation of Prime Minister Chirac. In 1974 she became the first female minister of health. To her still-greater surprise, in the end, she was the only woman minister. Simone Veil was known for being a trailblazer, unafraid to work in a traditionally male milieu, but nevertheless this appointment was a big deal.

When Simone became health minister, abortions were not legal in France. That did not mean they did not take place. Backstreet abortions were a scourge of women's health, and medical-travel companies openly advertised buses that would take women abroad to other European countries where they could obtain abortions in local chemists' shops. The threat this posed to women's well-being was recognised not only by Veil, but also by other members of the government.

Simone Veil's struggle to pass the abortion law in France in 1974 was marked by intense opposition and personal attacks. As minister of health, she believed that legalising abortion was essential to protect women's health, dignity and freedom. Simone was driven by her conviction that women should have the right to control their own bodies, seeing the reform as a matter of public health and social justice and a fundamental issue of women's rights and women's health.

The opposition she faced was fierce, especially from conservative politicians and religious groups. During debates in the French

National Assembly, she faced hostile rhetoric, including comparisons to Nazi atrocities. Despite this, Simone remained firm. On 26 November 1974, Simone made a historic speech at the National Assembly. She appealed to both reason and compassion, framing abortion as a decision never taken lightly, and the legalisation of abortion as a necessary step to protect women's health and dignity. By presenting abortion not as a matter of morality but as a matter of public health, she made steady progress. The law, passed in January 1975, had a profound impact, significantly reducing deaths and complications from unsafe abortions and marking a major step forward in women's rights in France. Today, it stands as a cornerstone of her legacy, and is still known as the *Loi Veil* (Veil Law).

Following the end of her term as health minister, she continued to make history, becoming the first woman to serve as president of the European Parliament in Strasbourg, from 1979 to 1982. She was a strong supporter of the European integration process, which she saw as a guarantor of peace. She headed the Foundation for the Memory of the Shoah from 2000 to 2007, before becoming its honorary president. Among her many distinctions, she was decorated with the Order of the British Empire in 1998, elected member of the Académie Française in 2008 in the 13th chair, and received the Grand Cross of the Legion of Honour in 2012. Recognised as one of France's most revered figures and often referred to as a 'secular saint', Simone Veil was the fifth woman to be interred in the Pantheon, buried there alongside her husband on 1 July 2018.

Simone Veil's impact on French society, particularly through her advocacy for women's rights, health reform and European unity, places her alongside iconic French feminists like Simone de Beauvoir and Gisèle Halimi. While de Beauvoir focused on existentialist philosophy and the emancipation of women in her writing, Veil pursued practical and systemic change within the spheres of law and policy, ultimately reshaping French society through her work on reproductive rights and family law. Halimi, a contemporary of Veil's and an equally fierce advocate, championed legal defence and gender equality; both women's work intersected in the push for abortion rights and equal representation under French law. Together, Veil, de Beauvoir and Halimi form a powerful trinity in French history, embodying intellectual rigour, justice and activism.

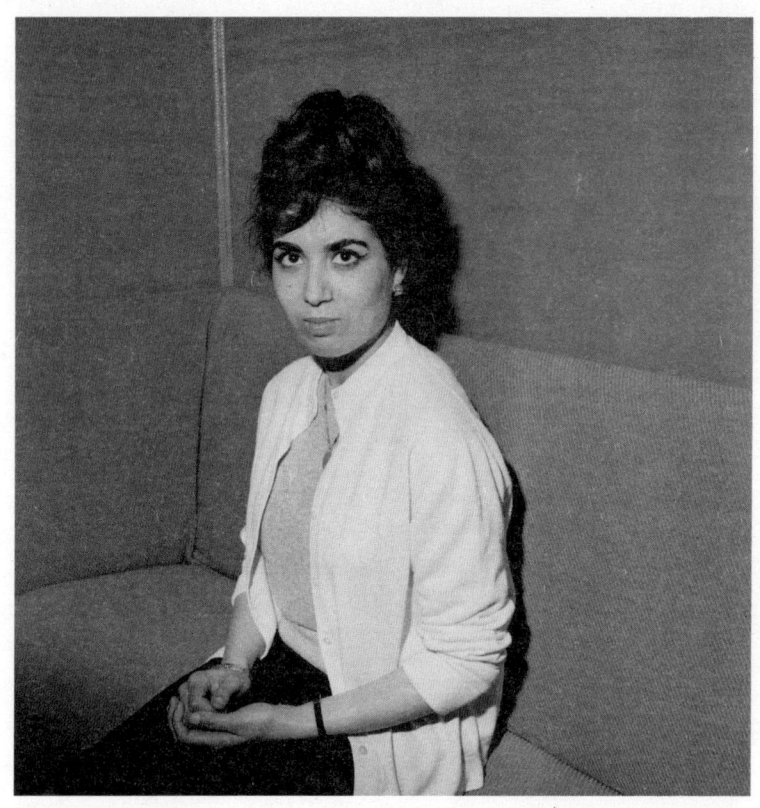
Djamila Boupacha, photographed on 14 March 1963.

# 20

# Djamila Boupacha

## 9 February 1938–present

'We must shout the truth to the rooftops.'

Gisèle Halimi

On 2 June 1960, an article appeared in *Le Monde* that shocked the French public. Shocked, actually, is an understatement.

It was written by Simone de Beauvoir, the renowned feminist and existentialist philosopher and the long-term partner of Jean-Paul Sartre, whose book *Le Deuxième Sexe*, or *The Second Sex* as it is better known in English, was often credited with launching second-wave feminism.

In her article she detailed the abuse, rape and torture of a young Algerian woman, accused of attempting to commit a terrorist attack against colonial French forces in Algeria. De Beauvoir did not mince words, and while her language was not overly florid or emotive, the French public were horrified by what they read. The victim had confessed to planting a bomb in a café, which did not explode. But the confession was extracted under torture. Without de Beauvoir's article, this young woman's case might only have passed through corrupt colonial courts in Algeria and never appeared on the radar of the French public, but following this piece in *Le Monde*, it was suddenly a matter of national debate. De

Beauvoir's writing was graphic but precise. It had its desired effect. It was a call to arms and galvanised the French public to demand justice for Djamila, and to reflect on the colonial regime they were indirectly supporting in Algeria, inviting them to interrogate their consciences. In Algeria, the authorities were furious, and ordered that day's copies of *Le Monde* seized, to prevent the public accessing the article. They were afraid of its potential impact.

Many French people knew about the situation in Algeria, but few had really engaged with the issue, nor been confronted by the realities and brutalities of what their country was doing in North Africa. De Beauvoir's article – entitled simply 'Pour Djamila Boupacha' – was a wake-up call to the French people, and the beginning of the turn of the tide of public opinion against the continued occupation of Algeria.

This chapter is really about three women, two of whom are famous throughout France, and sometimes beyond: Gisèle Halimi and Simone de Beauvoir – and the third is Djamila, whose name is often forgotten even among French Algerians. Djamila was a victim of colonial violence and injustice, and Gisèle Halimi and Simone de Beauvoir the lawyer and the feminist writer who rallied to her cause. Gisèle and Simone were included in the opening ceremony of the 2024 Olympics, as female luminaries of France, but Djamila was ignored.

\* \* \*

Djamila Boupacha was born in 1938 in Saint-Eugene, a small town now called Bologhine, on the northern coast of Algeria, a deeply divided country at the time. It was run by French colonial authorities who – often brutally – oppressed the native Algerian population, treating them as a subclass of citizens under the French settlers, known as *les pieds-noirs*. This period in Algeria was marked by social and racial inequality between the predominantly Muslim local population, mainly of Berber and Arab descent, and white Christian *pieds-noirs*, who enjoyed more rights, liberties and opportunities than their Algerian neighbours, and also a Jewish minority. Although Algeria was considered a part of France, the local Algerian community was subjected to second-class citizenship, with limited legal rights. Under French law, they were classed as neither French nor foreign until 1962. Algerians, while given French documents, were in turn classed as 'indigenous', 'French subjects' then 'Muslim French from Algeria', all rungs below the simple status of 'French' enjoyed by their white neighbours. French settlers, who comprised a small fraction of the population, controlled most of the wealth and power.

By the time of Djamila's birth, Algeria had been under colonial rule for more than a hundred years. The conquest had taken place in 1830, and after a few years as a colony Algeria became a *département* of France. After paying a visit to Algeria in September 1860, Emperor Napoleon III – of Franco-Prussian War infamy – had the audacity to give the country increased rights and freedoms, and treat it as a semi-independent client state for a decade, but his capture at Sedan put paid to that.

In 1865, French citizenship was offered to native Algerian Muslims and Jews for the first time, on the condition that they accepted being governed by the French civil code in all matters – including where their own religious laws contradicted it. Unsurprisingly, this was not a popular offer, and by 1870 only 194 Muslims and 398 Jews had taken advantage of it. In 1870 the new French provisional government decided to resolve the situation for Algerian Jews by decreeing them to be citizens governed by French law at a stroke. While Muslims were considered French subjects, they were broadly denied official citizenship and had no voting rights. After thousands of Algerian soldiers served in the First World War, some rules about applying for citizenship were relaxed, most notably for soldiers, or those with sons in the armed forces.

At the same time as the local population was suffering these indignities, hundreds of thousands of European migrants moved to French Algeria, and French culture and values were being imposed. Some Algerians were allowed to receive French education – few at first, but gradually more and more. During the years of colonisation, the native Muslim population declined sharply, the result of scarcity, disease, warfare and mistreatment. The society that formed in the aftermath of this settlement was starkly divided and deeply unequal. Tensions and resentment at the injustice simmered, and they would come to a head during the childhood and adolescence of Djamila Boupacha.

Djamila grew up witnessing the injustices of this colonial system. Discrimination was embedded deep in French Algerian society. Though Djamila was able to train as a nurse, she was never allowed to qualify due to her status as 'indigenous'. These experiences contributed to her radicalisation, compounded by the rise of the Algerian nationalist movement, and led to her entry in to political activism.

In 1954 the Front de Libération Nationale (FLN) was founded. On All Saints' Day it conducted around seventy attacks against colonial police, military forces and some civilian *pieds-noirs*. In its manifesto, it declared it would fight for independence 'by all means'. It was a bloody start to the Algerian War of Independence, a brutal and prolonged conflict with atrocities committed by both sides. By the age of fifteen, Djamila had joined the FLN. She adopted 'Khelida' as a codename and served in the militant wing of the FLN for seven years, growing increasingly radicalised as the war wore on.

Then on 27 September 1959, just under nine months before the publication of Simone de Beauvoir's article, the sun shone on a grand square – the Place de la Grande Poste – in the capital city, Algiers. Children played; friends lounged in cafés. French colonial troops were present too, never far away. For all that the square was a popular meeting point, it was also a potential target. Three years earlier, a bomb had been planted in the Milk Bar – an ice cream parlour – just a few minutes' walk away. It had exploded, killing three people. On 27 September, a young militant sought to repeat the scene; a bomb was planted in the Brasserie des Facultés, a favourite haunt of French troops and officials. It was concealed in a beach bag, but it was discovered and defused by French army bomb experts – the plot was foiled and no one was hurt. No one was seen planting the bomb, and at first it was unclear who the culprit was. This bomb, which was never detonated, launched the story of Djamila Boupacha, and her unlikely partnership with Gisèle Halimi and Simone de Beauvoir.

Less than five months later, on 10 February, fifty French colonial agents conducted a raid on the house of an Algerian family suspected of orchestrating the attempted terrorist attack, arresting several members. One of them, aged twenty-two at the time, was Djamila Boupacha. When Djamila was dragged from her bed in February 1960 and imprisoned, girls her age in Paris were cutting their hair and wearing miniskirts and listening to rock music. She was fighting for the liberation of Algeria. At the time of her arrest, the evidence against her was flimsy at best. There was no witness who could testify to her involvement in the plot. There was no proof that linked her specifically to the manufacture or placement of the bomb, and in any case, it did not explode and no one was killed. Yet the colonial authorities were still seeking capital punishment. In order to make a case against her, a confession was needed, and it was duly extracted by the French authorities tasked with finding and punishing a culprit. A scapegoat was needed, and Djamila would do.

The colonial agents beat her, they beat her father, they beat her sister's husband and carted them off together to a detention facility. There she was stomped on, which broke her rib. Then they stripped her, strung her up and attached electrodes to her face, her breasts, her genitals. They shocked her, punched her and burned her with cigarettes. All in the name of justice, to extract the required confession. After all, a confession would excuse the obvious lack of evidence. Nothing else would be needed.

Still defiant, she was suspended above a bathtub and repeatedly immersed in the water. The soldiers crowed that they would not rape her, for fear of giving her too much pleasure.

But they did rape her, penetrating her violently with a beer bottle, resulting in her bleeding out and losing consciousness. While in this state, they showed her to her father – then aged seventy – who after several rounds of torture had been rushed to hospital. Following his release he continued to be held in a detention centre, with no charges ever brought against him.

Countless others were subjected to similar abuse, and hundreds of French officers went unpunished for these crimes. During the Algerian War, torture and rape were commonly used by the French military as tools of suppression against the resistance, which was also very violent in its fight for liberation. But systematic rape can never be justified as a tool of war, and nor can collective punishment against civilians – even if authorities supported by Western governments claim it is in the name of justice and counter-terrorism. Rape, in particular, held a particular power as a terror tactic in conservative Algerian society, where a woman's virginity was highly valued. French authorities used sexual violence to destroy the morale of both the female fighters and the broader community, exploiting the shame of the act. Many victims and their families remained silent, unable to publicly acknowledge what had happened. In the aftermath of Djamila's trial, and as the true horrors of the colonial regime in Algeria came to light, more and more soldiers spoke about the acts they witnessed and took part in.

One conscript, Henri Pouillot, revealed having witnessed around one hundred rapes of Algerian women over a ten-month period. He wrote a book, *La Villa Susini*, about his experiences at a notorious interrogation centre: 'Women were raped on average nine times out of ten, depending on their age and physique,' he recounts. 'We arranged, during the roundups in Algiers, to capture one or two of them solely for the needs of the troops.

They could stay one, two, or three days, sometimes more.' Pouillot split the rapes into two categories: 'Those that were intended to get people talking, and the "comfort" rapes, to let off steam.' He asserts that the French men had complete freedom: 'There were no prohibitions. Rape was a torture like any other, it was just a complement that women offered, unlike men.'

While the abuse Djamila suffered might have become grimly commonplace in the corrupt regime in Algeria, Djamila's next steps were not commonplace at all. What set Djamila's case apart was not the violence she endured, but her decision to speak out.

Injured and traumatised, yet still outraged by what she was forced to endure, she decided to sue the government for these crimes committed against her. She retracted her confession, and accused her jailers of torture, and of forcing her to confess under torture.

Her case was referred to Gisèle Halimi, a rising lawyer with a reputation for defending the voiceless and dispossessed, and an uncompromising champion of justice, particularly for women and minorities. She herself was Maghrebi, of Jewish Berber origin and born in Tunisia. When Gisèle Halimi first met Djamila Boupacha in Algeria's notorious Barberousse Prison, the young woman was silent and withdrawn, struggling to speak about the abuse she had been subjected to. Halimi later described the moment when Djamila unbuttoned her blouse, revealing her breasts, marked with cigarette burns, and showed Halimi her ankles and wrists, bruised and swollen from many beatings and being suspended with chains and restraints. Though initially hesitant to discuss the sexual violence she had experienced, Djamila eventually confided in Halimi about the rape, saying, 'You know, I was a virgin. And then they took a beer bottle and … it was terrible. But now, it's over. They have made me into something else, I am no longer anything.' Halimi kissed and held Djamila as she described, falteringly, what had happened to her. Djamila had begun their interview with a steely façade, pronouncing that she would fight for her country. By the end of her interview with Halimi she was visibly distressed. As Halimi left, she reminded her that while she had told her parents about the torture, and her father had even seen and heard her suffering, she had withheld from them the details of her rape, as it was too awful to speak of to them.

Halimi had long been involved in Algeria's struggle for independence, and Djamila Boupacha was not the first accused FLN militant she had defended. She quickly realised that Djamila's trial was not just about one woman's guilt or innocence; it was an opportunity to expose the atrocities committed by the French military in Algeria. She knew she needed to bring powerful allies on board to amplify the case and put France itself on trial. She was swinging the spotlight from the question of Djamila's guilt or innocence, and onto the methods through which her confession was extracted. She positioned herself as not Djamila's defender, but prosecutor of France.

Immediately after her first meeting with Djamila Boupacha, she phoned de Beauvoir, who listened in grim silence as Halimi explained that Djamila, accused of carrying a bomb, was now condemned to death despite her weapon never being used – it was claimed she had decided not to detonate the bomb on seeing that there were civilians present. De Beauvoir responded without hesitation, asking Halimi directly, 'What do you want me to do?' Gisèle asked Simone to do what she did best: to write. She said to her, *'pour sauver Djamila, il faut lancer un cri'* ('To save Djamila, you have to shout'). De Beauvoir did just this, publishing 'Pour Djamila Boupacha' in *Le Monde*, two weeks before the trial was set to take place.

The attention brought to the case by Halimi and de Beauvoir's involvement transformed Djamila's trial into a moment of political reckoning for France. With de Beauvoir's intellectual and public influence, the case quickly gained national and international attention. Artist Pablo Picasso, philosopher Jean-Paul

Sartre, writer Aimé Césaire, former Resistance fighter and concentration camp survivor Germaine Tillion and other prominent figures joined the cause, and the 'Boupacha Committee' was formed to campaign for Djamila's release and demand justice for the crimes committed against her. They requested the transfer of the investigation to France, and made sure the case stayed in the spotlight, to avoid it slipping away into mires of corruption and secrecy, holding numerous press conferences throughout the trial. De Beauvoir and Halimi's partnership went beyond just this trial; it was a fusion of feminism and anti-colonialism, highlighting how the fight for women's rights intersected with the fight against imperialism.

As the movement progressed, in 1962 Halimi and de Beauvoir published a book together, *Djamila Boupacha*, featuring a portrait of her by Picasso on the cover. The book was a testament to their commitment and featured medical expertise from gynaecologists demonstrating the toll of violence on the colonised female body during the Algerian War. The book was reviewed by the then minister of culture, Françoise Giroud, as 'the story of a crime' – a factual file that could be consulted by anyone and allow them to draw their own conclusion. Giroud asked a haunting question posed to Boupacha: '*Pendant que votre nation est en train de se faire, la nôtre va-t-elle se défaire …?*' ('While your nation is being made, will ours be unmade …?)

Boupacha's granddaughter, Sophia Khali, later shared a personal memory of attending an exhibition in Algiers with her family, where Picasso's portrait of her grandmother was unveiled, and remembered her grandmother talking to many people at the event. Too young to understand the background of the image, she remembers just knowing that she should be proud of her grandmother, without learning why until much later. She felt the pride her father had in his mother and felt that too herself. She recalled that in Picasso's drawing, the weariness in Djamila's eyes stood out, a reflection of the pain she had endured. The artwork itself represented a softened image of Algerian women fighters, capturing both their suffering and their dignity. Picasso's image echoed the wider fight for justice, linking the FLN women's struggle with broader global ideals of human rights and resistance.

Gisèle Halimi centred her defence on challenging the validity of confessions obtained under torture. With Djamila Boupacha's consent, she publicly exposed Boupacha's rape and filed a complaint against unidentified perpetrators. For the first time in a trial of this nature, gynaecologists were called as expert witnesses. Halimi was unable to attend the initial trial before the military tribunal, so she delegated her colleague in Algeria, Pierre Garrigues, who was tragically assassinated in Algiers on 1 March 1962. It was a frightening time for the lawyers involved in defending Boupacha, as animosity towards Algerians and the FLN ran deep. Halimi's son, Jean-Yves, recounted this time as a period of uncertainty and fear for his family. He described how his mother, anxious about the volatile political situation, woke him and his brother in the middle of the night to leave quickly, fearing they would be targeted. In a moment of maternal calm, she assured her young son that they were simply going to a party. Despite the hardships of that period, Jean-Yves expressed gratitude for his unique childhood, influenced by his mother's commitment to justice.

Facing legal challenges, Halimi filed a complaint against General Ailleret, the senior commander of the armed forces in Algeria, and against Pierre Messmer, the minister of the armed forces, for violating her client's constitutional rights, and refusing to supply photographs of the soldiers who had allegedly tortured Djamila to protect their identities. These charges brought significant media attention to the case. Halimi also succeeded in having the trial relocated to Caen with the help of the Boupacha Committee. Halimi and de Beauvoir also drew attention to the case of Djamila's father, Abdelaziz Boupacha, detained without charges at the Beni Messous camp. After a particularly brutal interrogation, Abdelaziz Boupacha was said to have shouted: 'De Gaulle has forbidden torture!' The captain's response, in de Beauvoir's paraphrase, was: 'Let De Gaulle do what he pleases at home, here, we are the ones in charge.' De Beauvoir suggested his real words were too filthy to reproduce.

As Djamila stood trial, she did so not just as a member of the FLN but as a symbol of all the women and men who had suffered under French rule. Her time in prison in France was gruelling. Conditions were poor, and while there was no torture, Djamila voluntarily undertook hunger strikes in solidarity with her countrymen. Halimi ensured that Djamila's voice was heard and that her suffering was acknowledged in court. The military attempted to portray her as an isolated and extreme case and mentally unstable. They bribed and intimidated witnesses to testify against her, and asserted that Djamila had not been tortured and was crazy, but this backfired.

The trial was a piece of theatre. A key witness who had been manipulated by the colonial authorities withdrew her testimony against Djamila, and instead testified in her favour, saying that she had witnessed her torture in the Algerian prison. The judge was sympathetic, thorough and discerning, but with a distinct mean streak, and almost seemed to enjoy and relish hearing about Djamila's plight. Nevertheless, he gave her the time and space to make her case, enabling her to prove the validity of her claims. He presented her with the type of electric dynamo used to pump electricity through her body, and made her watch as he tried the torture instrument out on the clerk of the court. Likewise, when she began to describe the torture technique of the 'hung pig', whereby the victim is trussed up like an animal carcass on a stick and thrust naked into freezing water, he summoned one of the journalists in the court to demonstrate the pose on a broom handle Halimi found in the courthouse. The man remained clothed and there was no icy bathtub in sight, but the visual image of the brutality was seared into the minds of all who saw it.

Finally, he invited Djamila to identify her torturers from a set of passport photographs. This she duly did, selecting the real culprits from a pile of decoys. The judge was delighted with the brilliance of her memory.

However, wheels were in motion that were bigger than Djamila's case. The Algerian War of Independence was rapidly drawing towards a successful conclusion, propelled by a finally prevailing call for peace and justice and self-determination for the Algerian people. A verdict was never reached on Djamila's case in France, as before the conclusion of the trial, she was granted amnesty under the Évian Accords and released on 21 April 1962.

*Le Monde* reported her release in these words:

> Rennes, April 23 (AFP). – Djamila Boupacha, the young Algerian woman arrested in 1959 for having planted a bomb in the Brasserie des Facultés in Algiers, was released at 4 p.m. Saturday from the central prison of Rennes, where she had been detained for three months. She was immediately taken in charge by her lawyer, Gisèle Halimi.
>
> Under police escort, Ms. Halimi's car, in which the young girl was seated, took the road to Paris, escorted by two motorcycle gendarmes.
>
> Ms. Halimi said that Djamila Boupacha's residence could not be disclosed 'because she is sentenced to death by the OAS'.

The OAS (Organisation Armée Secrète) was a far-right French nationalist terrorist organisation that opposed Algerian independence and carried out numerous terrorist attacks to hinder the independence process – it was founded in 1961 in response to the referendum on Algerian independence. The OAS was sinister but capable, and depicted in the 1973 thriller *The Day of the Jackal* as plotting an elaborate assassination of Charles de Gaulle. They made many attempts on de Gaulle's life – and famously almost succeeded in ambushing de Gaulle and his wife with machine-gun fire in Petit-Clamart in 1962.

Despite these very real threats, Djamila was overjoyed at her release and expressed her joy at being freed and her wish to be able to return to Algeria. This momentous day – after two years in custody, numerous abuses and hunger strikes – came just two months before Algeria gained its independence. Her release was a victory not merely for her, but for all who had fought against the brutality of French colonial rule.

The Évian Accords, signed in March 1962, formally ended the Algerian War and marked the beginning of Algeria's independence from French rule. The agreement included France's recognition of Algeria's right to self-determination, leading to a referendum in July 1962 in which Algerians overwhelmingly voted for independence. The accords allowed a limited continued French military presence for a transitional period, particularly at strategic sites like the Mers El-Kébir naval base, and established cooperative economic terms that permitted French access to Algeria's oil and gas resources. Additionally, the accords guaranteed cultural ties, maintaining French-language education and cultural institutions in Algeria.

The publicity surrounding Djamila Boupacha's case deeply shocked the French public and increased anti-war sentiment, highlighting the human rights abuses that were being committed in the name of colonialism. This, combined with other high-profile incidents of torture and brutality, began to sway French and international opinion against the war. While Boupacha's case did not directly initiate the Évian Accords, it contributed to mounting pressure on the French government to seek a negotiated end to the conflict. The widespread awareness and condemnation of French practices helped accelerate the momentum towards peace negotiations, ultimately leading to the signing of the accords in 1962.

Provisions were also made for the protection of the European settlers and Harkis, Algerians who had fought for France, giving them the choice to stay in Algeria with assurances of safety or relocate to France as citizens. However, these protections were inconsistently applied, and many Harkis faced retribution or were unable to relocate safely. The accords also granted amnesty for crimes committed by both sides, ensuring that French and FLN forces would not face prosecution for wartime actions. This amnesty was part of a broader effort to close the chapter on colonial violence and build a cooperative postwar relationship between France and the newly independent Algeria.

Despite her prominence during the war, Djamila's role in post-independence Algeria reflected a complex and deliberate navigation of public life. While many female combatants felt sidelined in the new Algerian state, Djamila remained an iconic figure of the independence struggle. In the immediate aftermath of independence, she worked in the Office of Women's Employment and participated in official delegations abroad, including to Britain. However, she was also vocally opposed to being used as a mere symbol, publicly resisting such roles. In the years that followed, Djamila married a fellow resistance fighter and had three sons, but her story, like that of many women who fought for Algeria, faded into the background. Her withdrawal from public life appears to have been a conscious choice, though her legacy remained significant. In 2022, President Abdelmadjid Tebboune appointed her as a senator in honour of her contributions, an offer she publicly declined due to objections to his regime.

Other women who fought for Algeria's liberation, like Djamila Bouhired and Zohra Drif, took active roles in post-independence politics and even opposed subsequent governments, participating in protests. However, many felt deeply betrayed by the post-independence leadership, which often marginalised their contributions. Recognition of the sacrifices these women made has been slow and fraught. It was only in 2021 that France agreed to unseal archives related to the torture of Algerian militants, and in 2023, President Emmanuel Macron publicly acknowledged that Djamila had been tortured during the war, a significant moment in France's reckoning with its colonial legacy.

Djamila's story reflects both the resilience and the complex postwar reality faced by women who had risked everything for Algeria's freedom, only to confront new challenges in the years that followed. She remains a true icon of the Algerian struggle for independence, and the suffering inflicted upon the Algerian people.

Brigitte Bardot in *La femme et le pantin* by Julien Duvivier, 1959.

# 21

# Brigitte Bardot

## 28 September 1934 – 28 December 2025

'The male is an object to her, just as she is to him.'
Simone de Beauvoir

A group of musicians play, and the feverish rhythm of mambo music swells in the air, filling a room in a quiet beach bar. A woman – Juliette – in a long green skirt and black leotard is dancing. Her tousled golden hair swings loose around her shoulders. She moves, slowly at first, sensuously, her hips swaying playfully, arms rising, her body pulled deeper and deeper into the rhythm. She tosses her hair with abandon, whipping it round and round her as she pirouettes and sways. The Black musicians increase the tempo, delighted with their unexpected dancer. They are energised by her presence, and she responds with her whole body. She becomes more and more lost in the music; there's a wildness about her. Her speed increases, her breath shortens. From the side-lines her lovers from her conservative French town look on in a mixture of shock, horror and pure desire. Their jaws tense above their neat collars, they swallow. She is too much for them. They order her to stop. Her lip curls, she tells them '*non*'.

# A HISTORY OF FRANCE IN 21 WOMEN

In a single movement she sweeps her hand up the front of her skirt, throwing open the buttons to give herself more freedom to move, and to reveal her thighs and the leotard beneath. She dances harder, faster. Her skin glows with sweat. She turns to a mirror, running her hands over her own body, watching herself, biting her lips, tossing her hair, flushed.

She spins again. Hair flying. Breathing ragged.

In moments, she looks ecstatic, in others, almost in pain, as she approaches a frenzy.

The room watches, helpless, angry, in thrall.

She is magnetic.

\* \* \*

Brigitte Bardot looked great. It caused a scandal.

*Paris Match* called her 'immoral, from head to toe'. Simone de Beauvoir described her as 'a locomotive of women's history'. In 1996 the *Guardian* called her 'the most famous French woman since Joan of Arc'.

The scene described above is the climax of the 1956 Roger Vadim film *Et Dieu ... Créa la Femme* (*And God Created Woman*), and it catapulted the then little-known Brigitte Bardot to stardom, for her portrayal of the brazenly sexual protagonist Juliette. Although the film was banned in many territories, the world could not look away.

Since she burst onto screens in the 1950s, 'BB' has courted controversy, beginning by pushing the boundaries of sexuality on screen, and more recently convicted of hate speech. Her rise to stardom, and activity since, charts some of the most crucial cultural changes of modern times in France.

As I was putting the finishing touches to this book, Brigitte Bardot, aged ninety-one, died at home in St Tropez, after a private battle with cancer and watched over by her husband of three decades. Her funeral was attended by close family and invited guests, including her visibly moved son Nicolas, and Marine Le

## BRIGITTE BARDOT

Pen. President Emmanuel Macron was rejected from proceedings, given Bardot's open disdain for his presidency. The coffin was modest, made of wicker, and topped with yellow and orange flowers. Her son laid a wreath marked '*à maman*', and well-wishers lined the streets for her funeral procession, many with their pets.

In the years leading up to her death, I had tried and failed to get an interview with this elusive screen icon. She had, famously, been a recluse for decades, choosing an introverted life with her husband and a small menagerie. Nevertheless, despite having not appeared on screen since 1973, Brigitte Bardot's fame – and the cult surrounding her – never diminished. In the aftermath of her death, reams and reams of articles and photo essays celebrating – and critiquing – her life were printed across the world.

Brigitte Bardot had a life trajectory that almost felt medieval: a woman in the spotlight, seen for her sexuality and power, who then suddenly withdraws to a monastic-like existence. It feels a bit like Eleanor of Aquitaine or Diane de Poitiers; the woman at the very centre of a glittering court tires of the world and retreats from it. She was the darling of international cinema, and then – just as suddenly as she arrived – she disappeared.

BB retired voluntarily at thirty-nine years old with almost fifty films to her name, the undisputed icon of 1960s French cinema, and an international sex symbol. She was sick of the spotlight, and ready for a new chapter.

The film that put the twenty-two-year-old BB on the map and catapulted her to international fame was the 1956 release *Et Dieu … Créa la Femme*, directed by Roger Vadim, the man who at that time was her husband, married to his muse. He cast Bardot in the lead role of Juliette, a woman with high sexual energy and a restless spirit, who cannot be tamed despite the best efforts of her conservative neighbours and lovers. Her impulsive physicality and freedom upend the social order around her. Her beauty and sensuality are emphasised throughout, through her costumes, and suggestions of nudity.

*New York Times* critic Bosley Crowther wrote:

In the French film *And God Created Woman* ... Exhibit A is 'B. B.,' the currently beloved Brigitte Bardot. This round and voluptuous little French miss is put on spectacular display and is rather brazenly ogled from every allowable point of view. She is looked at in slacks and sweaters, in shorts and Bikini bathing suits. She wears a bedsheet on two or three occasions, and, once, she shows behind a thin screen in the nude. What's more, she moves herself in a fashion that fully accentuates her charms. She is undeniably a creation of superlative craftsmanship. But that's the extent of the transcendence, for there is nothing sublime about the script of this completely single-minded little picture.

His views echoed that of the wider French public. Critics were not impressed with the film. One critic in *Le Monde* wrote:

Roger Vadim, who wrote the screenplay and directed it, wanted, he tells us, to depict the psychosis in which post-war youth find themselves plunged. Shall I admit that when I saw the film I didn't find much of the author's intentions? Why would this girl in love with a handsome guy symbolize the children of our half-century better than another? Is it because she sleeps with her brother-in-law? Because she dances the mambo? Because she is indolent and lazy? Because she is naked under her bodice? It is really not enough.

And many were furious at Bardot's beauty and the fact that her body, her youth, her lips, her sexuality were so brazenly the focus of the film. People in multiple countries – considering it indecent – campaigned to have it banned.

Her presence was magnetic – bold, carefree and unapologetically sensual, at a time when actresses were expected to be either sweet ingénues or untouchable femmes fatales. She was something else entirely: a modern woman who didn't just accept her desires but flaunted them, to the secret delight of 1950s audiences.

Her portrayal of Juliette – perhaps the antithesis of Shakespeare's original – sent shockwaves through the prudish society of the time. Audiences in France were scandalised and incredulous – some laughed during the screenings – but American audiences, ever thirsty for a bit of French daring, couldn't get enough. Bardot in *Et Dieu … Créa la Femme* pushed boundaries, flipping the script on what was considered 'acceptable' for women on screen. The Americans ate it up.

*Et Dieu … Créa la Femme* was the most successful foreign film of all time in the United States. While it was panned critically in almost every territory, the numbers spoke for themselves, and it was a hit in France, the UK and other territories. The script may have been rubbish, but something – or rather someone – resonated with audiences.

Suddenly, Bardot was everywhere – on magazine covers, in fashion spreads, setting trends with her tousled hair, smouldering eyes and cheeky bikinis. She was no longer just an actress; she was a cultural force, redefining what it meant to be a woman in the 1960s. From *La Vérité* (*The Truth*) to Godard's *Le Mépris* (*Contempt*), she kept pushing and kept surprising, and the world kept watching.

Simone de Beauvoir was struck by Bardot's impact. She penned a lengthy essay, 'Brigitte Bardot and the Lolita Syndrome', analysing Bardot's impact on societal perceptions of femininity. De Beauvoir observed that Bardot's portrayal in *Et Dieu … Créa la Femme* presented a new archetype of womanhood – liberated, unapologetically sensual, defying traditional norms. For her, Bardot propelled forward a more authentic expression of female sexuality. Bardot's Juliette was a free-spirited individual, well intentioned, embracing her desires without shame. This representation resonated with the existentialist themes de Beauvoir often explored, emphasising personal freedom. That said, she fully recognised the misogyny implicit in the hyper-sexualisation of this character, always under the male gaze, and written and directed by a man: 'She is a force of nature, dangerous as long as she is not disciplined, but it is up to man to tame her.' It is perhaps ironic that de Beauvoir's treatise first appeared in the American men's magazine *Esquire*, alongside pin-up-style pictures of Brigitte. It's unclear whether de Beauvoir was merely writing for her audience, but even she seems to fall victim to Bardot's seductiveness at points, writing, 'The line of her lips forms a childish pout, and at the same time those lips are very kissable … her walk is so lascivious that a saint would sell his soul to the devil merely to watch her dance.'

Through her essay, de Beauvoir articulated that Bardot's performance in *Et Dieu … Créa la Femme* was not merely a cinematic milestone but a cultural shift. It signalled a move towards acknowledging and celebrating women's autonomy, complexity and sexuality. While on the surface Bardot and de Beauvoir's careers and contributions were radically different, both contributed to reshaping the narrative of gender, sexuality and freedom.

While men could hardly tear their eyes away from Brigitte's curves, and some women felt furious at her immodesty (and perhaps threatened by it), other women smelled something new in the air, something a bit like freedom.

The world over, women started copying Brigitte Bardot. Her make-up, her hair, her cinched waist, her sexual freedom became an aspiration for women across not only France but the world. Fourteen years after the film's release, Brigitte Bardot was chosen to pose for the bust of Marianne, the symbol of France. She had become the archetype of beauty, freedom and sexuality too: it was the first Marianne with visible nipples. It was more than a film, but the beginning of a revolution. Bardot left a mark that would linger on in pop culture for decades, turning her into the ultimate symbol of sexual liberation, the woman who wouldn't apologise for who and what she was – a psycho-sexual being, who was not all that interested in marriage and motherhood.

\*   \*   \*

Born in Paris on 28 September 1934, into a wealthy and traditional family with strict Catholic values, Brigitte Bardot was perhaps an unlikely candidate for international bombshell and sex-kitten status. Her father, Louis Bardot, was a successful engineer and factory owner, who, despite his stern demeanour, indulged in hobbies like poetry and amateur photography. Her mother, Anne-Marie Mucel, came from an equally respectable background but secretly harboured dreams of an artistic life. She had always longed to dance and was well connected in the fashion and ballet circles of Paris, later to play a crucial role in shaping Brigitte's career.

Brigitte was not an only child; she had a younger sister, Mijanou Bardot, born in 1938, who would also dabble in acting before eventually stepping away from the spotlight. The two sisters grew up in the family's elegant flat on Rue de la Pompe in the affluent 16th arrondissement, surrounded by the comforts of Parisian high society. The family would remain in Paris during the Second World War and endure the Nazi occupation of the capital. The girls were young, but the time was not without trauma, and Brigitte would later recall waking in a sweat, panicking that Paris had been destroyed. She was nine years old when France was liberated.

From a young age, Brigitte was subject to a rigorous schedule. Her father believed in discipline and strict rules; her mother encouraged her daughters to explore their creative sides. At her mother's insistence, Brigitte was enrolled in ballet classes, where she learned discipline, grace and poise. Ballet offered her an escape from the rigid expectations of her upbringing, and by the age of fourteen, she had already won a prize at the prestigious Conservatoire de Paris.

Anne-Marie's ambition for Brigitte did not stop there. Recognising her daughter's striking beauty and potential, she leveraged her social connections to secure modelling gigs. One of her early breaks came through Jean Barthet, a renowned hat designer and family friend. Brigitte's unique blend of modelling and ballet skills – dancing to *Swan Lake* while showcasing Barthet's hats – captured attention and led to photo shoots for popular women's magazines like *Les Cahiers du Jardin des Modes* and *Les Veillées des Chaumières*. By the age of fifteen, Brigitte's face was already becoming familiar in Parisian fashion circles. In 1949, Bardot appeared on the cover of *Elle* magazine for the first time.

It was around the time of her first *Elle* cover that she first met Roger Vadim, who for better or worse would be pivotal in her rise to fame. The relationship was problematic. The world of postwar France was a confused one, plagued by shortages and turmoil. Charles de Gaulle resigned in 1946, and wars were continuing in Vietnam and Algeria, in which France would later be revealed to be on the wrong side of history. Existentialism and new ideas about sexuality and romantic relationships were also circulating. There was a feeling of chaos in the capital as Brigitte Bardot went through adolescence and her country and her city recovered from the occupation. It is unclear when exactly she became involved with Vadim – allegedly she was sixteen and he was twenty-four – but she may have been as young as fourteen and, understandably, her parents did not support the romantic relationship between this adult man and their teenage daughter.

The story goes that Vadim, then starting his career in film, saw her *Elle* cover, was entranced and showed it to his boss who agreed to screen-test her.

Her parents, of course, said *non*, and a family argument ensued. Her grandfather reportedly ended the discussion; gesturing to his precocious granddaughter, he announced that if 'this little girl was to become a whore, it would *not* be because of a screen test'. This is often taken out of context – apparently what he meant was that a screen test alone was not going to corrupt the girl, but, of course, those eager for gossip are eager to interpret it another way.

Against her parents' wishes, the relationship with Vadim bloomed, partly in secret, partly in the open, and Brigitte became determined to pursue a career in film. By 1951, aged seventeen, she had secured her first film role in *Le Trou Normand* (*Crazy for Love*). But for all this success, the year was particularly hard for her as well. She had an unwanted pregnancy, which she aborted, and when her parents tried to separate her from Vadim, she tried to gas herself in the family apartment.

On 21 December, just a few months after turning eighteen, she married Vadim, with her parents' begrudging consent. The union would later be seen as a turning point in her life, one that catalysed her transformation from a young, well-bred Parisian girl into a cinematic icon known for sensuality, independence and unapologetic defiance of social norms.

Her rapid rise to fame was accompanied by a whirlwind of personal and professional transformations, and a constant struggle between her public image and private desires. By 1956, Bardot was on the brink of international stardom. This year marked the release of *La Lumière d'en Face* (*The Light across the Street*), in which she played a lead role that contrasted with her emerging sex-symbol image by portraying a faithful wife rather than the seductress role she was better known for. However, it was her performance in *Cette Sacrée Gamine* (*That Naughty Girl*) that cemented her playful, sexy persona, a mix of innocence and flirtation that would captivate audiences worldwide.

Then, she went blonde – and the French bombshell was born. She bleached it just in time for the Cannes Film Festival and the shooting of *Et Dieu … Créa la Femme*. Critics drew comparisons between Bardot's dishevelled sensuality in her performances and the more tightly controlled, choreographed sensuality of Marilyn Monroe. While Monroe's allure was carefully staged, Bardot's energy and sexuality seemed to burst forth naturally, epitomised by the famous mambo scene in *Et Dieu ...*, where her blonde mane became wilder as she danced. Bardot herself acknowledged the significance of this change, writing in her memoir *Initiales B.B.* that bleaching her hair was a 'turning point in the evolution of [her] persona' – the moment she became a lioness.

During the height of her fame in 1956, Bardot met Marilyn Monroe at the Royal Command Performance in London. She was captivated by Monroe, later recalling, 'I only had eyes for her: Marilyn. Gorgeous, blonde in a gold dress ... I wanted to be "Her".' However, Bardot's burgeoning fame was not without its complications. On the set of *Et Dieu ... Créa la Femme*, she began an affair with her co-star Jean-Louis Trintignant, despite him being married to actress Stéphane Audran, and of course being married to Vadim herself. According to cinema scholar Ginette Vincendeau, Bardot and Trintignant would live together for two years, a period marked by intense passion but also the strain of public scrutiny.

By April 1957, her marriage to Vadim had reached an amicable end. Vadim himself reflected on their relationship with surprising candour, stating that he preferred a wife with a spirit of adventure, even if it meant infidelity, over one who simply loved him alone. In 1958, they reunited professionally for *Les Bijoutiers du Clair de Lune (The Jewellers of Moonlight)*. Around this time, the intellectual elite began to take notice of Bardot's cultural impact. Marguerite Duras wrote an article titled 'Brigitte Bardot, Amoureuse', exploring the cultural phenomenon Bardot had become in postwar France, a symbol of youth, rebellion and liberated sexuality. It was this year that Raymond Cartier, editor of *Paris-Match*, devoted eight pages to examining 'the Bardot case'. He brought in psychologists, anthropologists and sociologists to dissect the roots of the Bardot phenomenon, exploring what it revealed about the psychology of the modern masses and the shifting social norms of the era. The goal? To see if any insights could be used to push back *against* this wave of change.

The following year, Bardot continued to solidify her position as a leading actress with *Babette s'en va-t-en Guerre* (*Babette Goes to War*), directed by Christian-Jaque. On 18 June 1959, Bardot married actor Jacques Charrier, her co-star in the film. That same year, Simone de Beauvoir published *that* influential essay, highlighting Bardot's ambiguous sexuality that could be both innocent and provocative. In it, she hinted that Bardot's marriage could be an attempt to rehabilitate her image to make herself more palatable to the French public.

Despite her public success, the tumult in Bardot's personal life rumbled on. In 1960, she gave birth to her son, Nicolas-Jacques Charrier, but her pregnancy was traumatic. Bardot famously did not want to become a mother, writing in her memoir that she viewed her pregnancy as an invasion. She likened her unborn child to a 'cancerous tumour' and even confessed to punching herself in stomach in a desperate attempt to end the pregnancy. Abortion was not yet legal in France, and she had no choice but to have the baby. These revelations, shared in her later memoirs, shocked the public and further fuelled her image as a woman who defied societal norms. They seriously damaged her relationship with her by then ex-husband and her son, who successfully sued her over the book for invasion of privacy. She and Jacques Charrier divorced in 1963, and Brigitte voluntarily gave up custody of her son.

The early 1960s saw Bardot expanding her artistic pursuits. In 1962, she starred in *Vie Privée* (*A Very Private Affair*), directed by Louis Malle, which marked the beginning of her singing career with the recording of her first song, 'Sidonie'. Her breathy and playful singing style drew mixed reviews – but as always brought attention.

Bardot's film career reached new heights in 1963 with Jean-Luc Godard's *Le Mépris*, where she played a woman caught in a disintegrating marriage. By the mid-1960s, she was branching out into new genres with films like *Viva Maria!* and *Masculin-Féminin*, embracing the spirit of the French New Wave. During this period Bardot's love life remained as intense as her professional one. In 1966, she met German millionaire Gunter Sachs in Saint-Tropez, and after a whirlwind romance filled with grand romantic gestures – including Sachs showering her home with thousands of roses from a helicopter – they married in Las Vegas that July. But old habits die hard, and the relationship was tested by reports of her infidelity; it was alleged that she began an affair with singer Mike Sarne shortly after their wedding. It was at this time that she came out in public support of Josephine Baker and used her public profile to raise money for the down-on-her-luck icon.

Indeed, she did not let being married put the brakes on her love life. In 1967, she went on a date with the provocative musician Serge Gainsbourg and demanded he write her a love song. The relationship lasted three months, but Gainsbourg wrote her two songs: 'Bonnie and Clyde' and 'Je t'aime … moi non plus'. They recorded them together, with a sound engineer later recalling the passionate 'heavy petting' that went on in the recording booth, sounds that made it into their final version of 'Je t'aime … moi non plus'. However, after Sachs heard the recording, he and Bardot had it pulled from broadcast. Gainsbourg later re-recorded the song with his new girlfriend, Jane Birkin, and released it. By 1969, after multiple affairs, her marriage to Sachs came to an end. There were no regrets on his side at least; Sachs famously remarked, 'A year with Bardot was worth ten with anyone else.'

In 1973, at the age of thirty-nine, she announced her retirement from acting after completing her final film, *L'Histoire Très Bonne et Très Joyeuse de Colinot Trousse-Chemise* (*The Edifying and*

*Joyous Story of Colinot*). Having grown disillusioned with fame, the nature of which was profoundly changing, she chose to step away from the spotlight. The second half of the twentieth century marked a dramatic shift in what it meant to be famous, driven by the rise of mass media, television and global celebrity culture. Unlike the carefully curated personas of earlier stars like Sarah Bernhardt, who controlled their public image through theatre and posters, fame in the age of film and television became more intrusive and unrelenting. Brigitte Bardot exemplifies this transformation – initially celebrated as a symbol of liberated femininity and French allure, she quickly found herself trapped by the very image that made her famous. Unlike Bernhardt, who cultivated her legend through art and intellect, Bardot became a modern celebrity in the age of paparazzi and tabloid sensationalism, where personal life and public persona became inseparable. Bardot was hounded by the press and recalled that even back in 1960 during her pregnancy she could scarcely make it to a doctor's appointment without photographers jostling her and tracking her for a photograph of her pregnant body.

Her post-acting years marked a dramatic shift in focus. In 1986, Bardot released her version of the shelved track 'Je t'aime ... moi non plus' and established the Brigitte Bardot Foundation for the welfare and protection of animals, dedicating herself to animal rights, a cause that became her life's mission.

However, her outspoken nature meant that she soon stirred up controversy. In 1992, she married Bernard d'Ormale, a former adviser to far-right leader Jean-Marie Le Pen. This association with the far right drew heavy criticism, especially after Bardot voiced support for Le Pen in her memoir, *Initiales B.B.*, published in 1996. Despite impressive sales and winning an award, the book came under fire for its provocative content. As mentioned, Bardot's ex-husband Jacques Charrier and their son Nicolas sued her for 'hurtful remarks', including her statement that she would have preferred to give birth to a puppy than her son. Jacques and Nicolas endeavoured to force the removal of the passages about them, but were unsuccessful. However, Bardot was found guilty of defamation and ordered to pay the pair compensation. In any event, the real significance of the case was that it highlighted the extent of her fractured relationship with her only child. She wrote that she felt 'suffocated' by fame.

The late 1990s and 2000s saw Bardot repeatedly facing legal issues over inflammatory, often hateful comments and a general disregard for law. In one more comic incident, she took it into her own hands to castrate her neighbour's donkey for being overly amorous with hers, resulting in a lawsuit (which she won). In 1997, in a far more serious incident, she was fined for inciting racial hatred due to her criticism of the Muslim practice of slaughtering sheep during Eid al-Adha. She doubled down on her rhetoric in 1998, stating in court that Muslims were 'obsessed with throat-cutting'. Her statements did not stop there; in 2008, she was fined €15,000 for sending a letter, deemed Islamophobic, to then interior minister Nicolas Sarkozy. In her letter she requested that the animals sacrificed for Eid be anaesthetised before slaughter, before going on to claim that the country was being destroyed by the Muslim population.

In 2018, Bardot stirred controversy yet again by denouncing the #MeToo movement, calling it 'hypocritical and ridiculous', and dismissing many harassment claims as women seeking attention. More recently, in 2021, she was fined a reported €20,000 for calling the people of Réunion 'degenerates' and accusing them of having 'savage genes', ostensibly due to the practice of decapitating live animals in religious festivals, and general animal rights violations on the island. While many may have agreed with her on her animal rights advocacy, her love of animals often appeared to be a thin mask for real hate speech.

Bardot remained a polarising cultural figure – admired for her beauty and boldness, criticised for her offensive statements. Her life after stardom was as colourful and controversial as her years in the spotlight, marked by a fierce commitment to her beliefs, regardless of the cost. These issues, and her marriage to a far-right political adviser, exemplify the fractures in modern France. It was partly for her views, which many condemn, that I chose to include her in this book. At the time of writing, she was one of only two women I included who were still living, and still active in politics. She supported Marine Le Pen openly, which, while incomprehensible to me, resonated with hundreds of thousands of French voters. She symbolised France's popular sexual awakening of the 1960s, but also the political fragmentation, right-wing politics and stark divisions of this century. She was – and always had been – unapologetically individual.

Through it all, Brigitte Bardot remained impenitent, standing by her convictions regardless of public backlash, or fines. Despite her many controversies, she became a symbol of both the liberation and complexities of womanhood in the twentieth century, her life reflecting the contradictions of fame, freedom, privilege and the illusion of perfection.

# CONCLUSION

Women have always been at the heart of France's most defining moments, shaping the country's politics, arts, sciences and society – but all too often their contributions have gone unrecognised. The twenty-one women in this book reveal that France's transformation – whether in times of war, intellectual awakening, artistic innovation or social upheaval – was profoundly influenced by the ambition, resilience and talent of women.

These women were often outsiders in their time. Many fought against rigid structures designed to keep them silent. Some, like Paulette Nardal, Josephine Baker, Simone Veil and Djamila Boupacha, were doubly marginalised, by their gender and their origins – yet their impact on France's intellectual and political history was weighty. Their struggles remind us that progress has never been handed to women; it has always been demanded, hard-won and defended.

Their lives also expose the tensions and contradictions in France's national story. The Revolution's promise of *égalité* famously excluded women; the golden age of French intellectualism often relegated women to being muses rather than thinkers; and even today the recognition of women's contributions is still an ongoing battle. The exclusion of figures like Émilie du Châtelet from most major museum spaces, or the continued relative obscurity of Paulette Nardal, shows that the work of reclaiming women's place in history is far from finished. It took until the 1990s for the first woman – Marie Curie – to be interred in the Pantheon for her own achievements. Simone Veil followed in 2018, and Josephine Baker in 2021, her name now carved into the stone of the French Republic.

And yet, progress has undeniably been made. This book hopes to be part of that progress. I do not claim it to be a complete history of women in France – such an endeavour would be sure to fail. But it is a testament to the fact that no history of France is complete without its women. Their voices, struggles and triumphs continue to shape the nation. A nation's history is not a fixed narrative but a conversation – one in which women's voices must be heard.

Writing this book has been both a privilege and a personal journey. I started it intentionally to coincide with my move to Paris, seeking a new project that would help me get to know my new city and dig into its history and culture. I had lived in Paris before, but this time the move was meant to be permanent, and I wanted to invest. The process of researching and writing this book, of excavating the lives of so many fascinating women, has made me see Paris differently. I see the city through clearer eyes.

The streets of Paris bear the imprints of these marvellous women and are alive with their memories. When I take coffee in the Jardin du Palais-Royal, I see Colette smoking a cigar from her window at 9 Rue de Beaujolais, overlooking the park. When I walk along Quai Malaquais, I think of George Sand barricading her window with a mattress to protect her daughter from the bullets of the June Uprising. When I cross Place de la Concorde, I feel a chill thinking of Olympe de Gouges facing the guillotine. Climbing the

## CONCLUSION

hill of Montmartre, I remember Bloody Week, Louise Michel and her cats. On Rue Cuvier I think of Elisa, of Paulette Nardal and grimly of the fate of Sarah Baartman. I see them all: moving through salons, prison cells, courtrooms, theatres, barricades, cafés and courtyards – each leaving her mark on this glittering, blood-soaked, complicated city, and this equally complicated country.

And what of the future? The women in this book are part of a lineage not yet complete. Their lives show us what is possible when women dare to speak, to create, to dissent and to lead. They have cleared many obstacles from the path of a new generation of French women, and, while many remain, the future and the goal are clearer. The next generation of women in France will shape new revolutions – of thought, of policy, of imagination. They will write themselves more fully into the story of this country. Whether in classrooms, courtrooms, laboratories, ministries or the streets, they will continue to reshape and advance the country. The twenty-first century has brought with it a slew of challenges and threats, posing pressing questions around women's safety and rights. Women's voices will be a vital part of the answer.

# ACKNOWLEDGEMENTS

No book would be complete without a note of thanks to everyone who helped pull it together. Firstly, I am grateful to my agent, Rachel Conway, for her help and guidance in the early stages of the project, and of course to my editors, Sam and Hannah at Oneworld, whose contributions have helped make this book better. Paul and Kathleen also deserve special thanks, Paul for his patience and skill corralling all the materials into a finished product, and Kathleen for her meticulous care in smoothing out my prose.

The next thank you must go to Belinda Jack and Estelle Paranque for being generous with their time and feedback, even when juggling their own deadlines. A book spanning so many periods and regions needs many pairs of eyes to get it right, I really benefited from the advice and research of scholars specialised in different periods. Thanks are also due to Grace Hart for her diligent help with research, and similarly to Bella de Geus for her notes on Colette.

In addition to being a professional endeavour, this book was a personal one, the project that accompanied me building a new life in Paris and deepening my relationship with the country I now call home. Paris is famously hard to break into, and without many good friends helping me along and opening doors for me – both my life here and this book would be much the poorer. Thank you very much to Anna for taking me under her wing when I first arrived and driving me around on her scooter, to Frederique, Maud, and Sherlock for being the best neighbours a new arrival could hope for, and to Léa for her consistent friendship since we met during my first Parisian internship aged nineteen. Alexis and Felix helped me settle in and get to know the city, and Xavier accompanied me to several far-flung places for research. There are so many others who have been great supports to me in Paris and during the writing process, Erin, Grace, Nancy, Marie, Audrey, Emilia, Ysé, Emilie and Clemence to name a few – and not least Tristan – who has been a variously sardonic and joyful guide around Paris, and made the city feel like home. He deserves special thanks for driving me across the country to visit the Château de Chenonceau and George Sand's house at Nohant, all with an unruly German Shepherd in tow. Shadow has – as always – been a faithful companion throughout.

Last but not least, my parents have given me so much support in launching my writing career, my life here and, indeed, in introducing me to France and French culture. From financing remedial French tutoring in my childhood and my gap year course at the Sorbonne, to bringing me on holidays to France every summer, they laid the groundworks for this book. Mum schlepped out to Fontainebleau to visit Eleanor of Aquitaine's final resting place with me, and Mum and Dad both accompanied me to Empress Josephine's house at Malmaison. Above all I am grateful to them.

# KEY SOURCES AND SUGGESTED READING

For this book – a whistlestop tour of French history through some of the country's fiercest women – I've been deeply grateful for the excellent research of others. The following texts were especially useful, and I think readers eager to learn more will enjoy them too. This list isn't exhaustive, but it's a strong start. On top of this, some museums and historic sites I visited made a lasting impression, and I recommend to everyone that they visit the George Sand House at Nohant and Josephine Baker's Chateau de Milandes to name just two. These places are rich in atmosphere and treasure troves of information.

## 1. Balthild of Chelles
Paul Fouracre and Richard Gerberding, *Late Merovingian France: History and Hagiography 640–720* (Manchester University Press, 1996).

Jo Ann McNamara (ed.), *Sainted Women of the Dark Ages* (Duke University Press, 1992).

Henry von Blumenthal, *The Life and Times of Saint Hubert* (Longcross Press, 2021).

## 2. Eleanor of Aquitaine
Sara Cockerill, *Eleanor of Aquitaine: Queen of France and England, Mother of Empires* (Amberley Publishing, 2019).
Marion Meade, *Eleanor of Aquitaine: A Biography* (Penguin, 1991).
Katherine Pangonis, *Queens of Jerusalem: The Women Who Dared to Rule* (Weidenfeld & Nicolson, 2021).
Alison Weir, *Eleanor of Aquitaine: By the Wrath of God, Queen of England* (Vintage, 2008).

## 3. Béatrice de Planisolles
Malcolm Barber, *The Cathars* (Routledge, 2013).
Emmanuel Le Roy Ladurie, *Montaillou: Cathars and Catholics in a French Village 1294–1324* (Penguin, 1978).
René Weis, *The Yellow Cross* (Penguin, 2001).

## 4. Christine de Pizan
Claire Breay and Julian Harrison (eds.), *Medieval Women: Voices & Visions* (British Library Publishing, 2024).
Charity Cannon Willard, *Christine de Pizan: Her Life and Works* (Persea Books, 1984).
Charlotte Cooper-Davis, *Christine de Pizan: Life, Work, Legacy* (Reaktion Books, 2021).
Christine de Pizan, *The Book of the City of Ladies*, trans. Rosalind Brown-Grant (Penguin Classics, 1999).

## 5. Joan of Arc
Helen Castor, *Joan of Arc* (Faber & Faber, 2014).
Daniel Hobbins (trans.), *The Trial of Joan of Arc* (Harvard University Press, 2007).
Régine Pernoud, *Joan of Arc: By Herself and Her Witnesses* (Scarborough House, 1990).
——— *The Retrial of Joan of Arc: The Evidence for Her Vindication* (Ignatius Press, 2007).

# KEY SOURCES AND SUGGESTED READING

## 6. Catherine de' Medici
Leonie Frieda, *Catherine de Medici* (Weidenfeld & Nicolson, 2011).
Estelle Paranque, *Blood, Fire & Gold* (Ebury, 2022).

## 7. Émilie du Châtelet
David Bodanis, *Passionate Minds: The Great Enlightenment Love Affair* (Little, Brown & Co, 2006).
Émilie du Châtelet, *Foundations of Physical Science* (Routledge, 2018).
Judith P. Zinsser, *La Dame d'Esprit: A Biography of the Marquise du Châtelet* (Penguin, 2006).

## 8. Olympe de Gouges
Olympe de Gouges, *The Declaration of the Rights of Woman and of the Female Citizen* (originally published 1791; various modern editions available).
Sophie Mousset, *Women's Rights and the French Revolution: A Biography of Olympe de Gouges* (Routledge, 2017).
Joan Wallach Scott, *Only Paradoxes to Offer: French Feminists and the Rights of Man* (Harvard University Press, 1996).

## 9. Joséphine Bonaparte
Henry Foljambe Hall, *Napoleon's Letters to Joséphine* (Leonaur, 2010).
Andrew Roberts, *Napoleon the Great* (Penguin, 2016).
Andrea Stuart, *The Rose of Martinique: A Biography of Napoleon's Josephine* (Grove Press, 2004).
Kate Williams, *Joséphine: Ambition, Desire, Napoleon* (Hutchinson, 2013).

## 10. George Sand
Belinda Jack, *George Sand* (Yale University Press, 2010).
George Sand, *The Story of My Life*, Dan Hofstadter (trans./ed.) (Folio Society, 1984).
Naomi Schor, *George Sand and Idealism* (Columbia University Press, 1993).

## 11. Louise Michel
Alistair Horne, *The Fall of Paris* (Penguin, 2007).
Louise Michel, *Mémoires* (Gallimard, 2021).
———— *The Red Virgin: Memoirs*, Bullitt Lowry & Elizabeth Ellington Gunter (trans./ed.) (University of Alabama Press, 1981).

## 12. Berthe Morisot
*Berthe Morisot: Shaping Impressionism* (Dulwich Picture Gallery & Musée Marmottan Monet, 2023).
Anne Higonnet, *Berthe Morisot* (HarperCollins, 1990).
Sebastian Smee, *Paris in Ruins: The Siege, the Commune and the Birth of Impressionism* (Oneworld, 2024).

## 13. Sarah Bernhardt
Sarah Bernhardt, *My Double Life: The Memoirs of Sarah Bernhardt by Sarah Bernhardt* (originally published 1907; available via Project Gutenberg).
Collectif, *Sarah Bernhardt: Catalogue Exposition Petit Palais* (Petit Palais, 2023).
Robert Gottlieb, *Sarah: The Life of Sarah Bernhardt* (Yale University Press, 2010).
Petit Palais, *Sarah Bernhardt. Et la femme créa la star* (Beaux Arts Ed, 2023).

## 14. Colette
Colette, *Complete Works* (various editions).
Michael LaPointe, 'The Brilliance of Colette, a Novelist Who Prized the Body Over the Mind,' *The New Yorker*, 15 November 2022.
Jean-Yves Tadié, *Colette: A Biography* (Gallimard, 2012).
Judith Thurman, *Secrets of the Flesh: A Life of Colette* (Knopf, 1999).

# KEY SOURCES AND SUGGESTED READING

## 15. Coco Chanel
Lisa Chaney, *Coco Chanel: An Intimate Life* (Penguin, 2011).
Justine Picardie, *Coco Chanel: The Legend and the Life* (HarperCollins, 2023).

## 16. Paulette Nardal
Jennifer Anne Boittin, *Colonial Metropolis: The Urban Grounds of Anti-Imperialism and Feminism in Interwar Paris* (University of Nebraska Press, 2010).
Annette K. Joseph-Gabriel, *Reimagining Liberation: How Black Women Transformed Citizenship in the French Empire* (University of Illinois Press, 2019).
Shirley Moody-Turner and James Davis (eds.), *The Black Press: A Literary Tradition* (Routledge, 2012).
Léa Mormin-Chauvac, *Les Sœurs Nardal: À l'avant-garde de la cause noire.* (Autrement, 2024).
Paulette Nardal, *Beyond Negritude: Essays from Woman in the City*, Sharpley-Whiting, T. Denean (eds.) (State University of New York Press, 2009).

## 17. Joséphine Baker
Jean-Claude Baker and Chris Chase, *Josephine: The Hungry Heart* (Cooper Square Press, 1993).
Phyllis Rose, *Jazz Cleopatra: Josephine Baker in Her Time* (Anchor, 1989).

## 18. Édith Piaf
Simone Berteaut, *Piaf: A Biography* (Da Capo Press, 1994).
Carolyn Burke, *No Regrets: The Life of Edith Piaf* (Bloomsbury, 2012).

## 19. Djamila Boupacha
Simone de Beauvoir, 'Pour Djamila Boupacha,' *Le Monde*, 3 June 1960.

Simone de Beauvoir and Gisèle Halimi, *Djamila Boupacha* (Gallimard, 1962; English translation, 1963).

Natalya Vince, *Our Fighting Sisters: Nation, Memory and Gender in Algeria, 1954–2012* (Manchester University Press, 2015).

**20. Simone Veil**

Simone Veil, *A Life*, Tamsin Black (trans.) (Haus Publishing, 2009).

**21. Brigitte Bardot**

Brigitte Bardot, *Initiales B. B.* (Grasset, 1996).

Marie-Dominique Lelièvre, *Brigitte Bardot: Plein la vue* (Denoël, 2009).

Barnett Singer, *Brigitte Bardot: A Biography* (McFarland, 2012).

Ginette Vincendeau, *Stars and Stardom in French Cinema* (Bloomsbury, 2000).